Staging the revolution

MANCHESTER
1824
Manchester University Press

Staging the revolution

Drama, reinvention and history, 1647–72

Rachel Willie

Manchester University Press

Copyright © Rachel Willie 2015

The right of Rachel Willie to be identified as the author of this work has been asserted by her in accordance with the Copyright, Designs and Patents Act 1988.

Published by Manchester University Press
Altrincham Street, Manchester M1 7JA, UK
www.manchesteruniversitypress.co.uk

British Library Cataloguing-in-Publication Data is available

ISBN 978 0 7190 8763 9 *hardback*
ISBN 978 1 5261 3956 6 *paperback*

First published by Manchester University Press in hardback 2015

This edition first published 2019

The publisher has no responsibility for the persistence or accuracy of URLs for any external or third-party internet websites referred to in this book, and does not guarantee that any content on such websites is, or will remain, accurate or appropriate.

Contents

List of figures	*page*	vi
Acknowledgements		vii
List of abbreviations		x
A note on dating and on spelling		xi
	Introduction: Of 1647, theatre closure and reinvention	1
1	The paper stage	25
2	Fairs, ghosts, tyranny and usurpation: debating the body politic on the paper stage	52
3	Reinventing the masque: Shirley's and Davenant's protectorate entertainments	80
4	Heroic drama on the commonwealth and Restoration stage	117
5	Ideas of panegyric in early Restoration comedy	157
	Epilogue: Of 1688 and reinventing the past	188
	Bibliography	210
	Index	237

List of figures

1 *A Dialogue Betwixt the Ghosts of Charles the I Late King of England: and Oliver the Late Usurping Protector* (London, 1659), RB 77181, frontispiece. Reproduced by permission of the Huntington Library, San Marino, California   page 43
2 *A New Meeting of Ghosts at Tyburn Being a Discourse of Oliver Cromwell. John Bradshaw. Henry Ireton. Thomas Pride. Thomas Scot, Secretary to the Rump. Major Gen. Harrison and Hugh Peters, the Divills Chaplain* (London, 1660 [1661]), A.10 (7), frontispiece © The Governing Body of Christ Church, Oxford (2014)   44
3 *A Messenger from the Dead, or Conference Full of Stupendious Horrour, Heard Distinctly, and by Alternate Voyces, by Many as that Time Present. Between the Ghosts of Henry the 8. and Charls the First of England, in Windsor-Chappel, Where They Were Both Buried.* (London: 1658), P1597, frontispiece. Reproduced by permission of the Folger Shakespeare Library   45
4 John Ogilby, 'Of the rebellion of the hands and the feet', in *The fables of Æsop paraphras'd in verse, and adorn'd with sculpture*, 3rd edn (London, 1673), Douce A. 694, Vol. 1 pp. 136–9 (p. 137). Reproduced by permission of the Bodleian Libraries, University of Oxford   149

Acknowledgements

As with many first books, this one had its genesis in my doctoral research, undertaken at the University of York. Here, I benefited in different ways from conversations with Michael Cordner, Mark Jenner, Helen Pierce, John Roe, Richard Rowland, Bill Sherman and Jonathan Wainwright. Helen Pierce and Mike Cordner both supplied me with material that (at the time) awaited publication, for which I am very grateful, and Mike helped me to fully comprehend how a generally non-reactionary parliament might have been driven to regicide. My fellow early modern graduate students, Tamsin Badcoe, Nick Moon, Varsha Panjwani, Kate Pond, Chloe Preedy and Amritesh Singh, proved excellent colleagues and friends. The greatest intellectual debt goes to Helen Smith and I would also like to thank especially Kevin Killeen and Martin Butler for their wisdom and patience with my wayward ideas.

Further afield, I was very lucky to come into contact with some very generous scholars. Conversations with Anne Coldiron, John Cunningham, Michael Dobson, Claudia Kairoff, Jennifer Keith, Ian Gadd, Jane Grogan, Jerome de Groot, Helmer Helmers, Gordon McMullan, Lucy Munro, Susan Wiseman, Maarten van Dijck and Mimi Yiu helped to inform my critical thinking. Carol Morley kindly provided me with an extract from James Fraser's diary, and Mark Rankin very generously shared with me *A Messenger from the dead*, (London: 1658), discussed in Chapters 1 and 2. As part of the Making Publics (MaPs) project, in 2009 I took up a summer fellowship at McGill University, which greatly influenced the ways in which I have been considering performance and the circulation of text in the nascent public sphere. Thanks especially to Paul Yachnin, Shankar Raman and Angela Vanhaelen, not only for giving me this fascinating and rewarding opportunity but also for continuing discussions after the project ended.

Tamsin Badcoe deserves considerable praise for reading the manuscript with unflagging good humour, and especially for identifying a worrying and unintended correlation between historical narrative and *Star Trek*. Thanks are also due to Natalie Pollard and Elizabeth Swann for comments upon parts of the piece, to Liam Haydon for his help with locating materials, and Barbara Eichner deserves special mention for her abilities at conceiving headline-grabbing titles. Julia Knaus proved an exemplary exchange student and an excellent checker of quotations.

Librarians at the Bodleian Library, the British Library, Guildhall Library, Huntington Library, King's College London Library, University of London Library at Senate House, York Minster Library, and the Borthwick Institute and J. B. Morrell Library at the University of York were all very helpful. Paul Carr at the BL deserves special thanks for checking a pamphlet for me and correcting an unforced error. In 2011, I was very lucky to be awarded a short-term fellowship at the Folger Shakespeare Library and I would like to thank all the librarians and fellows for welcoming me into a friendly and stimulating community and for allowing me to present work in progress. Thanks too to Kevin de Ornellas and to Helen Wilcox for inviting me to present papers at the Irish Renaissance Society and the Wales-wide Institute for Medieval and Early Modern Studies (IMEMS) respectively, and to all who were present for their helpful comments.

In 2011, I joined Bangor University and have enjoyed conversations with my new colleagues. It is a privilege (albeit an intimidating one) to work amongst such erudite and perspicacious scholars. Some of the material presented in this book has been reprinted from my 'Viewing the paper stage: civil war, print, theatre and the public sphere', in Angela Vanhaelen and Joseph Ward (eds), *Making Space Public in Early Modern Europe: Performance, Geography, Privacy* (New York and London: Routledge, 2013), pp. 54–75. Thanks to Routledge for allowing me to reprint this material. I am grateful to all at Manchester University Press for helping to transform this matter into a book and for their patience with its author.

Various people deserve thanks for offering me a bed/floor/sofa when I visited libraries and attended conferences: Anne and Peter Gill; Hayley, Sumedha and Sebastian Gunawarna; Rachael and Nick Hilliard; Lindsay McSporran; Nick Moon and Pragya Vohra; Ella Paremain; Natalie Pollard; Lizzie Swann and Tom McAuley were all kind enough to let me be an absent house-guest. My siblings, Rob and Hannah, were good

Acknowledgements

enough to feign an interest in what I do and serendipitous Fortune was occasionally kind. The greatest debt of gratitude goes to my parents, Andrew and Val Willie. Without their encouragement, their undutiful and daft daughter would not have had the confidence to undertake this project, nor the support to succeed in it.

List of abbreviations

BL	British Library
ELH	*English Literary History*
MLR	*Modern Language Review*
ODNB	*Oxford Dictionary of National Biography*
PMLA	*Publications of the Modern Languages Association of America*
PRO	Public Record Office
RES	*Review of English Studies*
SEL	*Studies in English Literature*
YES	*Yearbook of English Studies*

A note on dating and on spelling

In accordance with current scholarly practice, I have silently amended the calendar year to begin on 1 January and not 25 March as was the custom in seventeenth-century England. Thus, for example, Charles I was executed in January 1649 rather than 1648/9. Days of the year refer to Julian calendar dating as this was the calendar used in England at the time; England did not subscribe to the Gregorian calendar that was (and is) used by many of its continental neighbours until the eighteenth century. In presenting quotations, I have retained original spelling, but normalised j/i and u/v, and expanded abbreviations.

Introduction
Of 1647, theatre closure and reinvention

In May 1645, Colonel Blunt, a member of the parliamentarian army, faced a challenge. While civil war was being fought throughout the three kingdoms, and skirmishes at Pontefract castle were growing particularly vicious, Blunt had a different problem to overcome. His dilemma was how to prevent the people of Kent from partaking in May Day festivities. The incident is reported and commented upon in a parliamentarian newsbook. We are told that 'In Kent the countrey people (no where more) love old customes, and to do every yeer what they have done in others before, and much pastimes, and drinking matches, and May-Poles, and dancing and idle ways, and sin hath been acted on former May days'.[1] According to the parliamentarian newsbook, Blunt needed to suppress traditional holiday pastimes as they led only to drunkenness and vice.

Blunt's solution was novel. Rather than using his regiment to enforce sobriety upon the populace, he ordered the troop to provide another form of diversion:

> Colonell *Blunt* divided [the army] ... into two parts, and the one was as Roundheeds, and the other as Cavaliers, who did both of them act their parts exceeding well, and many people, men and women, young and old, were present to see the same.
>
> The Roundheads they carried it on with care and love, temperance and order, and as much gravity as might be, everyone party carefull in his action, which was so well performed, that it was much commended.
>
> But the Cavaliers they minded drinking and roaring, and disorder, and would bee still playing with the women, and compasse them in, and quarrell, and were exceedingly disorderly.
>
> And these had severall skirmishes one with the other, and took divers prisoners one from the other, and gave content to the Countrey people, and

satisfied them as well as if they had gone a maying in an other way, which might have occasioned much evil.[2]

Ingeniously, Blunt staved off riotous May Day revelry through putting on a civil war re-enactment; the first recorded dramatic reconstruction of the civil wars therefore occurred four years before the second civil war terminated in regicide. The reporting of this episode highlights tensions between the performance and the reasons for mounting the production. To prevent sin and revelry through disordered holiday pastimes, the parliamentarian army actively participated in an alternative entertainment. Revelry was prevented through the use of revelry, but the saturnalia and riotous element of previous festivities was removed and replaced with an entertainment that staged disorder and contained it. At the same time, the violence associated with war (and the realities of the ongoing warfare that tore families and communities apart) is contained by the battle being a staged act. Blunt replaces the old customs of maypole dancing and drinking games with a topical performance.

This transformation of current affairs into a form of entertainment indicates that some ideas relating to the civil wars were widely disseminated and understood in the 1640s, and Blunt could use these ideas to produce a different form of entertainment to the ones that the people of Kent were accustomed to experiencing. At the same time, Blunt consolidated ideas regarding roundheads and cavaliers. As David Cressy notes, contemporaries used the recent past to 'inform, remind and inspire the people who lived through it'.[3] Remembrance of these experiences was, according to Cressy, a collective undertaking, one that was always partisan and shaped people's understanding of their place in time and informed their futures. As I will show, this 'collective undertaking' was far from coherent and the past would continually be reinvented because the civil war and monarchical authority meant different things to different people at different times. However, remembrances of the civil war and ideas about what it meant to be a royalist or a parliamentarian would gain greater coherence and cultural verification in the centuries after the commonwealth.[4]

Blunt's May Day festivity is one example of how drama was used to create, interpret and disseminate recent history. Sober roundheads present a counterbalance to debauched cavaliers: the news report emphasises the virtuous behaviour of the roundheads in comparison to the violent, drunken and anarchical antics of the imposter cavaliers. Whereas the roundheads symbolise reliable and safe government, the cavaliers are portrayed as being a threat to women and (by extension) the family and commonweal. This feeds into traditional conceptions of May Day festivities, which often erupted into riots and where sexual licence was understood to be permissible.[5] Aware of its function as a dramatic representation, Blunt carefully constructs the civil war re-enactment to prevent traditional holiday pastimes and also as a way to mirror and develop anti-cavalier iconography. However, the licence afforded to May Day festivities does not disappear. Instead, it is refashioned as a way to present an unthreatening image of war: the roundheads who pretended to be cavaliers appear to have taken to their part with enthusiasm and in so doing present a comical entertainment for their viewing public. Polemic and drama conjoin through the depiction of roundheads and cavaliers. The newsbook suggests that many people in Kent viewed the entertainment, but the drama had wider cultural and political implications. Through the reporting of the re-enactment in the parliamentarian newsbook, knowledge of the performance reached a wider audience in print.

Blunt adopted the caricatures of cavaliers and roundheads found in some contemporary newsbooks and play pamphlets to produce a dramatic response to the civil wars. In this book, I explore a range of dramatic representations on both the page and the stage and look at the way in which drama was appropriated by both royalists and parliamentarians as a means of responding to the civil wars and reinventing the recent past. As will be shown, drama and its textual transmission played a key role in the construction of cultural memory and many of the representations enacted in live performances and in print gained cultural verification as a consequence of the debates played out in the mid-seventeenth century. Over the last twenty years, research into the production of drama during the commonwealth has done much to discredit the assumption that no drama was performed between 1642 and 1660. Susan Wiseman and Janet Clare, in particular, have done much to tease out the performances that have been hidden by Restoration narratives regarding the banning of drama in the commonwealth.[6] Drawing from these studies, I show how drama is used to respond to this historical moment. In so doing, I also build upon the growing interest in print culture and the history of the book that, in the last twenty years, has led to some exciting scholarship on textual exchange and the development of the newsbook in the mid-seventeenth century.[7] Within historical studies, the New British History with its focus upon an integration of the three-kingdom narrative of England, Ireland and Scotland has added to the richness of accounts of the turbulent seventeenth century and our understanding of how war was considered and responded to in the different nations that were governed by the Stuarts.[8]

Studies into both popular culture and court culture have likewise increased our understanding of the seventeenth century and complicated our ways of defining what culture is, as has the recent trend of considering the burgeoning public sphere.[9] In the last decade, critics have greatly enhanced perceptions of seventeenth-century history, popular culture and politics, and I draw from numerous sources to show how regicide, restoration and government are reinterpreted in the dramatic forms of the period.[10]

This book draws together all of these narratives to demonstrate the ways in which drama was adopted to negotiate the political moment of civil war, regicide, commonwealth and Restoration. By appropriating political discourses, dramatic narratives feed into historical narratives and produce their own versions of history. Drama is used both to create enduring constructions of kingship and to question what kingship means when established forms of government break down. The portrayals of roundhead and cavalier by Blunt and his regiment are just one of many dramatic responses to the civil wars and, while some tropes are shared, these multiple images are not uniform in their representation and are subject to appropriation and alteration throughout the period.

In this Introduction, I briefly outline some of the issues relating to the study of commonwealth and Restoration drama, tracing the sources of current critical orthodoxies that position parliamentary puritan anti-theatricalism against a royalist commitment to the stage. Early modern authority figures recognised that dramatic representations could be used as a form of political commentary. It was generally forbidden to figure a living monarch on the stage, and some satirical referencing of influential people could prevent a play from being licensed.[11] However, the representation of kingship was integral to the Stuart court masque, which allegorically praised (and sometimes covertly criticised) royalty.[12] As I will argue, attitudes to drama altered as a consequence of civil unrest and the stage was transformed into an overtly political tool, which reinvented dramatic form as much as it reinvented the events that it narrated. However, unlike previous studies, which locate this transition in theatrical culture at the outbreak of civil war in 1642 or at the Restoration of the monarchy in 1660, this book argues that a more important date for this shift is 1647. It was the October 1647 ordinance for theatre closure, confirmed by the ordinance passed in February 1648, that shows an altered perception of drama and not the earlier ordinance for theatre closure that was passed in 1642. This is emphasised by the proliferation of political play pamphlets printed from 1648. Unlike the 1642 ordinance for theatre closure, the 1647 ordinance politicises the very idea of drama.

Introduction

In her preface to her seminal study on drama and politics in the mid-seventeenth century, Susan Wiseman asks why it is that most books on 'Renaissance drama' end in 1642 and most books on 'Restoration drama' start at 1660.[13] This observation still rings true, with it commonly being assumed that the theatres were closed in 1642 because parliament judged plays to be morally bankrupt, and the playhouses remained closed throughout the civil war and commonwealth period. Some parliamentarian newsbooks certainly took a dim view of the morality of stage plays in the 1640s.[14] However, in many respects, locating the transition in theatrical culture between Caroline and commonwealth drama in the 1642 ordinance for theatre closure is misleading. At the outbreak of civil war in 1642, the theatres were closed temporarily because playgoing was considered an unseemly pastime while misfortune befell the land. It was stipulated that 'publike Sports doe not well agree with publike Calamities, nor publike Stage-playes with the Seasons of Humiliation'.[15] Reflection and quiet contemplation were more suitable ways of dealing with the civil war and comprehending how parliament and monarch took up arms against each other.[16] Such moves were fairly common: at the outbreak of plague, the theatres were closed to maintain public order and to prevent the spread of infection.[17] The decision by parliament in 1642 to close the playhouses was therefore a conventional reaction to unpredictable times and did not reflect parliamentarian antagonism to stage plays.

The ordinance for theatre closure in 1642, therefore, was not particularly noteworthy; it was a temporary measure. However, this temporary measure was to be reaffirmed in October 1647 and made permanent in February 1648, when the second and third measures for theatre closure were passed. They were not repealed until the Restoration of the monarchy in 1660. The passing of these ordinances coincided with radical voices becoming more audible in parliament and in the parliamentary army. The New Model Army met at Putney from October until November 1647 for several debates, which resulted in some arguing the case for a republic where each man was entitled to vote in biennial parliaments.[18] The radicals were vetoed, but Charles I's escape from Hampton Court in November 1647 led to the second civil war. A year later, in December 1648, Colonel Thomas Pride purged parliament of the moderates and instigated a more revolutionary parliament. This parliament would eventually execute its anointed king, an action that would have been unthinkable to the parliament that was sitting in 1642. The second and third measures for the suppression of stage plays therefore coincided with radicals in the army gaining a platform through which to voice discontents and the move towards radicalism in parliament. While there may not necessarily be a causal connection between these events, and regardless of whether or not the radicals were less tolerant of dramatic performance than their predecessors, the representation of parliamentarians as being against the Crown and the performance of drama quickly gained cultural verification.

Although the 1647 and 1648 ordinances for the suppression of drama coincided with this radicalisation of parliamentary beliefs, music, dance and drama were not prohibited under the commonwealth or protectorate. Oliver Cromwell was a great lover of music, belying the myth that all holiday pastimes were forbidden by puritans. We know that a consort of instrumentalists performed music during protectorate meals, dancing happened at the three weddings that took place at the protectorate court and Andrew Marvell wrote two songs that appropriated pastoral allegory and Platonic tropes from Caroline court masques for the marriage between Mary Cromwell and Thomas Belasyse, second Viscount Falconbridge.[19] However, parliament's contradictory and paradoxical approach to these pastimes meant that disgruntled voices could (and did) attack the commonwealth governments for their prohibition of all forms of entertainment. As Colonel Blunt's reaction to May Day in 1645 demonstrates, some festivities were considered improper and were banned or discouraged by some parliamentarians. The fact that Blunt selected improvised drama as the means through which to prevent May Day revelry, however, emphasises that dramatic representations were not necessarily perceived as sinful. Legally, the Restoration marked the reopening of the theatres, and thus royalism and drama become implicitly linked. However, as we will see, 'parliamentarians' and 'royalists' are both terms with multiple meanings, and supporters of both causes adopted dramatic tropes as a means of illustrating the political moment. This use of dramatic representation as a type of polemic has shaped future generations' perception of the place and function of drama in the mid-seventeenth century: the association of parliament with anti-theatricality and royalism with drama was a gradual one that developed throughout the commonwealth and Restoration period.

Royalists and theatre practitioners did not form a coalition against a puritan parliament. However, this did not prevent those who objected to theatre closure accusing parliament of closing the playhouses because parliamentarians were believed to be of the opinion that plays were sinful. Perhaps part of the problem later critics have faced in identifying parliamentarian sentiments regarding drama is that the ideas relating to the closure of the theatres seem to have become annexed to anti-stage pamphlets and sermons that date from the late sixteenth and early seventeenth centuries.[20] The views of parliamentarians are especially tangled with the anti-stage rhetoric of the lawyer William Prynne. In 1633, Prynne launched an attack on stage plays. As a consequence of his lengthy diatribe, he was fined £5,000, had his ears cropped and was sentenced to life imprisonment. Prynne's tract, *Histrio-mastix*, focuses upon the lewdness and profanity of stage plays and especially censures dramas that feature female roles, or, more significantly, women actors. In labelling women actors 'notorious, impudent, prostituted Strumpets',[21] Prynne had, by implication, attacked Henrietta Maria and her coterie of amateur actors at court.[22] While women actors from the continent sometimes toured England, professional acting companies in England comprised all-male casts, and an English woman actor did not appear on the public stage in England until William Davenant staged *The Siege of Rhodes* in 1656. As a versified eighteenth-century history of the civil wars emphasises, the mutilation of Prynne was (and continued to be) recognised as being a punishment for his critique of the queen:

> But Lawyer *Pryn*, who had been Cast some Years
> Before, and sentenc'd to resign his Ears,
> For writing and had exposing what had been
> Condem'd and censur'd as against the Queen[23]

The poem goes on to describe Prynne's further mutilation and branding with the letters 'S. L.' ('seditious libeller') as a consequence of his printing more unwelcome material in 1637. What is acknowledged in the above quotation is that Prynne lost his ears because he censured Henrietta Maria and her ladies performing in court entertainments and not because the state sought to defend the integrity of the public playhouses. Although it is known that the reasoning behind the brutality of the sentence had little connection with stagecraft and everything to do with statecraft, drama is nevertheless brought into the debate and used to emphasise longer-term puritan opposition to the theatre.

This prehistory (coupled with the sporadic condemnation of drama by preachers in the late sixteenth and early seventeenth centuries) has helped to shape the belief that drama and the Crown were tangibly connected and puritans and parliament were against both. In reality, opinions regarding drama were not homogeneous and, as Margot Heinemann has demonstrated in her study that examines Thomas Middleton's connection with critics of the Stuart court, there is continuity between early Stuart theatre and pamphleteering in the 1640s.[24] The ordinances for theatre closure in the 1640s disguised these diverse views beneath a layer of legislation, and this was consolidated by the increased printing of plays and play pamphlets from 1647 and throughout the commonwealth period.

In addition to printed plays, there are a few examples of plays being performed at taverns and intermittently at some of the playhouses in the 1640s and 1650s. Occasionally, soldiers broke up these performances. The third ordinance for theatre closure stipulates that performing drama would be punishable by public whipping in market squares on market day and monies received from acting would be confiscated and distributed amongst the poor of the parish. A repeat offender would be charged with being an 'incorrigible Rogue, and shall be dealt with as an incorrigible Rogue ought to be by the said Statutes'.[25] The audience members were to be fined five shillings each.[26] These productions would often take the form of short one-act dramas called drolls, which were interspersed with non-outlawed entertainments such as rope dancing and bear baiting, though sometimes the actors would perform full-length, five-act plays.[27] Documentation relating to these illegal productions is rare, but emphasises that commonwealth theatrical culture warrants further investigation. We know that continental acting companies toured England and played at fairs. James Fraser, who later became an episcopal minister, visited England from Scotland in 1657 and gave the following account of Bartholomew Fair:

> your eares are here entertained with variety of all sorts of musick, your eyes with sights and Showes that can be invented by art. Masks, stage playes, dancing on roapes, mountebancks tricks of all sorts fencing wrestling tilting Jousting and actors from France, Spain, High Germany and Italy are here to show their skill to the utermost; and all manner of wares and marchandise to besold, but bewarr ye be not cheated or your pockets pickt, and he hath good luck that is not.[28]

Although Fraser does not give any information relating to which plays were produced, it is clear that theatre, dance, music and other forms of entertainment were being performed for the delight of those attending the fair. Colonel Blunt's 1645 fears that old holiday pastimes would lead the people of Kent into drunkenness and sin is, in 1657, replaced with the warning to be cautious of the pickpockets and petty criminals who often prey upon individuals at fairs.

Fraser does not voice surprise that plays are allowed to be performed, which suggests that dramas were regularly staged at fairs and in the provinces despite the ordinance for theatre closure. The situation appears to have been different in 1644, when actors publicly remonstrated against the first ordinance for theatre closure. Their reason for protesting was because other forms of public entertainment such as puppet plays and bear baiting were not banned by the 1642 statute and plays had long been purged of any scurrilous material.[29] *The Actors Remonstrance* brings into focus the contradictions between banning the performance of drama while still allowing other forms of entertainment to be staged. Whereas Colonel Blunt used drama to prevent other recreational activities, the actors reflect upon the unfairness of losing their livelihood because drama is suppressed.

These contradictions are further emphasised by the fact that plays were performed regardless of the ordinances: parliament may have banned theatrical production, but seemed to have little inclination to enforce the law. A rich theatrical culture was therefore available at fairs and taverns, but the circulation of printed plays, play pamphlets and official documentation all enforced the belief that drama was outlawed. This was a thread that would be taken up by Restoration writers. As Steven Zwicker has pointed out, no period in literary history was more conscious of its cultural demarcation than the Restoration.[30] Writers were keen to represent it as a return to rightful government, but also the start of a new age of empirical philosophy and enlightened reasoning. Such representations of the Restoration become more entrenched when considering the Restoration stage, which is often conceived as being mainly royalist.[31] However, the performance history of Edward Howard's *The Change of Crownes* (1667) emphasises that, far from being a royalist entity, the Restoration stage was shaped and informed by the previous twenty years.

The prompt book of *The Change of Crownes* is, in many ways, an invaluable document. However, the empirical evidence that can be garnered from the text means that very little can be authoritatively asserted about the play's performance and the anecdotes complicate rather than elucidate our understanding of the drama. The prompt book is mainly written in a neat italic hand, but has annotations in other hands. The final page contains the signature of Henry Herbert (the Master of the Revels) and it also bears the date 'Aprill 13th 1667', the date on which the play was licensed.[32] The margins are littered with aides-memoires to the prompter regarding actors' cues, pointers to get ready for the next act and even the names of some of the actors who played some of the parts. Through both the marginalia and the text itself, the material practices of theatrical production thus seem to be presented in the prompt book. A relic of the Restoration stage, the manuscript of *The Change of Crownes* therefore seems to be an enlightening and important document. As will become apparent, this material evidence, when married with the narrative of the text's afterlife, means that the play inevitably intrigues and inspires interest in those plotting the vagaries of the Restoration stage.

The Change of Crownes often appears as a footnote to a wider narrative of how the Restoration stage was a royalist monolith and how tragicomedy (the purported genre of Howard's play) in particular was appropriated for the royalist cause. In many ways, the history of the text can be read as being in itself a tragicomedy. Abjured by an angry king, the play languished in notorious obscurity and the prompt book was believed to have been lost, until its rediscovery and publication in the mid-twentieth century. Before the manuscript resurfaced, it was known only through external evidence regarding how the play was received and how it angered the king when it was performed in 1667. The play was performed (probably once) in April 1667; Samuel Pepys was a spectator and commented upon the performance in his diary. In his diary entry for 15 April 1667, Pepys writes:

> I to the King's house by chance, where a new play; so full as I never saw it, I forced to stand all the while close to the very door, till I took cold, and many people went away for want of room. The King and Queen and Duke of York and Duchesse there and all the Court, and Sir W. Coventry. The play called *The Change of Crownes*, a play of Ned Howard's the best that I ever saw at that House, being a great play and serious; only, Lacy did act the country gentleman come up to Court, who doth abuse the Court with all imaginable wit and plainness, about selling of places and doing everything for money. The play took very much.[33]

Pepys was so enamoured with *The Change of Crownes*, that, the very next day, he planned a pleasurable excursion for his wife. Unfortunately for Pepys, the connubial outing was thwarted by a royal intervention:

> Up, and to the office, where sat all morning; at noon home to dinner; and thence in haste to carry my wife to see the new play I saw yesterday, she not knowing it. But there, contrary to expectation, find *The Silent Woman*, however, in; and there Knip came into the pit ... Knipp tells me the King was so angry at the

liberty taken by Lacy's part to abuse him to his face, that he commanded they should act no more, till Moone went and got leave for them to act again; but not this play. The King mighty angry; and it was bitter endeed, but very true and witty. I never was more taken with a play than I am with this *Silent Woman*, as old as it is – and as often as I have seen it.[34]

The saga continues, when on 20 April, Pepys reports that the King's Company were in disfavour again:

> the reason of no play today at the King's house – that Lacy had been committed to the porter's lodge for his acting his part in the late new play; and that being thence released, he came to the King's house and there met with Ned Howard, the poet of the play, who congratulated his release; upon which, Lacy cursed him as that it was the fault of his nonsensical play that was the cause of his ill usage; Mr. Howard did give him some reply, to which Lacy [answered] him that he was more a fool then a poet; upon which Howard did give him a blow on the face with his glove; on which Lacy, having a cane in his hand, did give him a blow over the pate. Here, Rolt and others that discoursed on it in the pit this afternoon did wonder that Howard did not run him through, he being too mean a fellow to fight with – but Howard did not do anything but complain to the King of it; so the whole House is silenced – and the gentry seem to rejoice much at it, the House being become too insolent.[35]

Judging by Pepys's response to the play, it would appear that the drama would have been a success, had Lacy not satirised the court and then concussed Edward Howard. Since the play angered Charles II, it was consigned to oblivion and, while Howard and Lacy might have blamed one another for the banning of the play, Pepys's account of events is partially verified by an entry in Joseph Williamson's journal:

> Lacy our famous Comedean is at length by great intervention released from his durance und[e]r the Groome Porter, whither he stood committed by his Ma[jest]ys particular ord[e]r, for haveing on his owne head added severall indiferent expressions in the part he acted in a late Play called The Change of Crownes, written by Mr Edw. Howard.[36]

Among his many roles, Williamson controlled the official newsletter, the *London Gazette*, but also gathered intelligence for the government.[37] He consequently had a network of sources of information through which to corrupt and corroborate London gossip. Although the play was removed from the repertory, external evidence suggests that its failure to garner royal approval was due to John Lacy's extemporising and not because of anything particularly contentious within the text as penned by Howard. However, contrary to Restoration practices, the play did not appear in print, which suggests that the drama itself gained a level of notoriety. Furthermore, although the playtext was licensed by Henry Herbert, it does not necessarily follow that the text itself would not be contentious. When the ordinances for theatre closure banned the performing of drama, they precipitated an interruption to the office of the Master of the Revels. With the reopening of the playhouses at the Restoration, the authority of the Master of the Revels over the London theatre was significantly curtailed. Herbert's powers to oversee the production of drama were therefore not as authoritative as they had once been, though some power was moved back to the office as the decade progressed.[38] Even before the civil war, Herbert had occasionally permitted plays that angered the monarch: in 1624, Herbert licensed Thomas Middleton's *A Game at Chess*, which ran for a record nine consecutive days before it was eventually suppressed.[39] In this context, Lacy's extemporising might have merely brought into focus elements of Howard's text that were critical of the court. Indeed, the sections that are believed to have angered Charles II have been circled in the manuscript, and there appears to have been some attempt to revise the first of the offending scenes. This has prompted its one editor, Frederick Boas, to print T. C. Skeat's cautious suggestion that they were circled with the intention that they would be revised as a way of permitting the play to be returned to the repertory.[40]

Sadly, there is no marginal note to mimic George Buc, who, as Master of the Revels in 1619, wrote 'I like not this' in the margin of the manuscript of John Fletcher and Philip Massinger's *Sir John Van Olden Barnavelt* to provide evidence as to which parts might be contentious; the simple encircling of scenes in *The Change of Crownes* neither corroborates nor negates theories of why the play was suppressed.[41] However, the comic subplot provides some clues as to why it was not performed after 1667 or printed during the Restoration. Lacy played the part of Asinello, a man who comes to court and hopes to bribe his way into office. In the text of the play, Asinello is summarily gulled by the courtiers and locked in the porter's lodge for his presumption. Such a topic might have proved an affront to the court in April 1667. In 1666, the great fire of London had destroyed much of the old part of the city, which was already in the throes of a plague epidemic. The city's woes were coupled with heavy wartime taxation, despite the politically embarrassing and economically unwise retrenching of the English fleet after the maritime successes of 1666. In the summer of 1667, this would turn into outraged incredulity and the downfall of Clarendon, the lord chancellor, as news was delivered that the Dutch navy had sailed up the Medway and set fire to the English fleet.[42] Although Howard's play was performed months before this event, the Dutch attack on the English fleet seemed to endorse ideas that were being propounded; in particular, the beliefs that corruption at court, the buying of offices and general laziness were the cause of maritime mediocrity and the mismanaged war with the Netherlands had all gained currency in 1667.[43] In satirically treating the sale of offices in the play's subplot, *The Change of Crownes* might therefore be considered as slightly tactless subject matter with which to entertain a beleaguered king.

Despite (or perhaps because of) Charles's response, one could assume that *The Change of Crownes* was a rampant success and, had Charles not banned the play, it would have become one of the major dramas of the Restoration. Pepys states that the play 'took very much', indicating that it seems to have been a success with its audience, though, given that Pepys was forced to remain near the door, he may not have had a good view of the audience. Whether the courtiers were as enamoured of the production as the citizens seem to have been is ambiguous; there is insufficient detail to assess the audience's response to the drama, and how different demographics and individuals within the audience may have reacted to the drama. Pepys writes of the Theatre Royal being full the night *The Change of Crownes* was performed. This does not necessarily mean that it was because the London citizens were keen to see the premiere of a very popular play: the playhouse might have been packed because members of the court were in attendance and consequently swelled the numbers of playgoers. While Pepys clearly enjoyed the play and claimed it was the best he ever saw, he is equally taken with the revival of Ben Jonson's *Epicoene* or *the Silent Woman* that he watched the very next day. Pepys is remarking upon personal taste rather than presenting a homogenised audience response and his personal opinion can, and does, modulate.

The entries in Pepys's *Diary* relating to *The Change of Crownes* are also illuminating with regard to how the Drury Lane theatre operated in the Restoration. In her excellent analysis of tragicomedy at the Restoration, Nancy Klein Maguire states that '[t]he reopening of the theatre reverberated as an unmitigated victory yell for the Royalists. Since Charles II recognized the propaganda value of theatre, and relished drama personally, nearly all of the new playwrights were politicians who became playwrights either to gain or enhance their political credibility.'[44] Howard certainly falls into this category; his tragedy *The Usurper* was first performed in 1664 and, in 1668, Pepys thought it 'a pretty good play, in all but what is designed to resemble Cromwell and Hugh Peters, which is mighty silly'.[45] This thinly veiled attack on the protectorate demonstrates the way in which courtiers wrote for the restored theatre. However, while it is true that more courtier playwrights were writing drama for the Restoration stage than had been the case with the Caroline stage, *The Change of Crownes* offers an example of what can happen when the 'propaganda value of theatre' goes awry. Edward Howard was from royalist stock and, as brother to the playwright and politician Robert Howard, and brother-in-law to the future Poet Laureate, John Dryden, had connections at court. Howard could use his connections to gain revenge upon Lacy for their private skirmish by petitioning the king to temporarily close the public playhouse where Lacy performed and thus deprive the hapless company of revenue. Pepys's observation that the 'gentry' rejoiced at the closing of the King's Men's theatre because they believed the playhouse was growing insolent only emphasises the ways in which drama could be appropriated to respond to the current political moment and not necessarily be used in praise of those in authority or in celebration of the restoration of the monarchy. Furthermore, 'royalism' itself is a far more fractured and fragmented term than it might at first appear, and those who were royalists were not above using drama as a way to voice discontentment with the monarch and his government.[46] Far from being a royalist monolith, the Restoration stage was a site where the body politic could and was represented and debated. Furthermore, as Lacy's extemporising emphasises, the playtext did not necessarily equate to the play in performance, and the manner in which actors chose to deliver (or corrupt the delivery of) lines affected the nuances of the piece.

The politics of Restoration drama are therefore fragmented, but the interplay between past and present on the Restoration stage is also of note. In the commendatory poems to Edward Howard's unsuccessful play *The Six Day's Adventure or the New Utopia*, Aphra Behn and Edward Ravenscroft favourably compared Howard's work to Jonson's and Samuel Clyat envisioned a time when Howard would supplant Beaumont and Fletcher. Other writers were less complimentary and accused Howard of borrowing too heavily from James Shirley. What this demonstrates is how early modern drama circulated in textual form and informed the Restoration stage. Twenty years after the controversy that surrounded the performance of *The Change of Crowns*, Gerard Langbaine published

Momus Triumphans, or The Plagiaries of the London Stage. This catalogue, which lists all the plays in circulation and their putative sources, has been eruditely analysed by Paulina Kewes in her influential book about the development of notions of authorship, canonicity and plagiarism in the Restoration. Before Langbaine, Francis Kirkman printed an earlier catalogue in 1661. Instead of being concerned with shaming authors who borrowed from earlier works as a way of producing contemporary drama, Kirkman's catalogue lists alphabetically and by genre nearly seven hundred plays that were in circulation at the Restoration. While the catalogue is not always reliable in terms of genre and some plays have been entered into the catalogue twice under different titles, or have been attributed to different authors, Kirkman's catalogue offers a valuable means of reassessing how Restoration drama borrowed from earlier dramas and the volume of drama that was available. Within the marketplace, themes and plots flowed freely between the stage and the page and playwrights borrowed from earlier playwrights and continental writers as they wrote new dramas. Howard himself alludes to this in the preface to his play *The Womens Conquest* (published 1671). Here, he echoes other playwrights of the period in offering a discourse on the art of playwriting. Paying homage to Beaumont, Fletcher, Jonson and other great playwrights of the past, Howard claims they have influenced his work:

> having made my self so far a party on the side of our former Poets, that I have composed this Play in some resemblance to theirs of the like nature, which in my judgement I have esteemed best. I have given it the name likewise of Tragi-Comedy, as I find they have done some of theirs, which I need not particularize to the Reader, because they are well enough known to be at this day no inconsiderable ornament and entertainment to the Stage[47]

From this, we can draw some important conclusions. Earlier drama was known at the Restoration through the circulation of the playtext. This means that Howard does not need to pontificate over the generic conventions of tragicomedy as the reading public knows what to expect of the genre. Howard freely acknowledges that, in writing *The Womens Conquest*, he has appropriated tropes from earlier dramas, and it is evident that he borrows from Jacobean and Caroline tragicomedy in writing *The Change of Crownes*.

The title *The Change of Crownes* comes from the plot twist that allows the tragedy of the piece to be averted. The King of Naples has died, but his eldest daughter Ariana is (to borrow from Shirley's *The Imposture*) being 'nunnified'.[48] Although she has not completed the process of nunnification, her younger sister, Artemia, is crowned queen. Incensed, Ariana fails to persuade Artemia to abdicate and returns to her cell to bemoan her fate. Meanwhile, Guarini, a duke and cousin to the princesses, expects to marry Artemia and Malvecchio, the Machiavellian adviser, encourages the match as a way of furthering his personal schemes. Artemia spurns Guarini's advances in favour of a match with the King of Lombardy, but angers Alberto, King of Lombardy, by choosing to marry Leonidas instead. Leonidas is a courtier at Naples, and pretends to the Crown of Lombardy. Guarini decides to depose Artemia and instate Ariana as queen as revenge for his loss of honour; Alberto invades Naples to atone for his loss of honour and all looks as though it could end very badly for Artemia and Leonidas. When all appears lost, it is revealed that Leonidas is really Carolo, Alberto's older half-brother. Carolo's death was faked and he was smuggled out of Lombardy because his wicked stepmother had ambitions to set her own son upon the throne. Alberto, as a dutiful younger brother, relinquishes his claim to the Crown of Lombardy and claims Ariana (with whom he has fallen passionately in love) for his wife. Chastened by Alberto's example, Artemia relinquishes the Crown of Naples to Ariana. Guarini apologises to all for his violent tantrum, accepts Artemia's betrothal to Carolo, the crowns are exchanged and all live happily ever after. There are no direct sources for the play but, at times, the plot echoes many Jacobean and Caroline tragicomedies, including, but by no means limited to, Shakespeare's *Cymbeline*, Shirley's *The Doubtful Heir* and *The Imposture* and Beaumont and Fletcher's *A King and No King* (which went into six editions in the 1650s and was revived five times in the Restoration decade).[49] This suggests a complex interrelationship between early seventeenth century drama and the Restoration stage.

Print culture and canonicity at the Restoration seems to imply that pre-civil-war plays had been relegated or promoted to the environs of the library, to be revived on the stage as high art or discreetly forgotten. In reality, as the history of *The Change of Crownes* demonstrates, a more complex interplay between stage and page was in operation. Playwrights were keenly aware of the drama that was staged in the early seventeenth century, and some playwrights and actors worked on both the Restoration and the pre-Restoration stage. This awareness of earlier drama and its circulation within the marketplace means that the assumption that the Restoration stage was a royalist monolith requires reassessment. Only through this reappraisal can the complex interrelationship between past and present performances on the stage and on the page be understood.

Introduction

Although the history of *The Change of Crownes* and its relationship to earlier plays emphasises that drama did not end in 1642 to be revived in 1660, this book argues that the notion that all parliamentarians were against stage plays was fostered in the Restoration. These notions were married with representations of roundheads and cavaliers, which often mirrored the images presented by Colonel Blunt in the civil war re-enactment he presented to the people of Kent in May 1645. Often counter-factual, these representations gained greater cultural verification as the decades progressed. In this way, the printed plays, play pamphlets and antiparliamentarian tracts printed in the Restoration and during the civil war and commonwealth period added to the fabricated history regarding the cultural conditions of the mid-seventeenth century.

Through fiction, civil unrest can be reduced to a minor skirmish that can be easily stopped. Play pamphlets and plays on both the stage and the page recast the current moment, partly as a way to comment upon contemporary events and partly to rewrite the civil wars, regicide, commonwealth, protectorate and Restoration. As I have already noted, the late 1640s mark a shift in conceptions of government, and I will draw on a range of non-canonical sources to show how dramatists respond to these changes from 1647 until 1672.

Charles I and Oliver Cromwell feature heavily in these textual and dramatic reproductions, particularly in play pamphlets from the late 1640s and 1650s. Shortly after the passing of the second ordinance for theatre closure in November 1647, there was a proliferation of tracts that commented upon the civil wars. A series of satirical play pamphlets were printed in 1648 and, while some play pamphlets were produced before 1648, the pamphlet wars that directly coincided with the civil war had not fully embraced the potential of drama as a way to comment upon topical events and the recent past until this time. The few play pamphlets that were printed prior to the 1647 ordinance for theatre closure therefore represent a prehistory of the subgenre. Consequently, although I begin in 1647, I take this prehistory into account when considering drama and play pamphlets. My narrative ends in 1672 before the popish plot and exclusion crisis added different dramatic and political textures to notions of civil war, regicide and Restoration. However, as a coda, I consider some eighteenth-century plays that historicise the death of Charles and investigate how, post-1688, the regicide was remembered and reinvented in a way that acknowledges the deposition of James II.

The book is thus broadly arranged chronologically, signalling specific genres and specific issues that arise at particular moments in the period.

In Chapter 1, I examine how drama was enacted in textual form upon the paper stage. I will outline how the paper stage can be conceived as a platform from which writers appropriated pre-civil-war drama and used it to comment upon the current political moment and how the playtext functioned for a broadly theatre-literate public. In so doing, I will consider how the nascent public sphere was used as a way to respond to the civil war and I will interrogate some of the theories of public-making that have informed perceptions of the early modern period. The work of Habermas in particular has shaped and informed critical debate regarding the early modern public sphere, but he has not been without his critics. In offering a reappraisal of the Habermasian public sphere, I provide a more fluid model of public-making that will inform the analysis of the rest of the book. From examining the public sphere and how the paper stage is used to produce public space, I will then move on to discuss how drama operates and participates in the public sphere. Whereas Chapter 1 examines the construction of the paper stage and how the paper stage is used to enact political grievances, Chapter 2 will explore a selection of play pamphlets and how the paper stage was used to present images of Charles I and Oliver Cromwell. While the regicide silenced some of the criticism levied against Charles, Cromwell was increasingly portrayed as a cartoon Machiavellian: the saint and martyred king met his polar opposite in the portrayal of a demonic lord protector. As we shall see, Colonel Blunt was not the only parliamentarian to have used drama as a way of reflecting upon and responding to the distracted times; royalists also appropriated the form for political ends. I investigate this dynamic further to show that these play pamphlets are not uniform in their depictions of Charles or Cromwell, but share and modify modes of attack and defence on the page.

As I have already noted, the paper stage was not the only stage available to actors and writers during the commonwealth period. While Fraser witnessed plays at Bartholomew Fair, Davenant staged entertainments at the Cockpit theatre in Drury Lane. Davenant, a prominent writer and producer of court masques in the 1630s and 1640s, reinvented himself in the 1650s and again in 1660. At the Restoration, he was granted management of one of the two acting companies that were permitted to mount productions in London. As I argue in Chapter 3, in the 1650s Davenant had reinvented the Stuart court masque to make it fit for the protectorate stage.

Through his protectorate entertainments, *The Cruelty of the Spaniards in Peru* (1658) and *The History of Sir Francis Drake* (1659), Davenant celebrates Cromwellian foreign policy and provides a counter-narrative to the image of Cromwell as the scheming politician that is present in many contemporary play pamphlets. On the protectorate stage, Davenant's new-modelled masques show what can happen to the court masque when the monarch, so integral to the Stuart masque, is removed. I will also address the only known masque that may have been performed at what might be considered the commonwealth 'court': James Shirley's *Cupid and Death* (1653). By drawing on John Ogilby's royalist translation of Aesop's *Fables* (1651), Shirley writes a masque that is paradoxically ambivalent about kingship and mediates much of the royalist bias present in Ogilby's text. Through being performed in private for the Portuguese ambassador and by appropriating (and neutralising) a royalist text, Shirley's masque marks a transition between the private court masques of the early Stuart period and Davenant's protectorate masques.

These different forms of drama demonstrate that responses to the political moment were diverse. Davenant's first protectorate entertainment, *The Siege of Rhodes* (1656 and 1663), was revised at the Restoration as a heroic drama, which emphasises that there was a belief that the drama needed modification to make it suitable for the changing times. In Chapter 4, I turn to examine how the text was made fit for a Restoration audience. In this chapter, I also address John Dryden's epic ten-act *The Conquest of Granada* (1670 and 1671) to see how early Restoration heroic dramas comprehended the previous twenty years and appropriated and reworked ideas of kingship that had circulated on both the paper and the real stages during the commonwealth. By relocating war and usurpation to another land, these plays endeavour to create a neutral territory through which to question notions of sovereignty. A response to *The Conquest of Granada*, but also to the brief fashion for heroic drama, the Duke of Buckingham's *The Rehearsal*, which was first performed in 1672, will also be discussed. Buckingham's burlesque of the heroic genre brings questions of governance back to England through figuring the trials and tribulations of the two kings of Brentford. Buckingham's play also has a metatheatrical concern with drama and calls for heroic drama to be consigned to oblivion so that better-quality plays may be produced. These restored plays will, for Buckingham, absorb the plotting believed to be endemic in the body politic and contain it on the stage. Buckingham may argue that the destabilising factors present in the body politic ought to be consigned to drama, but Restoration drama frequently returns to, and reinvents, these notions. In my final chapter, I examine some early Restoration comedy and how these plays rewrote the civil wars and addressed ideas of panegyric and the rhetoric of praise. Through dramatising the eve of Restoration, John Tatham's *The Rump* (c. 1660) directly engages with contemporary concerns, while Robert Howard's *The Commitee* (1663), and John Lacy's *The Old Troop* (1664) return to the civil war as their temporal location to question roundhead and cavalier virtues and vices. Blunt's 1645 civil war re-enactment is replaced at the Restoration by plays that recast the civil war in comic mode.

Far from disappearing during the civil wars, drama, both written and staged, was a medium through which civil war, regicide, commonwealth, protectorate and Restoration were debated. For Colonel Blunt, drama served as a way to prevent the people of Kent from partaking in May Day revelry in the 1640s; in addition, Davenant adopted dramatic forms to celebrate protectorate foreign policy in the 1650s. Furthermore, later playwrights wrote new plays that reimagined the civil war and discussed ideas of kingship in the 1660s and early 1670s. In print, plays on the paper stage also offered a way of reflecting upon the current moment. This was achieved by printing older plays that contained politically charged, topical, prefaces. Dramatic conventions were also grafted on to the pamphlet form as a way of responding to events of the 1640s and 1650s. Whilst writers at the Restoration were aware of the Restoration's function as a political demarcation and its place in literary history, writers during the civil war and commonwealth were also creating their own accounts of the period. Through the intertextual modification and adaptation of tropes, dramatists created, consolidated and ultimately destabilised their own endeavours to present a unified cultural and political response to recent history.

Notes

1 [John Saltmarsh and Henry Ironmonger Walker, (eds)], *The 20th. Weeke. Perfect Occurrences of Parliament And Chief Collections of Letters from the Armie* (London, 1645), sig. V1r (Friday 9 May 1645). For an alternative reading of this pamphlet, see Jerome de Groot, '"Welcome to Babylon" performing and screening the English revolution', in Mark Thornton Burnett and Adrian Streete (eds), *Filming and Performing Renaissance History* (Basingstoke: Palgrave Macmillan, 2011), pp. 65–82.
2 *The 20th Weeke*, sigs V1r–V1v.
3 David Cressy, 'Remembrancers of the revolution: histories and historiographies of the 1640s', in Paulina Kewes (ed.), *The Uses of History in Early Modern England* (San Marino: Huntington Library, 2006), pp. 253–64 (p. 254).

Introduction 21

4 See Epilogue.
5 Leah S. Marcus, *The Politics of Mirth: Jonson, Herrick, Marvell and the Defense of Old Holiday Pastimes* (Chicago and London: University of Chicago Press, 1986), pp. 151–2.
6 Janet Clare, *Drama of the English Republic: 1649–1660* (Manchester: Manchester University Press, 2002); Susan Wiseman, *Drama and Politics in the English Civil War* (Cambridge: Cambridge University Press, 1998); David Scott Kastan, 'Performances and playbooks: the closing of the theatres and the politics of drama', in Kevin Sharpe and Steven N. Zwicker (eds), *Reading, Society and Politics in Early Modern England* (Cambridge: Cambridge University Press, 2003), pp. 167–84.
7 Joad Raymond, *The Invention of the Newspaper: English Newsbooks 1641–1649* (Oxford: Clarendon Press, 1996); Raymond (ed.), *News, Newspapers and Society in Early Modern Britain* (London: Frank Cass Publishers, 1999); Nigel Smith, *Literature and Revolution in England 1640–1660* (New Haven and London: Yale University Press, 1994); Marcus Nevitt, *Women and the Pamphlet Culture of Revolutionary England, 1640–1660* (Aldershot: Ashgate, 2006).
8 John Kerrigan, *Archipelagic English: Literature, History and Politics, 1603–1707* (Cambridge: Cambridge University Press, 2008), maps New British History's three kingdom narrative on to literature of the period; Austin Woolrych, *Britain in Revolution, 1625–1660* (Oxford: Oxford University Press, 2002), and Trevor Royle, *Civil War: The Wars of the Three Kingdoms, 1638–1660* (London: Abacus, 2005), offer three-kingdom narratives relating to the civil war, commonwealth and Restoration. Conversely, John Adamson, *The Noble Revolt: The Overthrow of Charles I* (London: Weidenfeld and Nicolson, 2007), examines the period from 1640 until 1642 to argue that aristocratic discontent brought about the civil war.
9 John H. Astington, *English Court Theatre, 1558–1642* (Cambridge: Cambridge University Press, 1999); Clare McManus, *Women on the Renaissance Stage: Anna of Denmark and Female Masquing Culture in the Stuart Court (1590–1619)* (Manchester: Manchester University Press, 2002); Karen Britland, *Drama at the Courts of Queen Henrietta Maria* (Cambridge: Cambridge University Press, 2006); R. Malcolm Smuts, *Court Culture and the Origins of a Royalist Tradition in Early Stuart England* (Pennsylvania: University of Philadelphia Press, 1987); Andrew McRae, *Literature, Satire and the Early Stuart State* (Cambridge: Cambridge University Press, 2004).
10 Tim Harris, *Restoration: Charles II and His Kingdom* (London: Allen Lane, 2005); Laura Lunger Knoppers, *Constructing Cromwell: Ceremony, Portrait and Print, 1645–1661* (Cambridge: Cambridge University Press, 2000); Jonathan

Scott, *Commonwealth Principles: Republican Writing of the English Revolution* (Cambridge: Cambridge University Press, 2004); David Norbrook, *Writing the English Republic: Poetry, Rhetoric and Politics* (Cambridge: Cambridge University Press, 1999); Blair Worden, *Roundhead Reputations: The English Civil Wars and the Passions of Posterity* (London: Penguin, 2001).

11 N. W. Bawcutt, ed., *The Control and Censorship of Caroline Drama: The Records of Sir Henry Herbert, Master of the Revels, 1623–73* (Oxford: Oxford University Press, 1996), p. 72.

12 See Stephen Orgel, *The Illusion of Power: Political Theatre in the English Renaissance* (Berkeley: University of California Press, 1975).

13 Wiseman, *Politics*, p. xvii.

14 See, for example, *The Weekly Account: Number 5, October 4 1643* (London, 1643), sig. A4v (Monday).

15 *The Weekly Account*, sig. A4r.

16 *A Declaration of the Lords and Commons Assembled in Parliament, for the Appeasing and Quietting of all Unlawfull Tumults and Insurrections ... Also an Ordinance of Both Houses, for the Suppressing of Stage-Playes. Ordered by the Lords and Commons* (London, 1642), sigs A4r–A4v.

17 Andrew Gurr, *The Shakespearian Stage 1574–1642*, 3rd edn (Cambridge: Cambridge University Press, 1992), pp. 77–8.

18 For recent studies into the build up to (and aftermath of) the regicide, and reactions to civil war in the three kingdoms, see Woolrych, *Britain in Revolution*, and Royle, *Civil War*.

19 Percy A. Scholes, *The Puritans and Music in England and New England: A Contribution to the Cultural History of Two Nations* (Oxford: Oxford University Press, 1934), pp. 137–49. For details of Marvell's songs, see Nigel Smith, *Andrew Marvell: The Chameleon* (New Haven and London: Yale University Press, 2010), pp. 141–4.

20 See, for example, John Northbrook, *Spiritus est Vicarius Christi in Terra.* (London, 1577); Stephen Gosson, *The Schoole of Abuse* (London, 1579); John Rainolds, *Th'Overthrow of Stage-Playes, by the Way of Controversie betwixt D. Gager and D. Rainoldes* (1599).

21 William Prynne, *Histrio-mastix* (London, 1633), Facsimile edn, with a preface by Arthur Freeman (New York and London: Garland, 1974), p. 214.

22 Martin Butler, *Theatre and Crisis, 1632–1642* (Cambridge: Cambridge University Press, 1984), p. 84.

23 *The History of the Grand Rebellion*, 3 vols (London, 1713), II:209.

24 Margot Heinemann, *Puritanism and Theatre: Thomas Middleton and Opposition Drama Under the Early Stuarts* (Cambridge: Cambridge University Press, 1980), esp. pp. 200–57.

25 *An Ordinance of the Lords and Commons Assembled in Parliament, for the Utter Suppression and Abolishing of all Stage-Playes and Interludes. ... Die Veneris 11 Februarii 1647* (London, 1648), sig. A3r.
26 *An Ordinance*, sig. A3v.
27 Leslie Hotson, *The Commonwealth and Restoration Stage* (Cambridge, MA: Harvard University Press, 1928), esp. pp. 35–59.
28 James Fraser, *Triennial Travels*, 2 vols (University of Aberdeen MS 2538/1), I: fol. 37v.
29 *The Actors Remonstrance* (London, 1643 [1644]).
30 Steven N. Zwicker, 'Is There Such a Thing as Restoration Literature?', *Huntington Library Quarterly*, 69 (2006), pp. 425–49 (pp. 425–7).
31 See in particular, Nancy Klein Maguie, *Regicide and Restoration* (Cambridge: Cambridge University Press, 1992).
32 Edward Howard, *The Change of Crownes* (1667). Folger MS Add 948/V.b. 329, fol. 34r.
33 Robert Latham and William Matthews, eds, *The Diary of Samuel Pepys*, 11 vols (London: Harper Collins, 1995), 8:167–8 (15 April 1667).
34 Latham and Matthews, *Diary of Samuel Pepys*, 8:168–9 (16 April 1557).
35 Latham and Matthews, *Diary of Samuel Pepys*, 8:172–3 (20 April 1667).
36 *Diary, Chiefly of Public Events, by Joseph Williamson, from 4 March to 11 December 1668, full and important; containing many items of Court and Parliamentary news*, 22 April 1667. PRO, SP 29/231, fol. 14v.
37 Thomas O'Malley, 'Religion and the newspaper press, 1660–1685: a study of the *London Gazette*', in Michael Harris and Alan J. Lee (eds), *The Press in English Society from the Seventeenth to Nineteenth Centuries* (London: Associated University Presses, 1986), pp. 25–46 (p. 30); Alan Marshall, 'Williamson, Sir Joseph (1633–1701)', *Oxford Dictionary of National Biography*, Oxford University Press, 2004; online edn, Jan 2008 www.oxforddnb.com/view/article/29571 (accessed 9 March 2011).
38 John Loftis, ed., *The Revels History of Drama in English*, 8 vols (London: Methuen, 1976), 5:26–8; Hotson, *Commonwealth and Restoration Stage*, pp. 197–204.
39 Thomas Middleton, *A Game at Chess*, ed. T. H. Howard-Hill (Manchester: Manchester University Press, 1993), pp. 17–23.
40 Edward Howard, *The Change of Crownes*, ed. Frederick S. Boas (London: Oxford University Press, 1949), p. 5.
41 Joseph F. Stephenson, 'On the markings in the manuscript of *Sir John Van Olden Barnavelt*', *Notes and Queries*, 53 (2006), 522–4 (522).
42 Gijs Rommelse, *The Second Anglo-Dutch War (1665–1667): Raison d'état, Mercantilism and Maritime Strife* (Hilversum: Uitgeverij Verloren, 2006), chapter 7.

43 Steven C. A. Pincus, *Protestantism and Patriotism: Ideologies and the Making of English Foreign Policy, 1650–1668* (Cambridge: Cambridge University Press, 1996), pp. 363–5.
44 Maguire, *Regicide*, p. 3.
45 Robert Latham and William Matthews (eds), *The Diary of Samuel Pepys*, 11 vols (London: Harper Collins, 1995), 9:381 (2 December 1668).
46 Jason McElligott, *Royalism, Print and Censorship in Revolutionary England* (Woodbridge: Boydell and Brewer, 2007), chapter 5.
47 Edward Howard, Preface to *The Womens Conquest* (London, 1671), sig. A3v.
48 James Shirley, *The Imposture*, in *Six New Playes* (London, 1653), sig. B6r.
49 Maguire, *Regicide*, p. 58.

1

The paper stage

This chapter seeks to modify existing models of the relation between print and an emergent public sphere by considering the special case of drama printed between 1647 and 1660. Jürgen Habermas's notion of the emergence of a unified bourgeois public sphere, where people come together to critically share ideas and knowledge in spaces that are not governed by pressures from social or political authority, has inspired many scholars.[1] Habermas locates the development of the public sphere in the coffee houses of late seventeenth-century London and the salons of eighteenth-century France, but, as Brian Cowen notes, 'recent scholarship has ... relentlessly sought to push back the point at which one can trace the emergence of a distinct sort of "public sphere"'.[2] Scholars have demonstrated the importance of Habermas's ideas when considering textual transmission in the mid-seventeenth century.[3] Despite this influence, Habermas has not been without his critics. While historians have questioned Habermas's lack of attention to historical detail, other commentators have voiced dissatisfaction with the very notion of the unified public sphere.[4] These criticisms do not so much negate Habermas's theories and the application of these ideas to seventeenth-century literary history and culture; rather they emphasise that debates regarding the public sphere are ongoing as critics endeavour to define what it might embody.

The printing of drama occupies an ambiguous space within these discourses. For Habermas, public-making comes late to the theatre and only as a consequence of shifting cultural attitudes in the eighteenth century. By examining the material text as a performative mode, I will show that the political conditions of the mid-seventeenth century meant that drama played an active and tangible part in the public sphere. Precisely because the playhouses were closed, drama became important to the ways in which publics were conceived.

In her seminal study of pamphlet culture in early modern England, Alexandra Halasz pushes for the primacy of pamphlets and commerce in contributing to the emergence of the public sphere. Drawing from Habermas's assumption that the early modern playhouse did not have a place in the formation of the public sphere, Halasz argues that enacted drama assumes a role in the marketplace different from that of the more concrete presence of the printed playtext.[5] While this argument is insightful in terms of locating the place and function of print within the marketplace and the emerging public sphere, the removal of plays from playhouses poses further questions regarding oral and literate cultures. As Steven Mullaney argues, the reading of the printed text can be as much an event as the watching of a play. While they may be two very different experiences, the reader or author engages with the text or performance for a fixed period of time. Memory, whether of the performed drama or of reading the text, renders both experiences fixed in time and space, and privileging one over the other fails to account for the fluid interplay between oral/aural and literate cultures.[6]

Publishing and performing text is a way to publicly disseminate ideas and contribute to debate. The printing of newsbooks demonstrates the importance of print during the civil war. Precursors to the modern newspaper, newsbooks were initially published sporadically, with the more successful newsbooks later printed on a weekly basis. The booklets comprised eight to sixteen pages and detailed the weekly news. During the civil war they generally detailed military campaigns and political events. They circulated widely, though news would often be old by the time it reached the provinces. Between 1640 and 1660, the London bookseller George Thomason collected over seven thousand newsbooks, which testifies to the volume of newsbooks that were printed in the period. Some were printed at parliamentary command and others were printed with the endorsement of the Crown as each side sought to win the war of words as well as the physical war. Some newsbooks were printed without the consent of parliament or the monarch, but all combined proto-journalism with rumour and political bias.[7]

With the abolition of the Star Chamber in 1641, official endeavours to contain printing broke down. The pressures of the political and commercial moment meant that censorship became fractured. The Stationers' Register was the primary means through which ownership of copy was asserted, regulated and controlled. The Stationers' Company's charter permitted it to refuse the publication of unlicensed books and to seize illicit copy. Ironically, the Stationers' Register, the means through which control of copy could be asserted, can also become a means of testifying to the effectiveness of print in the public sphere; its endeavour to index licit copy points to the efficiency of publishing as a way to circulate ideas. Newsbooks and other forms of pamphleteering undermined regulatory authorities, but drama could also be appropriated as a form of textual protest.

While Habermas may question the place of the early modern theatre in the bourgeois public sphere, the printed play – and performed drama – was used to produce a space for public debate. The play pamphlet in particular became an important vehicle through which to voice discontent with the political order. Play pamphlets draw from newsbooks in their topicality and brevity, but they also appropriate the format of the playtext.

Although some playhouses intermittently functioned in the 1640s and 1650s, there is little evidence to suggest that play pamphlets were performed. Part newsbook, part play, this satirical form arose from the political and cultural moment of the civil wars.[8] The layout of some of these play pamphlets has some affinity with dialogues (a textual mode that has no connection with the stage), while other play pamphlets contain stage directions and woodcuts that provide a visual image to accompany the textual narrative. Through these additions, some play pamphlets experimented with the visual, aural and oral possibilities of their composition. The prologue to *The Second Part of Crafty Cromwell* (1648) ends with this quatrain:

> Here [sic] then with Candar; but be rul'd by me,
> Speake not a worde, what er'e you heare or see.
> For this Auther, bid me to you say,
> Heed live, to see this plaid another day.[9]

The author desires to see the play pamphlet performed another day, which suggests that it cannot be performed yet, but can be visualised in print upon the paper stage.[10] The reference to hearing the text could allude to its being read aloud, which Adam Fox believes to be the most common way of reading in the early modern period.[11] Pamphlets operated in a way similar to ballads, circulating at the margins of print and oral culture, and were read and disseminated among the literate and the illiterate alike.[12] The reference to the oral potential of the play pamphlet could therefore allude to the cross-fertilisation of drama and pamphlet culture.

Through the publication of playtexts, drama continued to circulate and be received by audiences through the construction of paper stages.

Performing plays may have been banned by statute, but the printing of plays proliferated in the 1640s and 1650s.[13] As we will see, the textual transmission of drama during the mid-seventeenth century was fluid and the paper stage was a far-from-coherent public space.

This textual theatrical space meant that drama was perpetuated in print, and it provided a literalisation of Thomas Nashe's presentation of the relation between page and stage. In his prefatory matter to the 1591 edition of Philip Sidney's *Astrophil and Stella*, Nashe writes of the poem as a 'paper stage,' inviting the reader to cast his or her 'curious eyes, while the tragicommody of love is performed by starlight'.[14] Describing 'dusky robes, dipt in the ynke of teares',[15] Nashe shifts between imagery that alludes to the stage and metaphors that invoke the page, a technique that presents Sidney's poem as functioning at the borders of dramatic and literary culture. Nashe follows the lead of Sidney's rhetoric to cast the reader as spectator on the starlit scene. Astrophil ('star lover') gazes upon Stella ('star') and the reader surveys the entire scene. The drama is punctuated by textual tears of ink. The material text conjoins with performativity and the reader becomes an audience to the drama that is staged in ink. By focusing upon the theatrical experience of reading, Nashe turns the page into a stage and the reader into an audience.

For Heinrich Plett, Nashe's portrayal of the paper stage presents early modern print culture as damaging the oral culture that preceded it. In his reading, print culture lacks some of the energy present in visual, theatrical representation and, to compensate, frontispieces and title pages from the early modern period sometimes contain elaborate pictorial representations that 'speak to the eye'. Combined with rhetorical poetics, pictorial images provide a way for the non-dramatic text to show dramatic action.[16] The metaphorical interchange of page and stage in mid-seventeenth-century drama becomes literal. The materiality of the paper stage combines with the narratives that it presents to its readers; the paper stage is transformed into an abstract public space where social and political concerns may be articulated and fictionalised. Through the various printing strategies detailed below, some printed plays and a vast majority of play pamphlets in the mid-seventeenth century presented themselves as paper stages that offered textual and pictorial representations of the civil war. Rather than marking the destruction of oral culture and, by extension, dramatic representation, the paper stage offers a place where drama may be silently vocalised. Readers are presented with a different mode of performance in which woodcuts provide the visual representations that were previously enacted upon the stage. The paper stage thus becomes an arena that simultaneously allows dramatic representation to hibernate until it can be reawakened in performative form and offers a platform where drama is staged in print.

Viewing the paper stage

The paper stage was used to perform drama metaphorically, but many plays were also printed for the first time from the 1640s. Included among these newly printed plays is the first folio of Beaumont and Fletcher's comedies and tragedies, which was printed for Humphrey Robinson and Humphrey Moseley in 1647. During the civil wars, Moseley appears to have specialised in printing royalist propaganda and preserving royalist texts.[17] The prefatory poems to the Beaumont and Fletcher folio read as though they pay homage to cavalier culture, with contributions from, among others, John Birkenhead, the editor of *Mercurius Aulicus* (the official royalist newsbook); Roger L'Estrange, the future Restoration censor; and cavalier poets such as Robert Herrick and Richard Lovelace.[18] Moseley had published some texts with Henry Herringman, who, after Moseley's death in 1661, purchased from his estate the copyright to some of Moseley's texts.[19] Unlike Moseley, Herringman does not seem to have focused upon printing royalist texts and was indeed responsible for the printing of the entertainments that were produced by William Davenant during the protectorate.[20] Moseley's and Herringman's printing presses therefore become the site of the printing of plays old and new. Despite the influence of ambiguous politics on printing, their efforts demonstrate how the practical considerations of material transmission directly affected production.

As Zachary Lesser has noted, not all publishers had a propagandist agenda.[21] The case of Herringman emphasises this, and in so doing highlights that the paper stage can be mercantile as well as political. Although Herringman reproduced the paratexts from Moseley's edition of Beaumont and Fletcher's works when he brought out a second folio in 1679 and, in the Restoration, had close connections with John Dryden (the poet laureate), political ideologies do not seem to have motivated Herringman's business decisions.[22] In the 1650s, Herringman printed dramas that celebrated Cromwellian foreign policy. At this time, he also printed texts by royalists.

However, the very act of printing drama can become a political action, despite appearances to the contrary. Herringman's apparent political apathy is mirrored by some other publishers, where prefatory letters present the printing of an old playtext as a form of social anthropology. The fifth impression of Beaumont and Fletcher's *Philaster*, printed in 1654 by William Leake, begins with a letter that plays with visual, oral and textual forms:

> This Play so affectionately taken, and approved by the seeing Auditors, or Hearing Spectators (of which sort I take or conceive you to be the greatest part) hath received (as appears by the copious vent of four Editions[)], no lesse acceptance with improvement of you likewise the Readers, albeit the first Impression swarm'd with errours, proving it selfe, like pure Gold, which the more it hath been tryed and refined, the better is esteemed; the best poems of this kind in the first presentation, resembling that all tempting Minerall newly digged up, the Actors being onely the labouring Miners, but you the skilfull Triers and Refiners: Now consider how currant this hath passed, under the infallible stampe of your judicious censure, and applause, and (like a gainfull Office in this age) eagerly sought for, not onely by those that have seen it, but by others that have merely heard thereof.[23]

The letter assumes that the play has gone into multiple editions precisely because it was well received in performance. Seeking to gain financial benefit from a past theatrical experience, the printed text is presented as a nostalgic memento of bygone performances, and thereby becomes an implicit critique of the policy to close the playhouses as it reminds the reading public that (by law) playgoing is no longer permitted. The circulation of four editions among the reading public does not supersede the staged event, but instead emphasises the fluidity of movement between the stage and the page and the expectations Leake has regarding the reception of the drama by the readers. Leake asserts that the play was well received in performance and conceives that an appreciative audience would wish to purchase a copy of the play. The play is refined through going into multiple editions; it is presented to new and future audiences who have the gift of appraising its artistic merit and create their own individual performances through reading the play. By invoking an imagined rather than a real performance, the printer uses the paper stage as a way to entertain the reading public, but also as a way to keep drama circulating. The ordinance for theatre closure means that staging drama on the page becomes a political act. Not only does this present a causal connection between the stage and the page, it also harnesses the paper stage as a space of indeterminate location at the margins of textual, visual and oral cultures.

Whereas Leake suggests that printed drama is a type of entertainment that reimagines that public space of performance, other plays invoke the

The paper stage 31

paper stage in more concrete ways to project dissatisfaction with the ordinance for theatre closure. A number of plays printed in the 1640s and 1650s are prefaced with lamentations regarding the state of the playhouse and provide a platform for public debate regarding the political moment. Aston Cokaine's prefatory poem to a collection of Caroline plays penned by Richard Brome and first printed in 1653 typifies these complaints:

> Then we shall still have *Playes*! and though we may
> Not them in their full Glories yet display;
> Yet we may please our selves by reading them,
> Till a more Noble Act this Act condemne.
> Happy will that day be, which will advance
> This Land from durt of precise Ignorance;
> ...
> Then the dull *Zelots*, shall give way, and flye,
> Or be converted by bright Poesie.
> *Apollo* may enlighten them, or else
> In *Scottish Grots* they may conceale themselves.[24]

For Cokaine, the paper stage is the temporary location for drama. Plays can be read until a time when they are permitted to be performed. The authority of the ordinance for theatre closure is upheld within the playtext, even if it was not enforced in the kingdom. Monarchy and the playhouse become implicitly connected as the poem looks to a future where Scottish covenanters (perceived as zealously opposed to drama) return from whence they came and the ordinance for theatre closure is repealed.

This engagement with print culture in the mid-seventeenth century creates the illusion of a unified space of opposition to parliamentarian intervention in the performance of drama. However, this unified public space was populated by multiple voices. As I have been arguing, when playtexts are printed with prefatory material, these paratexts operate in different ways. In the case of Moseley's edition of the Beaumont and Fletcher folio, the dedicatory verses point to an ambiguous cavalier culture through the texts being penned by prominent royalists; Leake's publications look to the profitability of printing plays, and Cokain laments the passing of the playhouse and celebrates the rise of the paper stage as a way for drama to continue. Other playtexts take on a more archaeological form, as is illustrated by a 1652 edition of John Ford's plays, printed under the collective title of *Comedies, Tragi-Comedies and Tragaedies*. In this volume, the reprint of *The Lovers Melancholy* is reproduced with the original title page, complete with the 1629 date of publication. The original letter to the reader and commendatory verses are also reproduced.[25] Although a copy of an older, unsold edition may simply have been bound up with more recently printed material as a way to make it saleable, it is presented to the reading public as a new edition. Here, the paper stage is used to document a past textual event. Whereas other textual productions flirt with performance to produce a new form of textual space for public debate, the Ford edition does not engage in civil war discourse. Instead it invokes performance by retaining the play in its temporal moment: representational absence becomes a form of presence, which only emphasises that the playhouses were closed. Publishers therefore appropriated the paper stage for different reasons, making it a space of multiple discourses.

What this emphasises is that the Habermasian notion of private people coming together and creating a unified space for rational public debate does not explain fully the ways in which the public sphere is formed. Habermas argues that the turn of the eighteenth century marks a change in the way in which individuals engaged with political discourse. Superseding a passive engagement with authority, people were now 'endeavouring to influence the decisions of state authority … [by appealing] to the critical public in order to legitimate demands'.[26] While the paper stage does create a space from which to engage with the critical public, this space is fictional, and, rather than legitimating demands, presents an image of culture and counter-culture. In so doing, writers construct enduring images of royalists and parliamentarians. These made-up publics emphasise the importance of storytelling and narrative when projecting ideas into the public sphere.

Storytelling is important to Hannah Arendt's theories of public-making and this is partly due to her notions of plurality. Arendt argues that the public realm is always political. Action within this politicised realm is important to her notions of identity. Arendt stresses that action requires freedom, or natality (the capacity to begin) and plurality. 'Plurality', Arendt writes, 'is the condition of human action because we are all the same, that is, human, in such a way that nobody is ever the same as anyone else who ever lived, lives, or will live'.[27] Because humans have individual identities, plurality is essential to the human condition: multiple perceptions and interpretations bind but also divide discourses in the public realm. For Arendt, the very word 'public' has a plural meaning: it signifies the world, but also the fact that all things that appear in public can be seen, heard and experienced by a multitude.[28] By bringing experiences into the public realm they are deprivatised and take on a collective meaning:

The paper stage 33

> The most current of such transformation occurs in storytelling and generally in artistic transposition of individual experiences. But we do not need the form of the artist to witness this transfiguration. Each time we talk about things that can be experienced only in privacy or intimacy, we bring them out into a sphere where they will assume a kind of reality which, their intensity notwithstanding, they could never have had before. The presence of others who see what we see and hear what we hear assures us of the reality of the world and ourselves[29]

Publics are located in shared sensory experience, and more importantly in language and the communication of experience. Storytelling, in particular, deindividualises experience, allowing it to assume an appearance in the public realm. While artistic creativity is a prime means of storytelling, any kind of relation is a form of storytelling. Through storytelling, fiction and politics conjoin. The printing of playtexts in the 1640s and 1650s established a platform through which experience (whether fictional or real) could be made public.

The playtext thus produced an unfixed public space, but play pamphlets emphatically entered civil war discourse. These play pamphlets extend the paper stage and use it as a platform through which to dramatise grievances. In so doing, play pamphlets often construct enduring (yet reductive) images and frequently project a fictional rendering of prominent political figures. In particular, the paper stage was deployed to produce impressions of Charles I and Oliver Cromwell that habitually made assumptions about private motives within the public realm.[30] While the regicide proved redemptive for Charles's public image, Cromwell was increasingly portrayed as a scheming Marchiavellian by royalists and radical republicans alike: the saint and martyred king met his polar opposite in the portrayal of a demonic lord protector. In *The Picture of a New Courtier* (1656), a supporter of 'the good old cause' (the ideal of universal suffrage in a republic) used the paper stage to attack Cromwell. We are presented with a dialogue between Mr Plain-heart and Mr Timeserver. Lamenting Cromwell's behaviour, Plain-heart lists the misdemeanours he perceives the Lord Protector to have committed since assuming office:

> First, his imprisoning of men contrary to law, at his own will and pleasure; ... Secondly, the King assumed a power to levy money upon the people without their consent in Parliament, and in this *Cromwell* is not wanting; for where the King raised a shilling without consent in Parliament, he raiseth ten to maintain himself and family ... Thirdly, The King dissolved but two

Parliaments in 20 years, but this strange Monster have destroyed 3 in lesse than 3 years ... Fourthly, The King sent out Fleets and Armies, with out consent in Parliament ... for all which he was judged an Offender, and lost his head as a Traytor to the Commonwealth: but in this, O.P [Oliver Protector] is not behinde his Predecessor (except in the punishment) ... Fiftly, The king stoped the free course of Law, that so his tyranny and Oppression might be the better hid from the eyes of men; and in this O.P hath kept pace with the King.[31]

Plain-heart presents a vision of a tyrant. Cromwell has succeeded in oppressing the nation to a greater degree than his monarchical predecessor. *The Picture of a New Courtier* creates an image of Cromwell where his plans for personal aggrandisement can only lead to national destruction. The reality of the climate of 1656 suggests that Cromwell did adopt some oppressive measures to maintain political stability; however, he also implemented some tolerant legislation and followed a fairly shrewd foreign policy. While the initial warring with England's old enemy Spain (which is alluded to in the fourth charge Plain-heart levies against Cromwell) was ill-advised, Cromwellian policy proved effective in other areas.[32] The play pamphlet inverts panegyric to produce a negative image of a tyrant who usurped parliamentarian or republican rule.

It is not just Cromwell who is attacked in *The Picture of a New Courtier*. Epitomising all that is bad about contemporary courtiers, Timeserver becomes the eponymous anti-hero of the piece. His 'manner [is] to be for anything that is profitable, although its contrary to equity and justice' (sig. B2v). Such representations echo pre-civil-war condemnations of the court favourite and, in being complicit in Cromwell's actions, the many timeservers whom Timeserver represents become the real villains of the piece. When considering his actions, Timeserver fears his fate:

Oh what will become of this courtly brood, when a Common-wealth will be in fashion? and a Parliament to call our actions into question? ... Oh misery to think! And grief to consider our condition: the earth will shake at the sound of our fall, and few will bewaile our sad disaster. (sig. D1v)

This republican imagines a future where all is resolved. However, unlike royalist play pamphlets that imagine a future where the Stuart line is reinstated, we are presented not with a wish for restored monarchical order but with a desire to establish republican rule. An apocalyptic future is foretold, where those who favoured personal gain above the interests of the republic will meet their final judgement.

Royalists also appropriated this type of literary presentation for political ends. For Laura Lunger Knoppers, these pamphlets are the ideal way through which to gain in print the victory over Cromwell that his detractors failed to achieve in reality, while simultaneously contributing to republicanism by creating popular images of Cromwell.[33] Through appropriating drama to produce fictionalised versions of Cromwell, Charles and other prominent mid-seventeenth-century figures in print, the authors of play pamphlets were emphatically entering into political discourse and offering a commentary upon the civil war period. Arendt argues that the public realm is a place where the individual can develop, but this appearance in the public realm is complicated by other-perception: 'The disclosure of "who" in contradistinction to "what" somebody is ... is implicit in everything somebody says and does ... it is more than likely that the "who", which appears so clearly and unmistakably to others, remains hidden from the person himself.'[34] Self-reflection and self-presentation become clouded by the reinterpretation and re-presentation of public figures within the public sphere. By fictionalising prominent mid-seventeenth-century individuals, the paper stage provides alternative narratives of their actions within the public realm. This establishes a complex discourse between self-perception, other-perception and the lack of control an individual has over the perception of their identity once they have been made public.

This sense of the deprivatisation of individuals within the public realm is emphasised in the publication of *Eikon Basilike* (1649). This text was published soon after the execution of Charles I, and was presented to its reading public as the private reflections of a suffering king who is martyred for the sake of his people. It went into multiple editions and achieves the impression of making private meditations public partly by drawing from piety tracts to present a subjective monarch, but also by presenting (in some editions) a frontispiece that shows Charles relinquishing his earthly crown for a heavenly one. Even texts such are these are not immune to the instability of text, context and individual interpretation. John Milton famously attacked the frontispiece to *Eikon Basilike* as being 'drawn out in the full measure of a Masking Scene, and sett there to catch fools and silly gazers'.[35] Milton's criticism of *Eikon Basilike* has been afforded much critical attention, and David Loewenstein tellingly highlights the way in which Milton attempts to negate the sense of the text's function as a private meditation by aligning the frontispiece with public performativity.[36] While *Eikon Basilike* was presented to its reading public as the private meditations of the decapitated king, the very act of printing undermines this subjectivity and deprivatises the act of meditation. Every form of public representation thus becomes an act of misrepresentation. When considering *Eikon Basilike*, this tension becomes more fraught as its authorship was continuously disputed and discredited from its moment of publication.[37] The public sphere becomes not just the site of the development of the individual but also the place where the individual may be debated and reinterpreted.

Play pamphlets, like devotional tracts, presented textual representations of individuals, but the performativity of drama means that the textual representations are enacted differently. Milton's critique of *Eikon Basilike* seeks to translate it into a performance precisely because drama has different resonances in the public realm. However, it also demonstrates fluidity in ways of perceiving generic constructs. This fluidity means that play pamphlets could be used to produce counter-images to official proclamations, declarations and meditations. Some play pamphlets also have an interest in theatrical culture and the playhouse, which emphasises how the ordinances for theatre closure blurred the distinction between politics and drama to an extent that was unprecedented. The oral potential of the play pamphlet could therefore allude to the cross-fertilisation of drama and pamphlet culture. Indeed, the *Actors Remonstrance* (1644) laments that some of the 'ablest ordinarie Poets, instead of their annuall stipends and beneficiall second-dayes, [are] being for mere necessitie compelled to get a living by writing contemptible penny-pamphlets'.[38] Not only did the textual production of the pamphlet form merge with that of the playtext, but theatre closure necessitated that playwrights became pamphleteers.

As I noted in my Introduction, the ordinances for theatre closure passed by parliament meant that royalists could appropriate the idea of the theatre to their cause. The play pamphlet therefore became an important vehicle through which to voice discontent with the political order and, as Susan Wiseman observes, one play pamphlet consciously references the purchasing of pamphlets and newsbooks by countrymen to 'make themselves merry at home'.[39] Formal performances of the play pamphlets might not have happened, but news was circulated and dramatic conventions were utilised in the dissemination of news.

In being printed, play pamphlets reached audiences who were familiar with drama: the readers understood the conventions of a play and could therefore respond to the images the play pamphlets produced. This form had a prehistory in the 1630s with the circulation (and possible performance) of play pamphlets that attacked William Laud, the Archbishop of

Canterbury, and his reforms in church worship.[40] In the 1630s and early 1640s, levellers such as Richard Overton used play pamphlets to voice political discontent, but, by the late 1640s, the paper stage was utilised by royalists and radicals as a platform from which to voice anxieties about authority figures.[41]

To voice displeasure against the King, in 1643 parliament sponsored the publication of *Tyrannicall-Government Anatomized*, a translation of George Buchanan's *Baptistes sive Calumnia* (c. 1542), a tragedy that narrates the demise of John the Baptist. *Tyrannicall-Government Anatomized* toys with performativity on the page as opposed to the stage by including a list of 'persons speaking' after the title page.[42] This emphasises that royalists were not the only faction to appropriate the paper stage as a means of forwarding a political agenda. The publication of *Tyrannicall-Government Anatomized* coincided with the issuing by parliament of parliamentary speeches, newsbooks, trial accounts and satires. As Elizabeth Sauer points out, these publications encourage play reading and merge the political and theatrical stages through the staging of debates.[43] The paper stage is a space where writers may voice and enact political grievances.

This emphasises the continuity between the pamphlet form as a disseminator of news, libel and satire and the theatricality of this type of writing; drama and satire are used to create polemic. Authorship seems of little concern to these writers: the title page of the first part of the anti-parliamentarian play pamphlet *Craftie Cromwell* (1648) claims that it was penned by Mercurius Melancholicus, the journal name of the pamphleteer who penned the royalist *Mistress Parliament* pamphlets,[44] although another author may have borrowed the pseudonym.[45] As Joad Raymond speculates, the 'shared cause' of royalism may have taken precedence over authorial continuity, leading to the inconsistent use of pseudonym.[46] This highlights an ambivalence regarding literary authorship and an endeavour to present a coherent and unified satirical narrative of events through the appropriation of pen names. The spatial fluidity of the paper stage is echoed by authorial fluidity, despite this attempt at using satire to create consensus within the public sphere.

Official and unofficial textual interventions added to this fluidity. Not all tracts that supported the Crown were printed by official royal printing presses. The contribution of other royalist 'voices' to the pamphlet wars adds nuance to the official line found in royalist newsbooks, which emphasises that the desire for a unified identity is complicated by the plurality of action within the public realm. The newsbook *Mercurius Aulicus* was printed from 1643 to 1645 with the support of the Crown,[47] but other texts, including tracts that were printed by parliamentarians and play pamphlets, have contributed to reductive images of what it meant to be a royalist (and, conversely, a parliamentarian) during the period. While authors may have shared tropes to influence royalist and parliamentarian opinions, these tropes were appropriated in different ways: the royalist or parliamentarian discourse is not as stable as contemporaries and some later critics have suggested. In spite of this, the crude pamphlets produced during the civil wars and the contributions to this pamphlet culture by people associated with them – whether as the authors, printers, readers or subjects of these texts – increasingly gained cultural verification.

The use of satire helped to create stereotypical images of royalists and parliamentarians. Satire has long been used as a tool of opposition.[48] Throughout the early Stuart period, libels were written against royal favourites such as Robert Carr and his wife Frances Howard, who were both sensationally implicated in the poisoning of the courtier and author Sir Thomas Overbury in 1613.[49] Another royal favourite made a rare appearance at the playhouse in an attempt to silence the satirists and quell a growing tide of negative opinion: shortly before his assassination in 1628, Robert Villiers, Duke of Buckingham, attempted to rehabilitate his public image by authorising and attending a performance of William Shakespeare and John Fletcher's *Henry VIII* at the Globe. His intention was to establish a connection between himself and the noble Buckingham of the play, but this attempt to influence public opinion went horribly wrong as the audience read the semiotics of Villiers's attendance at the performance differently and aligned the hapless duke with negative representations of Cardinal Wolsey.[50]

Mid-seventeenth-century commentators drew from this use of satire. *Leicester's Commonwealth* (a libel against Robert Dudley, Earl of Leicester and favourite of Elizabeth I, which first circulated under a different title in the 1580s) was reprinted in 1641, suggesting that an awareness of this inheritance of late Tudor and early Stuart satire influenced the writing of tracts in the 1640s.[51] Under the editorship of John Birkenhead, *Mercurius Aulicus* used satire in its representation of parliamentarians.[52] However, to describe the way in which royalists used satiric tropes to defend the court and attack parliament as merely borrowing satiric techniques underestimates the complexity of the treatment of satire in play pamphlets and newsbooks. Satiric imagery in older libels was continually reused and reappropriated in the period to comment upon topical events, and this suggests a connection with the past.[53] In using satire to uphold tradition, royalists flirt with what Ronald Paulson has identified as a conservative element within the development of satire. 'Depending on its emphasis – whether it is on nonconformity and deviation of the false society from old norms, or on its rigidifying of the old ways – the satire can be conservative or revolutionary, its aims to attack, release or to use it as a foil to stultification.'[54] While these observations are useful in considering royalist satire, they are complicated by the use of satire in the different genres: although biased, news claimed a basis in fact, a claim that hyperbolic libels and play pamphlets did not need to make.[55] Satire is used in different ways in the different texts: in newsbooks, it is appropriated to give a biased interpretation of factual occurrences; in play pamphlets, it is used to distort, fictionalise and re-enact events as a way to rewrite historical narrative. In rewriting historical narrative, past events can be revised: the past can be presented as writers believed it ought to have been and not as it necessarily was. Despite these sentimental and nostalgic elements within the appropriation of satire, it can be used less to uphold conservative values and more to protest against the present moment. Because of this tension between fiction and non-fiction, the extent to which satire is conservative or revolutionary becomes ambiguous. Satire was constantly being recycled and appropriated as a form of political commentary, but it was also used to tell stories. This emphasises the fluidity and plurality of language, and the pliability of the paper stage.

In identifying the origins of this kind of satire within popular culture, Nigel Smith and others have argued that a language was created in opposition to authority.[56] However, defining what this authority is becomes difficult during the civil war. In being loyal to the Crown, royalists were disloyal to parliament. Equally, parliament contained people who were not necessarily against monarchical government, even if they opposed Charles's leadership. Owing to this dissent in the body politic, satire ceases to be used to attack authority, but instead can be a form of defence against criticism. Rather than being a language of opposition (or indeed as a means to uphold tradition), satire offered a language of dissent and a way to present multiple perspectives that all added to the web of civil war discourse. Indeed, many royalists and parliamentarians occupied the middle ground, and responded to the events of the mid-seventeenth century in multiple and varying ways.[57] All of this indicates the difficulty of identifying supporters of the royalist or the parliamentarian causes in an age where there were no political parties, and an individual's political beliefs could be complex, contradictory and shifting.

As a consequence of this, the idea of these pamphlets giving voice to a 'language of opposition' comes under scrutiny. When those supportive of the Crown and those in favour of parliament both believe they are upholding the traditional values, order and government of England, it is difficult to consider what is being subverted. Nevertheless, these pamphlets often use satire to attack a type of authority, whether it is considered to be royalist or parliamentarian.[58] The focus of the satire shifts to condemn whichever authority figures are perceived by the writer of the satire to be abusing their power. In the 1630s and early 1640s, satire was used to attack Laud, and in the late 1640s and 1650s pamphleteers turned their attention to Charles and Cromwell. In play pamphlets, the image of the king is often juxtaposed with images of Cromwell. Knoppers argues that this creation of dichotomous visions of the two men ironically consolidates ideas of the lord protector; in trying to redeem Charles, royalists create an energetic Cromwell.[59] *The Tragicall Actors or the Martyrdome of the Late King Charles* (1660) neatly illustrates this. The title suggests that the play pamphlet seeks to be a panegyric to Charles I, yet the regicide is not depicted. Instead, the focus is upon Cromwell's perceived desire to usurp, and on the assistance he is given to achieve this goal. Alongside the image of Charles as blessed saint and martyr, royalists were satirically figuring Cromwell as the ultimate usurper.

The *Mistress Parliament* pamphlets (c. 1648) are perhaps the most famous example of the printing press being used to construct this image of Cromwell. Parliament, personified as a weak, feeble and heavily pregnant woman, is the focus of the narrative. She is figured surrounded by her gossips and easily beguiled by opportunists. Her long anticipated 'child of Reformation' proves to be a 'child of Deformation',[60] whilst Parliament herself is reduced from her noble state to succumbing to the whim of the army:

> Well, well, 'twas ill done, Ile besworne, to fright a Gentlewoman of her quallity and breeding, one that came of so ancient and Honorable a Family too, as the *Parliaments of England*? Who is it almost that has not known the *Parliaments* to be as honourable as ever was any Family in *England* (next to the King, God bless him) and hath done as much good for the kingdome: and now to be despised by every sause-boxe boy, and loose fellow to make Rimes as they call them, and sing-songs of her, making of her a Whore, ... telling her, that she hath ... followed the *Camp*, and become an Amunition–W, and turn'd up her tayle to every lowsy *Ill-dependent* Rascall in the *Army*; Sir *Thomas* himself, and king *Cromwell* too, a very Town-Bull.[61]

The narrative voice is far from sympathetic to parliament and casts scorn on Mistress Parliament's troubles, thereby exposing the house to ridicule.

In condemning those who mock parliament, the writer is ironically satirising his own work. Lamenting parliament's status as a fallen woman, the tract identifies her seducers. Chief amongst the disparate gallants are Thomas Fairfax and Oliver Cromwell. The fact that Cromwell is styled 'King Cromwell' demonstrates that, by 1648, the idea of Cromwell in full command of the army and pretending to the throne had become a commonplace that the reading public could understand. The future lord protector is represented as the seducer of a weak woman. The reference to Cromwell being a 'town bull' enforces his perceived lechery. Sexual politics and (in future *Mistris Parliament* pamphlets) bodily deformity are used as a means through which to parody religious schisms and deformity in the body politic.

An insatiate parliament thus gives birth to a distorted religion. Whether Cromwell is the father or godfather is not ascertained. Nevertheless, sexual intemperance is a theme through which royalists and radicals persistently attacked Cromwell and, as these tropes were repeated, they gained cultural verification. Penned by a leveller, *A New Bull-Bayting* (1649) directly figures Cromwell as a bull, and in so doing builds upon the imagery in the *Mistress Parliament* pamphlets.[62] This scope for obvious sexual satire is utilised by the play pamphlet, which lingers upon the bull's sexual intemperance. However, the bull references also allude to a type of authority, thereby legitimising Cromwell. In classical mythology, Jove was famed for abusing his authority and transforming himself into a bull to copulate with Europa.[63] Figuring sexual intemperance through bull imagery therefore paradoxically highlights that Cromwell held authority while seeking to undermine the fact that Cromwell had power.

Although the pamphlet attempts to reduce the political significance of Cromwell, it cannot refrain from discussing politics and the recent past. Whereas the 'stage directions' point the reader to assume the bull has been the subject of a baiting, the text of the play pamphlet glories in the death of Cromwell the politician. A decade after the printing of *A New-Bull Bayting* and the *Mistress Parliament* pamphlets, many anti-Rump tracts were in circulation, some of which directly repeated material from the *Mistress Parliament* pamphlets.[64] Although Cromwell has only a cameo role in the *Mistress Parliament* pamphlets, he was a figure with whom those opposed to the new regime would continue to concern themselves. This also emphasises the subtle shifts in representation that are present upon the paper stage. These shifts in iconography indicate the confused political perspectives of the period, and a desire to establish some form of coherency and unity through appropriating satire and dramatic conventions as a way of explicating politics in church and state.

This confusion is brought into focus by the use of woodcuts in several play pamphlets printed in the summer of 1659 that deal with Oliver Cromwell's death and imagined afterlife. Some of these play pamphlets reunite the ghost of the saint and martyred Charles with a demonic incarnation of Cromwell. Most of these pamphlets include a woodcut of ghostly figure(s) covered in a winding sheet and wielding a flambeau. For Knoppers, this is part of a shifting iconography in the wake of Cromwell's death, funeral and the months succeeding these events.[65] It also supplies an image to enhance the drama played out on the paper stage. The paper stage plays with visual, oral/aural and literate cultures as a way of conveying meaning. However, this meaning is not fixed and is subject to continuous reappraisal. This only emphasises the uncertainty of the political moment and how contemporaries sought to comprehend these events. Narrative and storytelling are important vehicles through which to allow views to take on a collective meaning, but pictorial representation attempts to concretise the abstract by providing a fixed visual image. The image provides a focal point for the narrative, but this attempt to consolidate thought is destroyed by the processes of print production.

Some of these woodcuts are ambiguous, which allows the reading public to interpret and respond to these images in multiple ways. The frontispiece to *A Dialogue Betwixt The Ghosts of Charles the I Late King of England: and Oliver the Late Usurping Protector* (1659, Figure 1) does not state which image represents Cromwell and which picture is of Charles. However, the larger nose of the left-hand image suggests an allusion to Cromwell's famously large protuberance. The partial nudity of the image on the left may also be an attempt to denigrate Cromwell by aligning him with radicals who publicly went naked.[66] Interestingly, this suggests that the woodcut used to define Charles in 1659 was, in 1661, recycled to portray Bradshaw in the frontispiece to *A New Meeting of Ghosts at Tyburn* (Figure 2). Furthermore, the same frontispiece is used in *A Messenger from the Dead* (1658), a play pamphlet that stages a conversation between the ghosts of Charles I and Henry VIII (Figure 3). Not only does the iconography of Cromwell's death and funeral alter in the build up to (and the aftermath of) Restoration, but the ghostly images of a martyred king (and a not-so-blessed monarch) were reused to illustrate a regicide. While this redeployment was probably motivated by the practicalities of the economics of printing rather than a political statement, it demonstrates the ephemeral nature of this type of imagery and how easily woodcuts

The paper stage 43

1 *A Dialogue Betwixt the Ghosts of Charles the I Late King of England: and Oliver the Late Usurping Protector* (London: 1659), RB 77181, frontispiece

can be inverted to provide an alternative meaning in the eighteen months succeeding Cromwell's death.

The paper stage and the public sphere

The visual, oral and aural possibilities presented by the paper stage demonstrate that the Habermasian notion of the public sphere as a site of inclusive critical discussion – the notion of communicative action that was to underpin much of Habermas's later writing – becomes an ideal that ultimately cannot be sustained given the multiple pressures from individual participation within the public realm. While the shared use of pseudonyms by royalists and a shared royalist cause point to a unified sphere, the desire for unity itself becomes a staged event that collapses under the multiple voices that interpret and reinterpret the roles of various individuals in civil war discourse.

The fabricated unity of the public sphere is undermined by the plurality of voices and perceptions that are generated by the very act of making things public. Assumptions made by those instrumental in the production of playtexts and play pamphlets regarding audience sensibilities combine with the refiguring of prominent figures upon the paper stage (and

> Here is *Cromwell* a Traytor bold
> Which by no mau would be controld.
> Which so much woe on this Land did bring.
> By murdering his Royall King.

> This is *Bradshaw* that divellish Fiend
> That brought his King to a fatal end
> For which cursed and damn'd act,
> He now doth suffer for his bloody fact

2 *A New Meeting of Ghosts at Tyburn Being a Discourse of Oliver Cromwell. John Bradshaw. Henry Ireton. Thomas Pride. Thomas Scot, Secretary to the Rump. Major Gen. Harrison and Hugh Peters, the Divills Chaplain* (London: 1660 [1661]), A.10 (7), frontispiece

the presence or absence of paratexts to printed plays). This is further distorted by the individual interpretations of the readership. This striving for unity becomes what Emmanuel Levinas, in conceiving selfhood, intersubjectivity and interactions with another person, considers to be a form of homesickness:

> The unity of the One in fact excludes all multiplicity, even that which is already adumbrated in the distinction between thinker and thought, and even in the identity of the identical conceived in the guise of consciousness of self where, in the history of philosophy, it would one day be sought.
>
> But the intelligence that is the intelligence of multiple ideas, which it reaches in act, is not absolutely separated from the One because of that multiplicity itself: that multiplicity remains a nostalgia for the One, a homesickness.[67]

The paper stage 45

3 *A Messenger from the Dead, or Conference Full of Stupendious Horrour, Heard Distinctly, and by Alternate Voyces, by Many as that Time Present. Between the Ghosts of Henry the 8. and Charls the First of England, in Windsor-Chappel, Where They Were Both Buried*. (London: 1658), P1597, frontispiece

Levinas's notion of the interaction between the 'I' and the other is useful when considering plurality and the public sphere. For Levinas, the 'I' first understands itself in relation to the other: ethics is predicated upon a face-to-face interaction with another being and 'I' always senses responsibility towards the other. The attempt for monism will always fail owing to the heteronomy of existence.[68] Arendt's notion of plurality being important to the human condition is, in Levinas, not only emphasised but further deconstructed as the unity of the self also comes under scrutiny. Self-perception, other perception and homesickness for an unattainable unity form the basis of an intersubjective, phenomenological notion of ethics. By locating ethical discussions within this framework, Levinas is gesturing towards a heterogeneous public sphere based not upon rational debate but upon mutual responsibility. The false unity of the public sphere that is implied by the paper stage becomes a form of homesickness for a unity that never was nor will be. For royalists, this homesickness manifests itself as a striving for unity in storytelling and the possibilities that the paper stage presents for representing a nation unified by the monarch and order in the body politic. The interventions of parliamentarians, combined with the lack of coherency in the representations penned by royalist writers, result in the fracturing of this desire for unity. Instead, the paper stage is appropriated in multiple ways for the edification of its reading public as those who are participating in the pamphlet wars demonstrate responsibility toward the other by appropriating a language of opposition to convey opinions.

Those who made use of the paper stage endeavoured to present a unified public sphere. This stage provided a platform where rational beings could appropriate drama as a way to present a language of opposition but also enabled the circulation in print of plays that were banned in performance. However, in reality, the reading public was introduced to multiple discourses that are pliable, fluid and constantly open to reinterpretation, reappropriation and reinvention. The paper stage created a unified public sphere of rational thought, but this was a false unity; the abstract public space that has been created is used in different ways. Whether acknowledging the function of the playtext as recording a past theatrical event, desiring to profit from the textual reproduction of plays that were well received in performance, lamenting the closure of the playhouse, or adopting satire and dramatic conventions as a way of creating a language of opposition, the strategies employed in the production of the paper stage became increasingly distorted under the weight of their own rhetoric. Rather than collapsing into multiple publics, we are presented with multiple voices participating in the public sphere and challenging the collective assertion of unity. The paper stage both asserts and negates these theories of public space, as printers, writers and readers used the textual reproduction and appropriation of dramatic conventions for mercantile and political ends. It is to the use of the paper stage as a space from which to voice political discontent that we will now turn.

Notes

1 See Jürgen Habermas, *The Structural Transformation of the Public Sphere*, trans. Thomas Burger (Cambridge: Polity Press, 1992).
2 Brian Cowen, 'English coffeehouses and French salons: rethinking Habermas, gender and sociability in early modern French and British historiography',

in Angela Vanhaelen and Joseph Ward (eds), *Making Space Public in Early Modern Europe: Performance, Geography, Privacy* (New York and London: Routledge, 2013), pp. 41–53 (p. 41).

3 See, for example, David Norbrook, *Writing the English Republic: Poetry, Rhetoric and Politics* (Cambridge: Cambridge University Press, 1999); Joad Raymond, *The Invention of the Newspaper: English Newsbooks 1641–1649* (Oxford: Oxford University Press, 1996); Marcus Nevitt, *Women and the Pamphlet Culture of Revolutionary England, 1640–1660* (Aldershot: Ashgate, 2006).

4 Harold Mah, 'Phantasies of the public sphere: rethinking the Habermas of historians', *The Journal of Modern History*, 72 (2000), 153–82; Nancy Fraser, 'Rethinking the public sphere: a contribution to the critique of actually existing cemocracy', in Craig Calhoun (ed.), *Habermas and the Public Sphere* (Cambridge, MA, and London: MIT Press, 1992), pp. 109–42; Michael Warner, 'Publics and counterpublics', *Public Culture*, 14 (2002), 49–90.

5 Alexandra Halasz, *The Marketplace of Print: Pamphlets and the Public Sphere in Early Modern England* (Cambridge: Cambridge University Press, 1997), esp. pp. 178–9.

6 Stephen Mullaney, 'What's Hamlet to Habermas? Spatial literacy, theatrical publication, and the publics of early modern public stage', in Angela Vanhaelen and Joseph Ward (eds), *Making Space Public in Early Modern Europe: Performance, Geography, Privacy* (New York and London: Routledge, 2013), pp. 17–40.

7 For an extensive study of the printing and circulation of newsbooks during the civil war, see Raymond, *Invention*.

8 For discussions of play pamphlets, see Susan Wiseman, 'Pamphlet plays in the civil war news market: genre, politics and "context"', in Joad Raymond (ed.), *News, Newspapers and Society in Early Modern Britain* (London: Frank Cass Publishers, 1999), pp. 66–83; Nigel Smith, *Literature and Revolution in England, 1640–1660* (New Haven and London: Yale University Press, 1994), esp. pp. 70–92.

9 Mercurius Pragmaticus, *The Second Part of Crafty Cromwell or Oliver in his Glory as Kind* (London, 1648), sig. A1v.

10 For a reading that argues for the performance, see Clare, *Drama*, p. 10. Raymond offers an alternative interpretation (*Invention*, p. 209).

11 Adam Fox, *Oral and Literate Culture in England, 1500–1700* (Oxford: Oxford University Press, 2000), p. 36.

12 See Fox, *Oral and Literate Culture*; Tessa Watt, *Cheap Print and Popular Piety, 1550–1640* (Cambridge: Cambridge University Press, 1993).

13 Louis B. Wright, 'The reading of plays during the puritan revolution', *The Huntington Library Bulletin*, 6 (1934), 73–108; Paulina Kewes, *Authorship and*

Appropriation: Writing for the Stage in England, 1660–1710 (Oxford: Oxford University Press, 1998), p. 27.
14 Thomas Nashe, 'Somwhat to reade for them that list', in *Syr P. S. His Astrophel and Stella* (London: Thomas Newman, 1591), sig. A3r.
15 Nashe, 'Somwhat to reade', sig. A3r.
16 Heinrich F. Plett, *Rhetoric and Renaissance Culture* (New York and Berlin: Walter de Gruyter, 2004), pp. 272–4.
17 Zachary Lesser, *Renaissance Drama and the Politics of Publication: Readings in the English Book Trade* (Cambridge: Cambridge University Press, 2004), p. 40.
18 *Comedies and Tragedies Written by Francis Beaumont and John Fletcher* (London, 1647).
19 C. Y. Ferdinand, 'Herringman, Henry (*bap.* 1628, *d.* 1704)', rev. *Oxford Dictionary of National Biography* (Oxford, 2004; online ed. Jan 2008) www.oxforddnb.com/view/article/37538 (accessed 12 October 2008).
20 *The Siege of Rhodes* (London, 1656); *The Cruelty of the Spaniards in Peru* (London, 1658); *The History of Sir Francis Drake* (London, 1659).
21 Lesser, *Politics of Publication*, p. 40.
22 See Ferdinand, 'Herringman, Henry'; *Fifty Comedies and Tragedies Written by Francis Beaumont and John Fletcher* (London, 1679).
23 Francis Beaumont and John Fletcher, *Philaster, or, Love Lies a Bleeding* (London, 1652), sig. A2r.
24 Richard Brome, *Five New Plays* (London, 1653), sig. A2r.
25 John Ford, *Comedies, Tragi-Comedies and Tragaedies* (London, 1652), sigs A2r–A4r.
26 Habermas, *The Structural Transformation of the Public Sphere*, p. 57.
27 Hannah Arendt, *The Human Condition*, 2nd edn (Chicago: University of Chicago Press, 1998), p. 8.
28 Arendt, *The Human Condition*, pp. 50–2.
29 Arendt, *The Human Condition*, p. 50.
30 See especially Joad Raymond, 'Popular representations of Charles I', in Thomas N. Corns (ed.), *The Royal Image: Representations of Charles I* (Cambridge: Cambridge University Press, 1999), pp. 47–73; Rachel Willie, 'Sacrificial kings and martyred rebels: Charles and Rainborowe beatified', special issue, *Etudes Epistémè* 20 (2011), www.etudesepisteme.org/2e/?sacrificialkings-and-martyred (accessed 29 December 2012).
31 I. S., *The Picture of a New Courtier, Drawn in a Conference, Between Mr. Timeserver and Mr. Plain-heart* (1656), sigs A2v–B1r.
32 Austin Woolrych, *Britain in Revolution, 1625–1660* (Oxford: Oxford University Press, 2002), pp. 693–6.

33 Laura Lunger Knoppers, *Constructing Cromwell: Ceremony, Portrait and Print, 1645–1661* (Cambridge: Cambridge University Press, 2000), chapter 1, esp. pp. 26–7.
34 Arendt, *The Human Condition*, p. 179.
35 John Milton, *Eikonoklastes*, in Don M. Wolfe *et al.* (eds), *Complete Prose Works of John Milton*, 8 vols (New Haven: Yale University Press, 1953–82), 3:342.
36 David Loewenstein, *Milton and the Drama of History: Historical Vision, Iconoclasm, and the Literary Imagination* (Cambridge: Cambridge University Press, 1990), p. 58.
37 Jason McElligott, 'Roger Morrice and the reputation of the *Eikon Basilike* in the 1680s', *The Library*, 6 (2005), 119–32 (121–2).
38 *The Actors Remonstrance, or Complaint: for the Silencing of their Profession, and Banishment from their Severall Play-Houses* (London, 1643), sig. A4r.
39 Laurence Price, *A New Dialogue Between Dick of Kent, and Wat the Welch-man* (London, 1654), sig. A3v; Wiseman, *Politics*, pp. 36–7.
40 Martin Butler, *Theatre and Crisis, 1632–1642* (Cambridge: Cambridge University Press, 1984), 234–50; Margot Heinemann, *Puritanism and Theatre: Thomas Middleton and Opposition Drama Under the Early Stuarts* (Cambridge: Cambridge University Press, 1980), pp. 231–6.
41 Wiseman, *Politics*, pp. 40–61.
42 *Tyrannicall-Government Anatomized* (London, 1642 [1643]), sig. B1r.
43 Elizabeth Sauer, 'Closet drama and the case of *Tyrannicall-Government Anatomized*', in Marta Straznicky (ed.), *The Book of the Play: Playwrights, Stationers, and Readers in Early Modern England* (Amherst and Boston: University of Massachusetts Press, 2006), pp. 80–95, esp. pp. 85–6.
44 Four *Mistress Parliament* pamphlets were printed in 1648, namely: *Mistress Parliament her Gossipping*; *Mistress Parliament Brought to Bed of a Monstrous Childe of Reformation*; *Mistress Parliament Presented in her Bed*; *Mrs. Parliament her Invitation of Mrs. London, to a Thanksgiving Dinner*. Sexual politics and bodily deformity are used as a means through which to parody religious schisms and deformity in the body politic.
45 See Lois Potter, *Secret Rites and Secret Writings: Royalist Literature, 1641–1660* (Cambridge: Cambridge University Press, 1989), pp. 12–16, on the problems of identifying authors of various journals, p. 91 on the false attribution of the first part of *Craftie Cromwell*.
46 Raymond, *Invention*, p. 207. Raymond makes his comment with regard to authorial continuity in reference to the differing pen name of the sequel to the first part of *Craftie Cromwell*. The second part is written under the pseudonym Mercurius Pragmaticus.
47 See *The English Revolution III: Newsbooks I: Oxford Royalist*, ed. Robin Jeffs

et al., with notes by Peter Thomas, 4 vols (London: Cornmarket Press, 1971), a facsimile edition of the Royalist newsbooks *Mercurius Aulicus, Mercurius Rusticus, Mercurius Anti-Britanicus* and *Mercurius Academicus*.

48 See, for example, Andrew McRae, *Literature, Satire and the Early Stuart State* (Cambridge: Cambridge University Press, 2004); Smith, *Literature and Revolution*, chapter 9.

49 See McRae, *Literature, Satire and the Early Stuart State*.

50 For a full account of this event, see Thomas Cogswell and Peter Lake, 'Buckingham does the Globe: *Henry VIII* and the politics of popularity in the 1620s', *Shakespeare Quarterly*, 60 (2009), 253–78.

51 Joad Raymond alludes to this in *Pamphlets and Pamphleteering in Early Modern Britain* (Cambridge: Cambridge University Press, 2003), pp. 20–5.

52 See P. W. Thomas, *Sir John Berkenhead, 1617–1679: A Royalist Career in Politics and Polemics* (Oxford: Oxford University Press, 1969).

53 Adam Smyth, '"Reade in one age and understood i'th'next": recycling satire in the mid-seventeenth century', *Huntington Library Quarterly*, 69 (2006), 67–82.

54 Ronald Paulson, *The Fictions of Satire* (Baltimore: Johns Hopkins University Press, 1967), p. 18.

55 McRae, *Literature, Satire and the Early Stuart State*, p. 26.

56 Smith, *Literature and Revolution*, esp. pp. 296–306.

57 A glance at journals kept by parliamentarians that recorded Charles's attempt in 1642 to enter the Long Parliament and arrest five MPs emphasises this. Roger Hill's entry for Tuesday 4 January 1642 accuses Charles of storming the building, accompanied by a mêlée of 'papists' and 'ill-affected persons', with the intention of arresting the five, or to 'fall upon the House of Commons and to cut all their throats' (Willson H. Coates *et al.*, eds, *The Private Journals of the Long Parliament*, 3 vols (New Haven and London: Yale University Press, 1982), 1:12). Conversely, Simonds D'ewes's more lengthy entries focus upon the episode as being a breach of precedent; D'ewes is concerned in maintaining the balance in government between king and parliament and his entries therefore lack an emotional reaction to events (*Private Journals*, 1:14–22).

58 Smith observes that 'Satire was encouraged by, and played a significant role in, the defamation of *all* kinds of authority' (*Literature and Revolution*, p. 306).

59 Knoppers, *Constructing Cromwell*, pp. 16–19, and *passim*.

60 This is emphasised on the title pages of two of the pamphlets: Mercurius Melancholicus, *Mistress Parliament Brought to Bed of a Monstrous Childe of Reformation* (1648); *Mistress Parliament Presented in her Bed* (1648).

61 Mercurius Melancholicus, *Mistress Parliament Brought to Bed of a Monstrous Childe of Reformation*, p. 4.

62 Elizabeth Sauer, *'Paper Contestations' and Textual Communities in England, 1640–1675* (Toronto: University of Toronto Press, 2005), p. 106.
63 *The. XV Bookes of P. Ovidius Naso, Entytuled Metamorphosis, Translated Oute of Latin into English Meeter, by Arthur Golding* (London, [1567]), book 2, sigs C4v–C5r.
64 See, for example, *The Famous Tragedie of the Life and Death of Mris Rump* (London, 1660). Raymond has convincingly demonstrated how these kinds of satirical civil war pamphlets are part of a rich inheritance of comic pamphlets going back to Elizabethan times (*Pamphlets*, esp. chapters 2 and 4).
65 Knoppers, *Constructing Cromwell*, pp. 159–64.
66 John Morrill has discussed Quaker nudity in his mapping of Quakerism's shift from radicalism to respectability; see Morrill, 'The suffering people: English Quakers and their neighbours c.1650 – c.1700', *Past and Present*, 188 (2005), 71–103.
67 Emmanuel Levinas, *On Thinking-of-the-Other Entre Nous*, trans. Michael B. Smith and Barbara Harshav (London: The Athlone Press, 1998), p. 134.
68 Levinas, *On Thinking*, p. 14, pp. 85–8.

2

Fairs, ghosts, tyranny and usurpation: debating the body politic on the paper stage

Charles I's image was a collaborative venture that was generated throughout his reign by the production of masques and other forms of entertainment.[1] From this genesis, Caroline iconography filtered through to popular print and, during the civil wars, was modified as a means of identifying Charles as a martyred prince. Conversely, the image of Oliver Cromwell began in the popular press; the play pamphlets that both appropriated and constructed the image of the royal martyr also developed a caricature of Cromwell as a Machiavellian schemer. Officially, the theatres may have been closed at the outbreak of civil war, but drama continued to circulate via the medium of play pamphlets. This chapter will examine ways in which some play pamphlets in the latter stages of the civil wars and during the commonwealth refigured Charles and Cromwell. Play pamphlets became one of the ways through which news was disseminated in the mid-seventeenth century. The form was appropriated as a way to debate kingship, allowing the hagiography relating to Charles to merge with the satirising of Cromwell. As the 1650s progressed, satirists would increasingly turn their attention to Cromwell, though memory (or false memory) of monarchy underpins many of these texts. Since the volume of material used to construct these images is vast and has been extensively covered in recent years, I will limit my discussions to the pamphlets that invoke the space of the fair to satirise Cromwell and ghost narratives that directly figure Charles or Cromwell.[2] Because fairs were the location of holiday pastimes and, as noted in the Introduction, spaces in which drama continued to be performed, their presence as an arena in which to discuss Charles and Cromwell is noteworthy. In representing a liminal space between the corporeal and the metaphysical, ghost narratives pretend to offer objective analysis of the recent past. Combined, these types of play pamphlet offer insights into how mid-seventeenth-century commentators contained conflict, whether by consigning discord to the space of the fair or by historicising war through the fabricated posthumous reflections of key figures. Pamphlets that address wider concerns will be omitted.

Crafty Cromwell attends the fair

As I have argued elsewhere, dramatic works such as *A Tragi-Comedy Called New-Market Fayre* (1649), *The Famous Tragedie of Charles I* (1649) and *Cromwell's Conspiracy* (1660) endeavoured to present an enduring image of Charles as the blessed saint and martyred king, but these narratives were destabilised by the ways in which similar rhetoric was used to represent deceased parliamentarians.[3] However, these representations of Charles also connected strongly with some anti-Laudian pamphlets of the 1630s and early 1640s and recognition of the bond between church and state is also present in earlier pamphlets. This relationship is illustrated in *New Lambeth Fayre* (1642) by Richard Overton, a prominent leveller.[4] Its sole 'character', a town crier, calls all to a sale of 'Romes Reliques'.[5] Religious tensions are brought to the fore in Overton's text: the Anglican church under Laud is perceived as being Roman Catholic, and the crier satirically advertises the sale of Catholic goods while simultaneously condemning both Catholicism and episcopal worship.

This connection between church and state is also emphasised in *A Tragi-Comedy Called New-Market Fayre* (1649), which uses the idea of a fair to turn kingly goods into relics.[6] Whereas *New Lambeth Fayre* attacked 'Romes Reliques', by 1649 the idea of relics was appropriated by royalists as a means of illustrating regal martyrology and to comprehend the regicide. The condemnation of popish superstition in earlier play pamphlets is replaced by nostalgic images in *New-Market Fayre*, and Charles is remembered through his material goods. What these two texts demonstrate is the ongoing cultural importance of fairs as sites of dissent and social unification. Echoing Robert Greene's 1590s cony-catching pamphlets, which purported to expose urban criminal roguery to unsuspecting newcomers to London, a 1641 pamphlet emphasises the heterogeneity of fairs:

> Hither resort people of all sorts, High and Low, Rich and Poore, from cities, townes, and countreys; of all sects, Papists, Atheists, Anabaptists, and Brownists: and of all conditions, good and bad, vertuous and vitious, Knaves and fooles, Cuckolds and Cuckoldmakers, Bauds, and Whores, Pimpes and Panders, Rogues and Rascalls, the little Loud-one and the witty wanton[7]

Once the pamphlet has listed the dramatis personae that are present at the fair, it then proceeds to outline how maidenheads are exchanged for material goods and also cautions against pickpockets and losing money through deception. Commodities might be sold at fairs, but plays are also performed. Furthermore, the everyday dramas enacted by those attending the fair can cause diversion for the observant onlooker. By using the location of the fair, the pamphlets play with performance space and the notion that fairs are a site of fluid and ambiguous social interaction. People may meet to sell their wares, but also to be spectators and actors and to observe and to be seen. As discussed in the Introduction, James Fraser's attendance at a fair and observance of a play demonstrates that fairs continued to be an ambiguous space where performance could take place. By appropriating the concept of fairs as the framing device for the narrative, these texts not only flirt with the space of the fair but play with the idea that monarchy and religion can be transformed into material goods which can be sold to the 'vertuous and vitious' alike. Since fairs are a place where rich, poor, good and not so good congregate, they present a highly charged yet non-partisan space where royalists and parliamentarians may meet, and many play pamphlets are concerned with this interaction. Alluding once more to Cromwell's perceived sexual virility, *A Bartholomew Fairing* (1649) opens with citizens' wives commenting upon Cromwell's sexual or political prowess:

> MRS WOOL[ASTONE]: He has a notable Head-piece, and another *Piece* too: Indeed he is a Man every inch of him. They call him *Iron-sides*; Alas, he is *flesh* and *blood* as other men are, and after the Conquest of *Ireland* and those wilde *Savages*, he will return and *do* wonderfully.[8]

Before this, the wives discuss approvingly ideas of free love that were professed by some Ranters – beliefs that many nonconformist religious groups were accused of practising by their detractors.[9] Cromwell's mortality is presented as the secret of his success: the wives equate sexual virility with military triumph, and prophesy that Cromwell will prove victorious in conquering Ireland. Charles's perceived divinity and its associated relics run parallel with Cromwell's lusty flesh and blood. It is Cromwell's vitality that allows him to achieve and retain power.

Cromwell returned from Ireland in May 1650, having led a very successful yet brutal campaign.[10] The writer of the second part of *New-Market Fayre* (1649) also touches upon this topic, and dreams that it may prove a suicide mission for the cuckolded spirit who is represented as inhabiting Cromwell's body. In the second part of *New-Market Fayre*, we are presented with a demon (conjured up by Hugh Peter, chaplain to the New Model Army). Cromwell becomes the polar opposite of representations of Charles, who as early as 1647, had been figured as a martyr for his people.[11] Unlike *A Bartholomew Fairing*, the second part of *New-Market Fayre* does not discuss Cromwell as a competent army officer, but figures him as a necromantic puppet. This demonic Cromwell lacks the sexual virility to satisfy his wife and (it is hoped) suffers from military impotence too. However, in producing this dramatic rendering of Cromwell and other parliamentarians, the play pamphlet exposes royalist defeat.

Through recreating parliamentarians, the prologue suggests that the play pamphlet is serving the medicinal purpose of purging the populace of a corrupt government. This process 'cannot choose but make proud rebels rage, / To see themselves thus acted on the Stage'.[12] Caricature and satire on the paper stage are adopted to gain victory over Cromwell. Supporters of the Crown may have lost the fight on the battlefield, but print offered a way to rewrite recent events and look to a future royalist victory. The victory anticipated by the citizens' wives in the opening scene of *A Bartholomew Fairing* is confirmed as being inevitable by their husbands:

> MR TR[Y-ALL]: I was afraid of *Ireland* once, I gave it
> For an unwholsome air, *Bogs* and *Quagmires*,
> But Collonel *Jones* hath clear'd it all again,
> With the States Thunder, *Powder*, and *Money*.
> MR WOOL[ASTONE]: It was a plot of *Crumwell's* all this while.
> (And *Munck* will justifie it) to loose so much:
> To make the businesse seeming desperate,
> To his eternall honour to restore it:
>
> (II:[i], sig. B2v)

The play pamphlet endeavours to diminish the complexity of suppressing Irish revolt, thereby overlooking Cromwell's military interventions in Ireland. In reality, the second part of *New Market-Fayre's* assessment of Cromwell's journey to Ireland appears to be more accurate.[13] Nevertheless, Cromwell's successes in Ireland were met with an ambiguous reception: some panegyric that was written upon Cromwell's return did not wholly praise Cromwell and salute his victories. The complex allegory of Andrew Marvell's *An Horatian Ode Upon Cromwell's Return from Ireland* (1650) has been discussed at length by numerous critics.[14]

The inclusion of references to Charles in this poem demonstrates that, while images of Cromwell may have entered discourses about Charles, Charles also appears in narratives about Cromwell. It is difficult to offer commentary upon Cromwell without alluding to the circumstances of his fame.

Although the invasion of Ireland may have been a pre-emptive strike to prevent rebellion against the English parliament in support of the Stuarts, England's claim on Ireland had always been problematic. Elizabethan tracts such as *A View of the Present State of Ireland*[15] demonstrate that a ruthless conquest was believed by most Englishmen to be the only way that Ireland could be settled and, despite increased immigration from Ireland to England leading to more interaction between the nations, English perceptions of the Irish increasingly focused upon the two nations' incompatibility.[16] For supporters of Cromwell, his successful military campaign could offer a way of praising Cromwell for achieving where the monarchy had failed.

Despite the tensions surrounding English interventions in Ireland, the author of *A Bartholomew Fairing* is dismissive of Cromwell's military abilities. In the play pamphlet, the conquest of Ireland is not to be applauded because it is not difficult to achieve. By claiming that Ireland is not a dangerous country, *A Bartholomew Fairing* attempts to undermine a context that was sometimes used by Cromwell's supporters to applaud him. According to the play pamphlet, the perils of Ireland have been overemphasised for financial reasons and Cromwell is really sojourning in Wales. Scotland, Ireland and Wales are brought into the narrative and, sixty years before the Act of Union between England and Scotland created the United Kingdom, we are presented with kingdoms that are disjointed:

> MR WOOL: *Crumwell* had powderd after *Ormond*, whiles
>   Good Sir *Arthur Haselrigg*, and *Lambert*
>   Rebuilt the wall betwixt the *Picts*, and us,
>   And kept them out of *England*, pent in Scotland:
>   This was the plot which none but sure ones knew:
>   This is the day to raise more money for't
> MR TR: It shall be levy'd what we say's law,
>   This, is the word, Do it, or *Crumwell* comes;
>   Wee'l fetch him with a whistle, if they boggle,
>   He lyes in Wales on purpose at a lurch:
>   (Upon pretence of waiting on the winds)

> But the truth is, it is to aw those here
> The Leveller, and the discontented party.
> Hee'l ... fright off *Ormond* with a whiffe of's tayl.
>
> (III:[i], sigs B2v–B3r)

Lest citizens refuse to pay for this military extravagance, Cromwell lies in wait to take the money by force. This recalls pre-regicide events: in December 1648, the army entered the city to take forcefully payment that the corporation of London had failed to hand over.[17] Although Fairfax was in command of the army at the time, the play pamphlet overlooks this and focuses instead upon Cromwell. The impending invasion of Ireland thus meets with recent history and is interpreted as a ruse for a possible invasion of London: in the play pamphlet, Cromwell may be absent in Wales, but the memory of what he can do awes both royalists and levellers into submission.

In the play pamphlet, Cromwell has gained the support of the city. In reality, London was quite hostile to the New Model Army.[18] *A Bartholomew Fairing* plays lip service to this antagonism in acknowledging that London harbours enemies to the new regime who need to be awed into submission. The play pamphlet also suggests that London's political support does not necessarily equate with financial assistance. *A Bartholomew Fairing* does not seriously contemplate Irish affairs. Instead, it focuses upon improbable threats from London: the city thus becomes an ambiguous space where both royalist and leveller dissenters may hide.

A Bartholomew Fairing alludes to levellers and royalists as harbouring anti-Cromwellian principles, demonstrating that Cromwell's detractors had disparate political views. With the breakdown of the censorship laws in the early 1640s, people of all political leanings printed commentaries on the distracted times.[19] Those sympathetic to the royal cause were not the only people to appropriate dramatic forms as a means of producing negative images of Cromwell: levellers and other radicals were equally wary of him.[20] In December 1653, Cromwell effectively launched a military coup, which led to him becoming lord protector of the commonwealth.[21] The first constitution shared power between parliament and protector, but the second constitution afforded Cromwell more control.[22] For some ardent republicans, this represented a betrayal of 'the good old cause', and Cromwell was as much an unpopular figure amongst some parliamentarians and parts of the army as he was to royalists.[23]

Endeavouring to afford Cromwellian rule a degree of constitutional legitimacy, some sought to establish Cromwell as king and even advocated providing Cromwell and his descendants with a dynastical legitimacy through an advantageous yet highly improbable marriage between Cromwell's daughter and the future Charles II.[24] In 1657, discussions over whether Cromwell should be made king were almost laid to rest; Cromwell refused the crown and would continue to be known under the caretaker title of 'lord protector'.[25] To his detractors, Cromwell was a king in all but name.[26]

Anticipating that Cromwell would assume the throne, political pamphlets that were supportive of the Crown would increasingly depict him following Machiavellian policies to further his ends. The use of Machiavelli within these pamphlets is not subtle: rather than offering a nuanced reading of Machiavelli's political writings, we are presented with an image of someone scheming to gain power. Represented as envying the Crown, Cromwell was perceived by royalists, levellers and his other critics as a person who ought not to be trusted.[27] These depictions partly stemmed from a perception that the New Model Army had acted duplicitously in their negotiations to end the war and establish Charles as a constitutional monarch; when Charles procrastinated and began making plans for a complete royalist victory, the army reassessed the situation. No longer content with re-establishing Charles as a king with limited power, some within the army encouraged parliament to proceed to a trial; since Charles had abdicated responsibility towards the people over whom he ruled it was no longer fitting that the populace should support him.[28] Executing the anointed king was a step that moderate parliamentarians were unwilling to take. Cromwell thus found himself advocating a radical agenda, although he himself appears to have been a conservative, as indicated by his role in the Putney Debates.[29] This bred mistrust amongst royalist and radical parliamentarians alike, which became manifest in print.

In 1648, the first and second parts of *Craftie Cromwell* were printed. These two play pamphlets discuss 'the Trayterous undertakings and proceedings of the said NOL, and his Levelling Crew'.[30] *Craftie Cromwell* satirically criticises Cromwell through episodic reflections upon recent events. Although the scenes of the first part of *Craftie Cromwell* appear unconnected, they are tied thematically. Each scene involves biased commentary upon recent history by fabricating episodes such as a conversation between merchants in the opening scene, or presenting Cromwell as resolving to take the crown after a nocturnal visitation by the ghost of Pym. Perhaps the most striking of these observations upon contemporary events is the conversation between two Jesuits:

CHIRL[ANDUS]: I have so much favour gain'd, to morrow I receive an Institution to be establisht in a wealthy Living which lately was Sequestred.

SYM[ANCHA]: Why, then our journy has been prosperous, and thanks is due from our most holy *Conclave*; what shall we pitch upon?

CHIRL: Not to divulge ourselves, 'tis dangerous, but this I propose as most emergent; we will assay ... to fan the fire of those grand differences which doe prognosticate a cruell Warre betweene those *Hereticks* on either side, the *Independents* and the *Presbyterians*, and so what SPAINE, nor ROME, nor HELL could bring to passe, we shall I hope effect.

(III:[i], sig. B1v)

Clerical livings sequestered from Episcopalians thus end up in the possession of Catholics. Under Laud, the Church of England had been condemned by radicals for its perceived covert Catholicism. The idea that religious schism can allow Catholicism to flourish is reinvented here to condemn parliament and the New Model Army: tropes found in anti-Laudian play pamphlets of the early 1630s and 1640s have been appropriated by royalist writers to attack Cromwell and his supporters. Not only the satiric potential of parliamentarian play pamphlets but the very subject of the satire has been adopted (and modified) by royalists. Joad Raymond's theory of a shared cause creating a collective authorial continuity can be taken to its extreme as parliamentarian propaganda was also appropriated by royalists.[31]

Following the conversation between the Jesuits, a Chorus offers a cautionary gloss on the action just witnessed. Strife between the Protestant denominations can lead only to a strengthening of the mutual enemy: "'Tis sure, that never Rome such footing had / Since Mary fell' (III:[i], sig. B3r). Bearing witness to the religious and political divisions that the writer argues assisted in the Counter-Reformation, the next scene portrays Colonel Hammond (jailer to Charles I) as being torn between obedience to parliament and loyalty to the Crown. It is this confusion over duty and loyalty that the play pamphlet seems to suggest Cromwell is manipulating and the pamphlet concludes with Cromwell sending orders to prepare a dossier that may be used to judicially murder Charles.

Charles, the royalist cause and moderate parliamentarians are the implicit tragic topics of the narrative. However, as Knoppers observes, these play pamphlets also bring into focus an image of Cromwell that afforded him a dubious legitimacy. The play pamphlets may attempt to lament the fate of Charles, but, by parodying his adversaries, *Craftie Cromwell* is ultimately unsuccessful as a eulogy for the monarch. This paradox is also found in the sequel to *Craftie Cromwell*, which continues to represent Cromwell as seeking power. In figuring a remorseful Fairfax, however, *The Second Part of Crafty Cromwell* alludes to the fact that there was no consensus amongst the army over how to proceed. Fairfax was conspicuous by his absence from Charles's trial. In addition to this, a veiled woman who disagreed with the proceedings interrupted the court. This woman was reputedly Anne Fairfax and (if so) her husband did not dispute her comments.[32]

History has read Fairfax's absence from the trial as demonstrating the lord general's silent censure of the trial and a mute expression of his doubts regarding the legality of the proceedings.[33] In 1650, Fairfax resigned his commission in the army and retired to the country.[34] This deed has added further fuel to the image of a repentant Fairfax, though Lucy Hutchinson blamed the resignation upon the meddling of Fairfax's 'wife and her Presbyterian chaplains'.[35] While both Hutchinson's theory and the account that cultural memory insists to be true have been discounted by some later historians (who have identified the resignation as being Fairfax's protest against the impending invasion by England of its former ally, Scotland),[36] this emphasises the way in which events are received and retold within the nascent public sphere.

War with Scotland was not the only action that met with Fairfax's disapproval: before Pride's Purge, the lord general had voiced his discontent with Ireton's wish to purge parliament and arrest Charles.[37] Fairfax undoubtedly had qualms about the handling of the political crisis during the latter stages of the war and attempted to postpone the regicide.[38] As early as 1648, there was rumour of disquiet amongst the army ranks over the direction events seemed to be taking.

The writer of *The Second Part of Crafty Cromwell* discusses royalist resignation to defeat; the inescapability of regicide becomes a means through which to attack some parliamentarian figures and partially exonerate others. While Fairfax is perceived as having reservations that civil war could culminate in regicide, Cromwell is imagined as desiring the deed to be performed. The trial of Charles is prefigured in *The Second Part of Crafty Cromwell* by the trial of Captain Burleigh. Court proceedings are perceived as being a formality when the state has already decided upon the defendant's guilt. Before the trial begins, the jury has come to a decision regarding the case:

> So cordiall we are unto the states, that had we each of us his Father here, standing in this mans stead, we would proclaime him guilty, right or wrong, ... we

did agree amongst our selves before to find him guilty of high [*sic*], were he as innocent as is the light.³⁹

The inference is that the trial of Charles will also conclude in finding an innocent guilty. Since Charles's most trusted advisers had been found guilty of treason, none of his supporters is safe from the arbitrary whim of parliament:

> All Lawes Devine, they basely abrogated.
> When Reverend *Laud*, was martyr'd by their power,
> All Regall sway, by heavens will created,
> When Noble *Strafford*, fell in evill houre,
> And that all human Lawes they may untie,
> Therefore ere long, must Learned *Jenkins* die.
>
> (III.[i] sig. B2v)

The Chorus lament the passing of Archbishop Laud, executed by parliamentary command in 1645.⁴⁰ This act is perceived as destroying the episcopal church, and the death of Thomas Wentworth, Earl of Strafford (executed 1641),⁴¹ is seen as the means by which secular, regal authority is lost. The perceived breakdown of the criminal justice system is thus identified as having occurred on the eve of civil war, and this breakdown is then exploited by Cromwell. The final episode of the play pamphlet is a parody of a coronation scene. The first task of the king-elect is to find a means to dispose of Charles, and the pamphlet ends with a cautionary tale for radicals and a quatrain of hope for royalists:

> CROMWELL: And if wee can the peoples pleasures gaine,
> wee may perchance, in peace and quiet Reigne,
> Else wee are lost, and O I greatly dread,
> At once to loose my Kingdome, and my head.
>
> (V:[i], sig. B4r)

The use of zeugma in the final line emphasises that the body politic cannot have two heads (a doctrine that both radical parliamentarians and the court were to be more stubborn about as civil war progressed). The precariousness of both Charles's plight and Cromwell's situation is confirmed: one must die for the other to succeed. While royalists were denied the witnessing of a suitably gruesome punishment for Cromwell, his death is heralded in a series of pamphlets that imagined Cromwell's afterlife.

Ghostly apparitions on the paper stage

After Oliver Cromwell's death on 3 September 1658, his son, Richard, succeeded him to the protectorate. Within a year, Richard had been overthrown, and by 1660 monarchy had been restored. The protectorate may have been dead, but royalists continued to create images of Cromwell and remember Charles. Whereas earlier play pamphlets satirically sketched reductive images of a usurping tyrant, later play pamphlets eagerly commemorate old Noll's death. Cromwell the man is succeeded by a ghost: unable to wield power in the material world, he is characterised as wanting to know whether his legacy is secured.

The conception of ghosts in the early modern period was confused; the Reformation's disownment of Catholic thoughts regarding purgatory mingled with debates relating to witchcraft. Protestant divines had to reinterpret biblical presentations of ghosts and did so through redefining or dismissing the evidence of apparitions.[42] Salvation depended upon being able to distinguish between apparitions as being angels or demons.[43] The ghostly narratives of the early 1660s play with and flatten this confusion by representing a demonic Cromwell. In *A Parly Between the Ghosts of the Late Protector and the King of Sweden* (1660), Charles X of Sweden (died 1660) deliberately journeys to hell in order to relate to his old friend and ally how events have unfolded. Charles X sought a military alliance with the Cromwellian regime as a means of enlarging Swedish dominions. Eager for a Protestant league to fight the Counter-Reformation in Europe, Cromwell welcomed Sweden's overtures.[44]

Beginning the dialogue between the two ghosts, Sweden relates briefly the recent events in England. The dialogue morphs into a cautionary tale about usurpation. Even after death, Cromwell is still depicted as desiring power and aspires to overthrow the devil. Before embarking on the deed, Cromwell seeks justification from Pym. This alludes to Pym's key role in drafting the Grand Remonstrance of 1641, a document that listed parliamentarian grievances against Charles, the presentation of which was one of the significant moments in the build up to war.[45] Knoppers observes that the similarity between the text and recent history satirically recasts the regicide as comedy.[46] It also implicitly brings the saint and martyred king into the narrative through the readers' memories of the actions that led to war. Although the pamphlet seeks to suppress events that some anti-Cromwellians might find troubling, it cannot refrain from alluding to them.

With Cromwell's dynasty deposed within months of his death and Sweden ruled by an infant king, the pamphlet suggests that monarchy can return to England and, with it, political stability.[47] This stability meets its opposite in the instability of the pamphlet type. At the beginning, it is clearly laid out as a play pamphlet. However, by the second page, the author becomes narrator by inserting a short digression. At the end of the pamphlet, any attempt to render a dramatic construction of either Cromwell or Charles X is abandoned. The writer of this pamphlet fails to sustain a coherent narrative of the recent past and also ineffectually appropriates the paper stage to represent Cromwell.

By the end of the pamphlet, Cromwell's punishment is complete. Through transforming a demon to look like Hugh Peter, Satan learns of the planned usurpation. Echoing (but also inverting) the necromantic possession of corpses by demons in the second part of *New-Market Fayre*, the pamphlet reinvents tropes found in earlier play pamphlets. Its concern with European affairs, however, complicates the narrative. Cromwell's foreign policy seems to have been popular at home and ultimately successful.[48] In figuring Cromwell and his European allies as imps of Satan, the pamphlet has trouble reconciling protectorate foreign policy with a desire to create a negative image of the ruler. The attempt to condemn Cromwell through his foreign policy highlights the inconsistencies between historical and textual realities; the inability of the play pamphlet to sustain dialogue form throughout adds to this instability. By the end of the piece, the pamphlet abandons dialogue form entirely and instead describes how the devils impatiently await the arrival of the surviving regicides.

A Parly Between the Ghosts of the Late Protector and the King of Sweden was not the only pamphlet to anticipate the deaths of the other notable radical parliamentarians. *The Case is Altered, or Dreadful News From Hell* (1660) depicts the ghost of Cromwell bribing his way out of hell to visit his wife. Cromwell desires to know what the Cromwellian legacy is and he also seeks a speedy reunion with his comrades:

> NOLL: I do intend for to streak out and appoint a place where *Haselrigs* bones, *Scot*, and *Vanes* shall be intered, for absolutely if they would dispatch and come away, with their advice and my own, we could usurp a power from the Devil, and live in a corner by ourselves, without interruption.[49]

Needing assistance to conquer some of hell, Cromwell eagerly anticipates the deaths of his friends. Post-mortem, the role of Cromwell is reduced: although the focus of the narrative remains on Cromwell, it also alludes to the role of other radicals in the regicide. Cromwell ceases to be the figure who manipulates events to his advantage, but instead requires the help of others to achieve a partial victory. By formulating an image of Cromwell as being in need of assistance, the play pamphlet does not negate earlier images of the lord protector. This is because Hugh Peter is often to be found in a supportive role as adviser to Cromwell (or controlling the action through necromancy). Peter is also represented as serving this function in *The Case is Altered*, though his encouragement is depicted as hastening the damnation of those whom he advises. *A Conference Held Between the Old Lord Protector and the New Lord General, Truly Reported by Hugh Peters* (1660)[50] sees Peter rewarded for his support by a damnably resplendent Cromwell. Once more, Cromwell escapes hell for a brief interlude in the material world. In contrast to the other representations of the ghostly Cromwell, Noll does not escape damnation for a short while, but has a day away from managing affairs of state:

> CROMWELL: I have been with my Sovereign Lord and Prince *Abaddon*, *Apollyon*, *Lucifer*, *Satan*, *Beelzebub*, Senior Don *Diabolo*, the Illustrous Emperour of *Plutonia*, in his infernal Dominions and Territories; where I am his substitute and *Grand-Vizier*, turmoiling my self with the Cares of his Government; ... But who would not be in Office, *Peters*? Believe me, though the trouble of my place be great, yet it is relaxation to me to consider, how I have outstripp'd in my Princes favour my fellow-Courtiers.[51]

Through sycophancy, Cromwell mounts a successful usurpation of the underworld. As lord protector of hell, it is within Cromwell's jurisdiction to reward Peter with a diabolical benefice. Before bestowing this gift upon his (still living) ally, Cromwell requests that Peter contrives a brief interview between the ghost and General Monck.[52] The interview inevitably proves outrageous to Monck, who reminds Cromwell of his misdemeanours:

> CROMWELL: Oh *George*! Reprove me not so bitterly. I'm bad enough already; to heare thee mention the name of a God and his feare, and his Saints and Martyrs, brings horror and despaire into my Conscience
> (sig. A4v, italics inverted)

Cromwell, chastened, returns to Hades. *A Conference* thus provides a rendering of Cromwell where his perceived ambitions have been realised. Charles, alluded to here as the saint and martyred king, is never far from discussions. The representation of Charles provides a parallel between a saintly king and a satanic lord protector.

Cromwell as a ghostly apparition would have had more pertinence in the summer of 1659 than at the Restoration; by the Restoration, political focus had shifted from the Cromwell's death and the immediacy of uncertain political times to celebrate (or commiserate) the return of the king. In 1659, however, the future was very difficult to discern, and play pamphlets therefore focused more emphatically upon the past. In imagining a posthumous reunion between Charles and Cromwell, *A Dialogue Betwixt the Ghosts of Charls the I, ... And Oliver* presents a more contrite Cromwell than is present in many other pamphlets. Addressing Charles, Cromwell acknowledges his manifold sins and wickedness:

> CROMWELL: O Sir, Pray forgive me, for you cannot imagine the tortures of conscience that I indure, when I call to mind all my ambitious and damnable Plots, to ruine you and yours, and to set my self in your sted; It was I that laid the Plot to draw your Subjects Obedience from you, under pretence of Religion and Liberty; It was I that after we had Routed your Army in the Fields, jugled you into the Isle of *Wight*; ... and then ... by my dam'd Policy and Power, broke off the Treaty, and all to get the Government my self.[53]

The pamphlet thus stages a full confession from Cromwell. The confession is not without a sense of pride: in suggesting that Cromwell has successfully negotiated the final years of the civil wars to gain power, the focus of recent events is concentrated upon him, and he vaunts the policies which led him to power. Charles, having been busy decomposing for ten years, is eager to know how the world has fared since his death. Cromwell's later allusion to his success in Ireland, however, leads the deceased monarch to reflect upon some of his more reprehensible deeds: '*Oh! Name* Ireland *and Deputy no more, for that puts me in mind of my weakness in subscribing to that wicked Bill, for putting* Strafford *to death*' (p. 5). As with *The Second Part of Crafty Cromwell*, the pamphlet cannot overlook Charles's actions in permitting Strafford to be executed. Here, the King's memory of Strafford's death is presented as a confession of guilt, paralleling Cromwell's explanations of how he gained power. Due to Cromwell's position as the focus of this narrative, Charles's torments are not elaborated upon. Conversely, Cromwell evinces grief when recollecting his past deeds:

> I had read too much of *Machivil* ..., my Guards were strong and all my own Creatures; And to tell you the truth my Reign was (as all Usurpers must be) more like to a Hell then a Heaven, my Palace being a Prison to me, I not daring

to stir out of it, without a guard sufficient to storm a City, and if I had had not Enemies, my own thoughts had been enough. (p. 8)

Unlike later ghostly visitations, Cromwell is not figured as an imp of Satan who endeavours to gain or retain power in hell. Instead we are offered an image in which Cromwell, seduced into craving power through reading Machiavelli's writings, experiences regret. Machiavelli influenced some seventeenth-century republican ideas, which suggests that the pamphlet is drawing on knowledge of republican thought.[54] However, here Machiavelli is figured as being at the root of seditious actions and we are warned that his influence can lead to damnation. Cromwell's earthly elevation thus prefigures the torments of hell and this representation of Cromwell cannot enjoy power because he is plagued by his conscience.

A Dialogue Betwixt the Ghosts of Charls the I, ... And Oliver thus presents an image of a scheming Cromwell experiencing the pangs of hell and a contrite Charles who, through sacrificing himself to atone for the sins of his nation, gains salvation. By reuniting the pair, the play pamphlet becomes a way of processing collective grief and staging reconciliation. The mentioning of Strafford, however, brings into focus tensions within the body politic. Strafford had been a controversial political figure, and his authoritarian rule as lord deputy of Ireland, unsuccessful steering of war with Scotland and the charge that he aimed to use Irish forces against English subjects, proved disastrous for both him and Charles. When Parliament attempted to try Strafford for treason, Parliament set a precedent that would eventually lead to the trial and execution of Charles. The proceedings against Charles's paternal grandmother, Mary, Queen of Scots, which culminated with her death in 1587, set a precedent for trying and executing an anointed monarch for treason but the charges against Strafford redefined the nature of treason. This made possible (albeit controversially) the trial of a monarch of the realm.

Medieval and Tudor statutes defined treason as a crime against the royal body. If convicted of treason, the unfortunate aspirant ruler could anticipate imaginative and brutal punishments, unless the mercy of the monarch rescinded the punishment to a simple decapitation. An attack, whether perceived or real, upon the royal body therefore would lead to the mutilation of the alleged traitor's body. What set the trial of Strafford (and later William Laud) apart from medieval and Tudor cases of treason was that both men appear to have had, to varying degrees, the support of their king. Their perceived treasons were not upon the king's body but against the body politic. The executions of Strafford, Laud and Charles punctuate the fractures within the body politic as well as emphasising the difficulties present in the post-Reformation conjoining of church and state. While the notion of the body politic had been used to instruct princes of Europe into rightful government in the twelfth century (and became a foundational concept in early modern notions of sovereignty), in the seventeenth century, crimes against the body politic were also crimes against the body natural.[55] In desiring to protect the body politic against the tyranny and abuse of office, parliament acknowledged that the body natural could be exposed to attack.

Alongside this ideological change came the controversial belief that a tyrant could be slain. This led to conflicting notions of the limits of monarchical authority and the role of the sovereign's advisers. Strafford's downfall was not only caused by parliament's desire to cure distemper within the body politic by amputating an irksome limb. Strafford had many enemies who were eager to blame the failures of Charles's personal rule upon the hapless earl. Conversely, Charles had promised to protect Strafford from parliament's wrath and swore that he would not authorise the exercising of capital punishment against the earl. When the trial collapsed, parliament passed a bill of attainder and Strafford released Charles from his promise. If this was designed to inspire mercy, it failed. Charles duly signed the death warrant and Strafford was dispatched. Some contemporary accounts suggest that Strafford met his death with dignity, but claimed his end served as a cautionary tale to all who put their faith in princes.

Biographies of Strafford narrate a complex and at times bafflingly contradictory character who seems to defy any form of consensus.[56] Strafford's friend Laud was also controversial, not least because his reforms in church worship were widely regarded as Catholic by the more Calvinist wing of the church. Both men, in their desire to show the impartiality of the law, prosecuted and antagonised noblemen and the wealthy. Regardless of whether their actions were just, each man attracted influential enemies, and having the confidence of the king did not mean that they had immunity from prosecution. In 1640, Laud was impeached for high treason. The numerous charges, both sacred and secular, pointed to Laud's alleged advocacy of Catholicism, incitement of violence and corruption of the king.

Depending upon political perspectives, Charles, Laud and Strafford thus present a trinity of tyrants or a triumvirate of martyrs. The execution of Strafford in 1641 did not prevent civil war, nor did the execution of Laud in 1645 address grievances in church and state. However, both Strafford and Laud inevitably enter civil war discourse as their detractors believed their advice had led to bad management within the body politic. Thus Strafford, Laud and Charles become inextricably linked.

Whereas Fairfax, Cromwell and Hugh Peter are frequently invoked in anti-parliamentarian tracts, some pamphlets that mourn the loss of Charles allude to Strafford and Laud. The reference to Strafford's fate in *A Dialogue Betwixt the Ghosts of Charls the I, … And Oliver* and Charles's mournful acceptance of his involvement in the lord deputy's downfall is therefore not atypical. However, these types of ghost narratives echo a more ambiguously royalist tract that was printed in 1658. *A Messenger from the Dead* presents an image of two dead kings. While later ghost narratives would either reunite a damned Cromwell with his collaborators, or stage a posthumous conversation between Charles and Cromwell, here we are presented with a debate between Charles and his great-great-uncle, Henry VIII. Like Charles, the Tudor monarch was buried at Windsor. This leads an indignant Henry to query why his grave has been disturbed by the body of a man who claims to have been the unhappy king of England:

> HENRY: What you a King! Did you ever wear a Crown on your head, who have not a head on your Shoulders?
> CHARLS: I have not alwayes wanted [i.e. lacked] a head, my Subjects, wo is me, did lately bereave me of it.
> HENRY: Your subjects! How could that be? What hainous crime have you committed, that could inforce your subjects to so great a violence?[57]

Henry assumes that tyrannical behaviour is the root of Charles's troubles. However, as the conversation progresses, it is apparent that, while Charles committed unwise actions, his greatest failing was to lose the love of his people. Chiming with Hobbesian principles that a sovereign governs with the will of the people, Henry laments that his niece (and Charles's paternal grandmother) found that the loss of her subject's allegiance sealed her downfall:

> The greatest prejudice that can arrive unto a Prince, is the loss of his peoples love. And thus my Neece *Mary* Queen of *Scotland*, having lost the affections of that Nation, amongst other things suffered for that Indiscretion by the loss of her head in England (sig A3V)

Reminiscing over the fate of his niece, the Tudor past collides with the Stuart future. When Mary, Queen of Scots, was executed, Henry had been dead for forty years and Charles was not to be born for another thirteen years. Seventy-one years after the beheading, the two ghosts remember an event that neither would have experienced in the corporeal world. Glossing over the official narrative that Mary was executed for plotting against the life of her cousin and Henry's daughter, Elizabeth, Henry implies that Mary was executed because her subjects lacked faith in her as a sovereign.

This revising of history transforms Mary's beheading from a controversial episode involving the body natural of two neighbouring queens to a debate over the role and function of the monarch within the body politic. Allusion to civil war is also made through the parallels that Henry is making between mid-sixteenth-century Scotland and mid-seventeenth-century England. Although Laud's attempts at uniformity in church worship were not well received in England and Ireland, when the reforms were inflicted upon Presbyterian Scotland it led to the bishops' wars. Religious controversy and frustrations with Charles's personal rule became two of the main points of contention in the build up to civil war, and war with Scotland precipitated civil war in the three kingdoms. Henry seems to be implying that, like Mary's, Charles's misfortunes began when he lost the support of his Scottish subjects and the inevitable conclusion of this indiscretion would be to lose the goodwill of the English.

Unable to heed the cautionary tale offered by his paternal grandmother, a narcissistic Charles focuses upon his own torments and cannot understand why his subjects should decapitate him. Charles blames Henry's instigation of arbitrary government and the religious reforms implemented by Laud for his tribulations:

> I would to God that Flattery had never been heard of in the Courts of Princes, would to God that I had never heard that we are above the Law, and are to give an account to God onley for what we have committed upon Earth, neverthelesse it doth administer some comfort to me, that I have made no innovation in Religion, I have been above my other Predecessors most gentle to the Catholicks, and came neerest to their Religion, and used my Supremacy with the greatest moderation. And because in my apprehension it was not fit for a Lay-man, I committed almost the whole Exercise of the Ecclesiastical affairs to the Arch-Bishop of *Canterbury*. (sig. C1r, italics inverted)

The notion of governance by God's ordinance and its foundations within the body politic is here critiqued. Tudor and early Stuart monarchs appropriated the notion that they ruled by divine right as a means of asserting their authority. Comparing himself to his forebears, Charles repents of listening to councillors who suggested that he could be judged only by God. Criticising the integral role that the favourite held in the late Tudor and early Stuart court, this construction of Charles proceeds to vaunt his belief that he took a laissez-faire stance in matters of religion. Charles repents of adhering to the words of flatterers and simultaneously abdicates responsibility over religious controversies, claiming that Laud held almost sole jurisdiction upon ecclesiastical affairs. Since reform in church worship had been one of several grievances that eventually led to civil war, this displaces blame for the schisms that ensued from Charles to Laud. Tolerance of religious difference ceases to be of benefit to the body politic and instead becomes the site of discord. Far from being a saint and martyred king, this representation of Charles ought not to boast of the trust he placed in a favourite to administer to matters of religion.

While Charles ought to have heeded religious controversy, Henry is identified as the creator of religious strife. Rather than being a defender of the faith, Henry admits to using the rhetoric of religion as a way to achieve his earthly desires:

> But could you by no printed papers, insinuate into the minds of your Subjects, how much you stood devoted to their safety and prosperity? When I was resolved to use my Arbitrary power, that I might appear unto the world to undertake nothing by force, I caused books to be dictated according to my own pleasure, which were presented to me as if they came from the Monks themselves. If any refused to subscribe unto them I caused them to be hanged up, especially the chiefest of them, to be a terrour to the rest. (sigs B1v–B2r)

Alluding to the way in which Henry used the printing press as a means of circulating texts that endorsed royal prerogative amongst the reading public, Henry suggests that Charles would have made a stronger prince had he played the tyrant but pretended otherwise. Arbitrary government can succeed only if the wielder of power is unwilling to compromise. Charles is punished in the material world precisely because he is a moderate ruler. In the ghostly realm, the body natural ceases to embody kingship: the body politic is redefined from a means of asserting divine right to embody a system that has the appearance of governance by contract and almost resembles constitutional monarchy. Henry, recognising differences in governance between England and Scotland, comments upon the place and function of the English parliament:

> The English were alwayes much addicted to their Parliaments, in which they found a constant redress for all their greivances, it is therefore less to be admired that they revolted from you (sig. B2r)

In this reading, civil war and regicide become the inevitable conclusion of Tudor and Stuart endeavours to impose a system of arbitrary government upon an unwilling populace. The English people, unwilling to continue to be oppressed by authoritarian rule, punish Charles for his failings as a king, but in so doing they also address complaints held against monarchy for the past one hundred and fifty years.

Charles, mourning his fate, queries how Henry was not punished for his transgressions. Prefiguring later pamphlets that imagine Cromwell damned while a resplendent Charles enjoys salvation, Henry receives posthumous punishments for his iniquities. However, the torments inflicted upon Henry are not limited to fire and brimstone. From hell, Henry witnesses his legacy. Alluding to his Bluebeard-style antics in his struggle to beget a male heir, Henry refers to the scriptural warnings:

> But in this great care of mine, and indeavour for posterity, not any of my race lived threescore years after my death ...
> Thus do I find true what the Kingly Prophet did foretell me. *The seed of the wicked shall perish Psalm 37.* and in another place. Thou *sha't destroy their fruit from the Earth, and their seed from the sons of men, Psalm 12.* (sig. B3v)

In death, Henry is presented with his tyrannies and the futility of his actions. Unable to heed the forewarnings of scripture and alienated by Protestants and Catholics alike for meddling in religious affairs for dynastic purposes, Henry can only accept his condition. This representation of Henry obfuscates our understanding of kingship. Throughout the seventeenth century, Henry was, to varying degrees, figured as the archetypal tyrant who was ripe for castigation.[58] Charles, though saved from the eternal punishments meted out to Henry, is not wholly blameless as a result of Henry's influence over future generations. The pamphlet constantly alludes to arbitrary government and the perception that Henry instigated authoritarian rule in England. Kingship is not positioned against the protectorate as a means of endorsing monarchy, rather the actions of Tudor and Stuart monarchs are critiqued and the regicide becomes a punishment for collective regal misdemeanours:

> HENRY: the jealous God, who visiteth the sins of the fathers on the children, doth most usually exact the punishment of the most enormous offences on the third or fourth Generation ... You are the third King from me, and do suffer punishment in the third Generation ... Neither do I beleive it is without the providence of God, that so direfull a revenge hath fallen on you, the most moderate, and the most innocent of them all, that so all might understand that not so much your sins, as the hereditary Evils, and the Wickedness annexed to your Crown and your titles, are taken vengeance of in your person
>
> (sigs C1r–C1v)

A hereditary Crown, it would seem, carries with it hereditary obligations. Charles's fate becomes an elaborate gloss on biblical exegesis and, in accordance with Christian scripture, the third generation receives punishment in the material world for the sins of the forefathers.

Henry's interpretation of the regicide, however, is not without its conceptual difficulties. Charles might be the third generation from Henry to wear the crown, but he is not directly descended from Henry. The body natural ceases to have any material value as the text focuses upon the office and sovereignty of the monarch within the body politic. Whereas parliament needed to redefine treason as an attack on governance rather than an attempt against the life of the sovereign in order to mount trials for treason against Strafford and Laud, the pamphlet dispatches of the corporeal altogether. Within the spiritual realm, genetics cease to be of importance: as inheritor of the crown, Charles also inherits the actions and misdemeanours of all who have been a monarch.

A Messenger From the Dead thus complicates our understanding of monarchy and what it means to be a just and an unjust ruler. Dismissing the body natural, the inheritance of the perpetual and corporate crown symbolises the continuance and unity of kingship. In refusing the title of king, Cromwell did not sever this connection. Instead, he redefined kingship to be the aspiration of a tyrant. However, Cromwell's adoption of the title 'lord protector' also presented its difficulties. As Shakespeare's *Richard III* warned the playgoing and reading public, lord protectors were not to be trusted. Tyranny may be associated with aspects of Tudor and Stuart governance, but lord protectors are also tainted with its implications. Furthermore, the place of the body politic becomes fractured as

Charles I's exiled son, although uncrowned in England, inherited the perpetual crown. The pamphlet may present two kings who, in their ghostly incarnations, lack corporeal bodies, but, in the material realm, both the body natural and the body politic become contested sites as the reading public endeavours to comprehend how governance could be structured in the absence of monarchy. Since precedence offered little assistance in defining the political order of the 1650s, critics of Cromwell turned to appropriate reductive notions of Machiavelli as the bogeyman who corrupted individuals to pretend the Crown. These ghost narratives seem to offer a cautionary tale that those who are seduced by power can expect only an afterlife of pain.

These play pamphlets might envisage posthumous punishments, but *The Court Career* (1659) allows Cromwell some corporeal joy and he presides over a lively court:

> [The court] was more frugal then frolick, unless at the *marriage* of some of our own *Relations*, and then *upse freze*, He was not modish that would not be drunkish. *Nol* himself knew then how to lay aside his staff o' state.[59]

These interludes add comic vigour and energy, which partially negate the negative representations of Cromwell.[60] In the months preceding the Restoration, Cromwell would be cast and recast: the point of political transition was also a point of iconographical change.[61]

Cromwell's image was not just a point of discussion in the twilight of the commonwealth but a constant concern throughout the 1650s and early 1660s; these images kept Cromwell's ghost alive.[62] However, they also brought Cromwell into all aspects of the rise and fall of the commonwealth and in so doing invoked the memory of Charles I. By sending Cromwell's ghost to reminisce with the martyred king (or gain intelligence from his fellow conspirators), the printed images of Cromwell experience the humiliation that royalists desired him to undergo as a consequence of the return of monarchy. The posthumous hanging, drawing and quartering of Cromwell's corpse symbolically allowed royalists to witness his punishment. In his diary, Samuel Pepys mentions the execution of Cromwell's corpse four times. Although Pepys's reporting is a little nonchalant, the fact that the exhumation and mutilation are referenced so often demonstrates that the event had iconographic (or iconoclastic) resonances for its observers.[63]

A New Meeting of Ghosts at Tyburn discusses some of the fates of the regicides and Cromwell's posthumous execution. Paralleling the contrite

Cromwell in *A Dialogue Betwixt the Ghosts of Charls the I, ... And Oliver*, the Cromwell at Tyburn laments his fate and declaims against Bradshaw, who 'gavest sentence on thy Matryr'd King' (sig. A2r). The remembrance of Charles's execution meets its counterpart in the depiction and reunion of those active in sentencing Charles. The author of *A New Meeting of Ghosts At Tyburn* may have wished to celebrate the execution of the regicides, but *Hell's Higher Court of Justice* (1661) seeks to materialise Cromwell's trial. Here, Cromwell is posthumously tried alongside his European allies. The trial is encapsulated in a commentary by Machiavelli, who opens the play pamphlet by lamenting that 'Hells floores by ... my Arts are embroidered / With Princes Thrones and Spirits of great men'.[64] The original cause of the troubles of the recent past is thus identified as Machiavelli. In using Machiavelli to frame the text, the author flirts with remembrance of performed drama. The Machiavellian usurper, so prevalent in Shakespeare's histories and Jacobean revenge tragedy, is here given body. It also echoes Marlowe's use of Machiavelli as the Chorus in *The Jew of Malta* (c. 1589/90). In appropriating Machiavelli in this way, the writer is acknowledging a theatrical inheritance and aligning Cromwell with past stage Machiavellians who have fallen under the influence of the Florentine writer. Cromwell is not absolved as a consequence of this, but is perceived as one of the statesman's more successful students:

> MACH: this I needs must say, you three have been
> Deeply concerned in all those wicked practices,
> The world of late have suffered by you *Sweden*
> Have done your part but yet fall short of these,
> And though the subtil *Mazarine* has been
> A cheif grand author of those miseries
> Yet *Cromwell* beares the bell away for hee
> In wickedness is cheifest of the three.
>
> (V:[i], sig. C4v)

The verse does not culminate in praise of Cromwell, but adopts the mode of panegyric to emphasise Cromwell's misdemeanours. Farcical as many of these dialogues are, they share in the iconography of Cromwell's posthumous execution. Both the play pamphlets and the ceremonial execution of Cromwell's corpse at the Restoration seek to materialise the punishment of Cromwell. The ceremonies and festivities that greeted restored monarchical rule celebrate the downfall of Cromwell as much as they applaud the return of the Stuarts.

Lois Potter has noted that royalist pamphlets and newsbooks were meant to irritate parliament.[65] Through shared tropes, themes were repeated, modified and exchanged between royalist and (sometimes) republican writers. On the paper stage, Cromwell's importance was restricted through presenting him as the antithesis of Charles. The afterlives of both were used to make key political points, demonstrating an anxiety to revisit and re-evaluate significant moments during the civil war and commonwealth period. The iconographic impact of regicide is unstable; endeavours to comprehend the event led to reductive images of Charles and Cromwell that established them as binary opposites. This is partly due to the availability of responses to the political moment being limited to satirical and/or hagiographical representation in the play pamphlet form. Some play pamphlets sought to celebrate Charles and denigrate Cromwell, but legally performed public drama in the 1650s responded to this trend by celebrating protectorate foreign policy. How drama operated on the protectorate stage will be discussed in Chapter 3.

Notes

1 See Graham Parry, *The Golden Age Restored: the Culture of the Stuart Court, 1603–42* (Manchester: Manchester University Press, 1981), pp. 184–203. See also pp. 58–62 on the disparity between the ideal present in the Stuart Masque and the reality of the Jacobean court. Richard Ollard mentions the masque within the context of Charles's attraction to image over reality in *The Image of the King: Charles I and Charles II* (London: Hodder and Stoughton, 1970), pp. 33–36. For a discussion of the politics and staging of court masques, see Stephen Orgel and Roy Strong, *Inigo Jones and the Theatre of the Stuart Court*, 2 vols (Berkeley and Los Angeles: University of California Press, 1973), 1:1–75; Jennifer Chibnell reassesses Orgel's and Strong's thesis ('"To that secure fix'd state": The function of the Caroline masque form', in David Lindley (ed.), *The Court Masque* (Manchester: Manchester University Press, 1984), pp. 184–203), while Clare McManus (*Women on the Renaissance Stage: Anna of Denmark and Female Masquing Culture in the Stuart Court (1590–1619)* (Manchester: Manchester University Press, 2002)) examines Anna of Denmark's key role in the formation of the Stuart Masque.

2 See Laura Lunger Knoppers, *Constructing Cromwell: Ceremony, Portrait and Print, 1645–1661* (Cambridge: Cambridge University Press, 2000); Elizabeth Sauer, *'Paper Contestations' and Textual Communities in England, 1640–1675* (Toronto: University of Toronto Press, 2005); Susan Wiseman, *Drama and Politics in the English Civil War* (Cambridge: Cambridge University Press,

1998); Joad Raymond, *Pamphlets and Pamphleteering in Early Modern Britain* (Cambridge: Cambridge University Press, 2003).

3 Rachel Willie, 'Sacrificial kings and martyred rebels: Charles and Rainborowe beatified', special issue, *Études Épistémè*, 20 (2011), www.etudesepisteme.org/2e/?sacrificialkings-and-martyed.

4 Butler provides a useful table of other play pamphlets (including anti-Laudian plays) printed between 1641 and 1642 (Martin Butler, *Theatre and Crisis, 1632-1642* (Cambridge: Cambridge University Press, 1984), pp. 289–91).

5 Richard Overton, *New Lambeth Fayre* (London, 1642), title page.

6 I discuss this pamphlet (and the material implications of its use of relics) at length in 'Sacrificial kings and martyred rebels'.

7 *A Bartholomew Faire* (London, 1641), p. 1

8 *A Bartholomew Fairing* (London, 1649), I:[i], sig. A2v.

9 See Christopher Hill, *The World Turned Upside Down: Radical Ideas During the English Revolution* (Harmondsworth: Penguin, 1975), pp. 306–23.

10 Woolrych, *Britain in Revolution*, p. 482; Royle, *Civil War*, p. 549.

11 Raymond, 'Popular Representations of Charles', in Thomas N. Corns (ed.), *The Royal Image: Representations of Charles I* (Cambridge: Cambridge University Press, 1999), p. 47–73.

12 Man in the Moon, *A Tragi-Comedy Called New-Market Fayre or Mrs. Parliaments New Figaryes* (1649), title page.

13 Woolrych, *Britain in Revolution*, pp. 462–80; Royle, *Civil War*, pp. 526–37; Antonia Fraser, *Cromwell: Our Chief of Men* (London: Bookclub Associates, 1974), chapter 13.

14 Some examples include, David Norbrook, *Writing the English Republic: Poetry, Rhetoric and Politics* (Cambridge: Cambridge University Press, 1999), pp. 243–80; John Kerrigan, *Archipelagic English: Literature, History and Politics, 1603–1707* (Cambridge: Cambridge University Press, 2008), pp. 233–4; Smith, *Literature and Revolution*, p. 8 and pp. 277–8; Nigel Smith, *Andrew Marvell: The Chameleon* (New Haven and London: Yale University Press, 2010), pp. 80–6 and *passim*.

15 This dialogue is attributed to Edmund Spenser and was entered in the Stationers' Register in 1598, though probably composed some time before this date. See *A View of the State of Ireland*, ed. Andrew Hadfield and Willy Maley (Oxford: Blackwell, 1997), xii.

16 Kathleen M. Noonan, '"The cruell pressure of an enraged, barbarous people": Irish and English identity in seventeenth-century policy and propaganda', *The Historical Journal*, 41 (1998), 151–77.

17 Woolrych, *Britain in Revolution*, p. 429.

18 Woolrych, *Britain in Revolution*, p. 347.

19 Press censorship has been covered extensively, but still remains conceptually fraught. For some studies, see Cyndia Susan Clegg, *Press Censorship in Elizabethan England* (Cambridge: Cambridge University Press, 1997), *Press Censorship in Jacobean England* (Cambridge: Cambridge University Press, 2001), and *Press Censorship in Caroline England* (Cambridge: Cambridge University Press, 2008); Annabel Patterson, *Censorship and Interpretation: The Conditions of Writing and Reading in Early Modern England* (Madison: University of Wisconsin Press, 1984).

20 John Morrill, 'Oliver Cromwell and his contemporaries', in John Morrill (ed.), *Oliver Cromwell and the English Revolution* (London and New York: Longman, 1990), pp. 259–281; Fraser, *Cromwell*, pp. 514–15.

21 Woolrych, *Britain in Revolution*, pp. 558–59; Royle, *Civil War*, pp. 653–9.

22 Woolrych, *Britain in Revolution*, pp. 564–67 and pp. 651–63.

23 Derek Hirst, 'The lord protector, 1653–1658', in Morrill (ed.), *Oliver Cromwell*, pp. 119–48 (p. 125).

24 Ollard, *The Image of the King*, p. 98; Underdown, *Royalist Conspiracy*, p. 220.

25 After Cromwell rejected the formal offer of the crown, speculation that Cromwell would accept the crown still continued. See Hirst, 'The lord protector', p. 122.

26 Woolrych, *Britain in Revolution*, pp, 580–1 and p. 593; Royle, *Civil War*, p. 666.

27 Knoppers, *Constructing Cromwell*, pp. 15–16.

28 Woolrych, *Britain in Revolution*, pp. 378–85; Royle, *Civil War*, pp. 415–17.

29 Woolrych, *Britain in Revolution*, chapter 13; Royle, *Civil War*, pp. 395–411. Interestingly, Woolrych emphasises Cromwell's conservatism, whereas Royle cites Cromwell as an example of a radical who was surprised by the army's discontent at parliament's failure to provide funds.

30 Mercurius Melancholicus, *Craftie Cromwell* (1648), title page.

31 See p. 37 above.

32 For a discussion of the disruption of the trial at the Higher Court of Justice and other women's responses to the regicide, see chapter two of Marcus Nevitt's *Women and the Pamphlet Culture of Revolutionary England, 1640–1660* (Aldershot: Ashgate, 2006).

33 In his memoirs, which were published posthumously, Thomas Fairfax absolves himself of any part in the events that led to regicide: scheming army agitators circumvented his leadership. Fairfax thus favoured being labeled a weak manager over being accused of treason. See *Short Memorials of Thomas Lord Fairfax, Written by Himself* (London, 1699), esp. pp. 93–128; Samual Rawson Gardiner, *History of the Commonwealth and Protectorate 1649–1656*, 4 vols (London: Longman, Green and Co., 1903) 1:249–50, 262–5.

34 Woolrych, *Britain in Revolution*, pp. 482–3; Royle, *Civil War*, pp. 572–4; Gardiner, *History*, 1:258–62.
35 Lucy Hutchinson, *Memoirs of the life of Colonel Hutchinson*, ed. N. H. Keeble (London: Phoenix Press, 2000), p. 240.
36 Woolrych, *Britain in Revolution*, pp. 482–3; Royle, *Civil War*, pp. 572–4.
37 Royle, *Civil War*, p. 480.
38 See Ian J. Gentles, 'Fairfax, Thomas, third Lord Fairfax of Cameron (1612–1671)', *Oxford Dictionary of National Biography* (Oxford: Oxford University Press, 2004) www.oxforddnb.com/view/article/9092 (accessed 10 August 2007).
39 Mercurius Pragmaticus, *The Second Part of Cratfy Cromwell* (London, 1648), IV.[i], sig. B3v.
40 Woolrych, *Britain in Revolution*, p. 295.
41 Royle, *Civil War*, pp. 116–27.
42 Gillian Bennett, 'Ghost and witch in the sixteenth and seventeenth centuries', *Folklore*, 97 (1986), 3–14 (6–7).
43 Bennett, 'Ghost and witch, p. 8.
44 Woolrych, *Britain in Revolution*, pp. 635–7.
45 Woolrych, *Britain in Revolution*, pp. 192–218; Royle, *Civil War*, pp. 150–3.
46 Knoppers, *Constructing Cromwell*, p. 175.
47 Woolrych, *Britain in Revolution*, p. 696.
48 Woolrych, *Britain in Revolution*, pp. 635–7, 694–5.
49 *The Case is Altered, Or Dreadful News from Hell* (London, 1660), sigs A3v–A4r.
50 Thomason dated this tract 19 August 1659, probably the date of purchase.
51 *A Conference held Between the Old Protector and the New Lord General* (London, 1660), sig. A2r.
52 George Monck was largely celebrated as bringing about the restoration of monarchy, and hence was depicted as a hero by royalist panegyrists (Woolrych, *Britain in Revolution*, pp. 763–6; Royle, *Civil War*, pp. 755–6). See also *The Return of the King: An Anthology of English Poems Commemorating the Restoration of Charles II*, ed. Gerald MacLean (Electronic Text Center: University of Virginia Library, 1999), http://etext.virginia.edu/toc/modeng/public/MacKing.html (accessed 26 January 2013), esp. section 3.3: 'Monk Marches on London'.
53 *A Dialogue Betwixt the Ghosts of Charls the I, ... And Oliver* (London, 1659), p. 5.
54 Jonathan Scott, *Commonwealth Principles: Republican Writing of the English Revolution* (Cambridge: Cambridge University Press, 2004), p. 40, chapters 5, 9 and 10.

55 Christine de Pizan, *The Book of the Body Politic*, ed. Kate Langdon Forhan (Cambridge: Cambridge University Press, 1994), p. xx. Pizan's complex late medieval text serves both as a warning to tyrants, but also advises subjects to obey their sovereign (pp. 90–5).
56 I am indebted to Ronald G. Asch's *ODNB* entry for this account ('Wentworth, Thomas, first earl of Strafford (1593–1641)', *Oxford Dictionary of National Biography*, Oxford University Press, 2004; online edn, Oct 2009, www.oxforddnb.com/view/article/29056(accessed 5 January 2012).
57 *A Messenger from the Dead* (London: 1658), sigs A3r–A3v.
58 Mark Rankin, 'The literary afterlife of Henry VIII, 1558–1625', in *Henry VIII and His Afterlives*, ed. Mark Rankin, Christopher Highley and John N. King (Cambridge: Cambridge University Press, 2009), pp. 94–114.
59 *The Court Career, Death Shaddow'd to life* (1659), sig. A4v 'upse freze': drunken carousing in the Friesian manner.
60 Knoppers, *Constructing Cromwell*, pp. 164–6.
61 Knoppers, *Constructing Cromwell*, p. 168.
62 Knoppers, *Constructing Cromwell*, and *passim*.
63 See *The Diary of Samuel Pepys*, ed. Robert Latham and William Matthews, 11 vols (London: Harper Collins, 1995), 1:309 (4 December 1660), 2:24 (28 January 1661), 2:26–7 (30 January 1661), 2:31 (5 February 1661).
64 *Hell's Higher Court of Justice* (London, 1661), 1:[i], sig. A3v).
65 Potter, *Secret Rites*, p. 16.

3

Reinventing the masque: Shirley's and Davenant's protectorate entertainments

When Cromwell gained control of England, Ireland and Wales in 1653, the protectorate established its own form of iconography, and this became increasingly monarchical in style as the decade progressed.[1] The investiture of the lord protector in 1653 and 1657 offered an alternative image to the spectacle of a royal coronation and counteracted that of the usurper that was presented in some play pamphlets. While commonwealth and protectorate governments appropriated some aspects of monarchy, the great form of courtly entertainment and monarchical iconography, the Stuart court masque, appears not to have been overtly adopted. In this chapter, I will seek to identify what happened to the Stuart court masque when court culture changed. In so doing, I will plot the transitions of this type of drama during the commonwealth.

Through looking at these transitions, I will explore some of the musicological differences between the masque form and opera to make the case that the entertainments William Davenant mounted in the 1650s are masques. Owing to the lack of clarity over their generic structure, these dramas have been variously labelled as the first English operas, semi-operas, heroic musical drama or 'pseudo masques'.[2] More recently, Lauren Shohet has insightfully labelled these works 'late masques', but this term warrants interrogation to show how changes in ideology have affected performativity.[3] After examining these shifts in masque production, the chapter will look at what the political iconography of the masque does at this specific moment in history. To begin, I will briefly outline Stuart masquing culture.

The early Stuart court was not an enclosed space comprising courtiers and royalty. Instead, the social circles that operated in and about the court were porous and connected with the city.[4] Despite this, audiences at court masques were usually aristocratic and diplomatic. By the Caroline period, a ticket system was in operation for attendance at masques, but its effectiveness is questionable.[5] Whether non-invited guests were minor aristocrats, gentry or citizens (or from all social groups) is equally debatable, but it seems most likely that any interlopers would have been middle-ranking nobility as they had more access to the court. Since masques circulated in print, we may expect that citizens had knowledge of Stuart court masques through printed texts of masques and through rumours of the entertainments. Since an element of the court masque is the apotheosis of monarchy through allegory, the aesthetics of masques are tightly bound with their politics. The print culture of these masques therefore offers an extension of court culture, where those beyond the court may gain knowledge of allegorical renderings of the monarch. Although the intended audience of the physical entertainment were a select group, knowledge of the masque and its celebration and affirmation of Stuart monarchy would reach a wider audience in print.[6]

Some of Ben Jonson's earlier masques may have been printed in quarto prior to their court performance, while others did not appear in print until the folio editions of 1616 and 1640.[7] Over time, masques began to be printed shortly after performance, and this seems to have been the practice adopted by writers of Caroline masques. The only masque known to have been performed for a diplomat during the commonwealth period follows the Stuart convention of printing a brochure through which the physical entertainment can be remembered. James Shirley's *Cupid and Death* was performed and first printed in 1653. Thomas Jordan's *Cupid his Coronation* was performed the following year in a non-court setting, but the state papers are frustratingly silent about these entertainments.[8] Unlike their Jacobean and Caroline predecessors, commonwealth 'court' masques do not appear to be well documented. *Cupid and Death* is thus of interest for the fact that any evidence of its performance exists at all: Matthew Locke's reworking of Christopher Gibbons's score for a 1659 performance is extant.[9] This marks a radical move away from the printing practices of Stuart court masques.

Music from earlier masques was often reworked to make it capable of being played by small amateur ensembles. The appearance in print of the music to these earlier masques is therefore haphazard owing to its being (re)arranged for different musical groups.[10] As the masques themselves were dramatic works with an amateur input from aristocratic dancers, music and choreography from earlier masques may have been recycled for later entertainments and different occasions.[11] Jonson and Inigo Jones famously argued over whether poetry or spectacle was the most important element of the court masque.[12] Through word setting, song supports the drama of poetry, and yet music also aids spectacle by being set as an accompaniment to dance. Consequently, music is present in both poetry and spectacle. In this respect, it is a necessary element of the Stuart court masque, but neither Jones nor Jonson deemed music to be significant enough to be meticulously recorded. It is worth considering this when, later in this chapter, we come to examine Davenant's protectorate entertainments. Literary critics have followed the lead of some musicologists in assuming that these entertainments are rudimentary operas, but the way in which music functions in each dramatic form is very different. In understanding this, we can lay to rest some of the aesthetic assumptions about Davenant's entertainments. This will help us to fully identify some of the political nuances of the dramas.

The extant score for *Cupid and Death* marks a transition in the recording of masquing culture. This transition prompts interesting questions: what does a court masque represent when (theoretically) there is no court and no monarch to be the order-restoring focal point of the entertainment, and why do we know so much about its music compared to earlier masques? The completeness of the score for *Cupid and Death* compared to the more fragmentary evidence of music in earlier masques is more surprising when juxtaposed with the lack of information regarding the masque's performance history. The title pages of earlier masques bear information about the date and circumstances of the performance. Often, there then follows a preamble regarding the splendour of the occasion, usually idealising the evening's entertainments and overlooking the drunken, gluttonous and debauched proceedings to which they were sometimes reduced.[13] The preamble and annotated text frequently describe in detail the staging of the masque, and the reader is directed to interpret the allegory of the performance as representing a positive image of Stuart monarchy. The information provided in these annotations varies, with some authors focusing upon different elements of the masque and others being more frank about the deficiencies of the performance.[14]

The text of *Cupid and Death*, however, does not contain any in-depth annotation. The title page to the first edition follows the convention established by Stuart court masques in providing details of its performance. We are told that the text is reproduced 'As it was presented before his Excellencie, the Embassador of Portugal, Upon the 26. March 1653'.[15] However, the next page does not provide specific information about the masque's performance. Rather than the intricate and often idealised renderings of the revels experienced at court, we are offered an apologia. Shirley's masque was intended not for courtly airing but as a 'privat entertainment' (sig. A2r), which happened to have been performed for the Portuguese Ambassador. Schoolboys may have acted the masque before the diplomat, as Shirley appears to have been a schoolmaster at the time.[16]

Such school productions were not without precedent. Anna of Denmark had watched a masque performed by schoolgirls at Queen's House, Greenwich in 1617.[17] Despite this, musicologists have not perceived the production of *Cupid and Death* before the Portuguese Ambassador as a court masque.[18] The fact that Portugal was seeking a treaty with the commonwealth at the time suggests that it might have been performed as a state (or state-approved) entertainment.[19] The lack of evidence in state papers means this cannot be asserted with any authority, but, if the masque was performed for a state occasion, the form of courtly entertainment most associated with Stuart monarchy and a key element of early Stuart kingship was reinvented for the commonwealth. Where the parameters of what signifies a court alter, courtly entertainments may also be subject to change.

Shirley's 'privat entertainment' was performed in an unknown, possibly courtly, space in March 1653.[20] The text of the masque is consequently not printed as a textual reproduction of a physical entertainment. Instead, the first printed edition of *Cupid and Death* is presented as a means of asserting authorial control. Although intended as a 'privat entertainment', it reached a wider audience in print. The letter from the printer to the reader presents a fairly conventional justification of its publication, but is still worth quoting in full:

> This Masque was born without ambition of more, than to make good a privat entertainment, though it found, without any address or design of the Author, an honourable acceptation from his Excellency, the Embassadour of *Portugal*, to whom it was presented by Mr. *Luke Channen*, &c.
>
> It had not so soon been published, for the Author meant all civilities to all persons, but that he heard an imperfect copy was put to the Press, with an addition before it, of some things, that should be obtruded by another hand, which the Authors judgement could not consent too.
>
> The Scaens wanted no elegance, or curiosity for the delight of the Spectator. The Musical compositions had in them a great soul of Harmony. For the Gentleman that perform'd the Dances, thus much the Author did affirm, upon sight of their practise, that they shew'd themselves Master of their quality. (sigs A2r–A2v)

The printer stamps authorial intent upon the work. He claims another hand would have presented the masque to a reading public had he not intervened, and authorial intervention is necessary to prevent an imperfect copy of the work being circulated. Such explanations for publishing were common in the sixteenth and seventeenth century. The sincerity of the claim is therefore dubious because it follows a well-established convention. Masques, however, tend not to be prefixed with these kinds of validation.[21] A credulous reader would note that the text appeared in print out of a desire to perfect the copy. The circumstances of the staged production are briefly sketched, but, in claiming ownership of the text, the printer seems to assert that Shirley is rejecting involvement in the enactment before the ambassador.

Such a reading of the masque's performance would be naive: Shirley had written masques for the Caroline court and therefore had knowledge of how to get a masque staged – even if the court had altered. The reference to Luke Channen (a dancing master, believed to have been involved in theatrical productions in the Restoration)[22] may therefore serve as an advertisement for Channen's teaching and choreographic skill, and is not necessarily a serious reference to his connections at Whitehall. Despite this, the letter directs the reader to think differently about why the text was printed and not to focus upon the performance, marking a transition in masquing culture. The spectacle is briefly mentioned, then dismissed. Particulars about what the scenery depicted, what machinery was used in the staging of the masque and what the allegory signifies are not given. We are thus presented with an allegedly authorial text while responsibility for the performance is placed beyond the author's control. However, without any direction as to how the allegory ought to be read, the authorial control that the printer affords to Shirley becomes problematic. Without direction to decode the allegory, the semiotics of the text are open to multiple interpretations. Of course, as numerous critics have long observed, while the iconography of the Stuart court masque may have been directed at praising the monarch, the form also encoded the possibility of covert criticism.[23] The problem of the multiple ways in which allegory may be interpreted is therefore not unique to *Cupid and Death*. However, both the source material for the masque and how this material is appropriated in *Cupid and Death* mean that the allegory is particularly difficult to decipher.

The masque is derived from two tales from Aesop. Both the fabulist tradition and the Stuart masque rely upon presenting allegory that can be (or, in the case of some masques, pretends to be) easily decipherable.[24] Fables use allegory to critique authority figures, whereas masques adopt

Reinventing the masque

allegory as a form of praise. Although an unsubtle reading of each genre would point to their appropriation of allegory for different ends, this shared use of allegorical representations means that fables can easily be transformed into masques. In 1651, for example, John Ogilby's translation of Aesop's fables appeared in print, and this text provided Shirley with his immediate source.[25] Since Davenant and Shirley had written dedicatory verses to Ogilby's *The Fables of Æsop Paraphras'd in Verse*, Shirley obviously had knowledge of his friend's work. Ogilby's entire verse offers a cautionary tale against civil war and the chaos that may ensue once monarchy is removed. Ogilby reinvents Aesop's fables to create a royalist commentary upon seventeenth-century events.[26]

Ogilby inverts the generic conventions of fabulist writing: he transforms the genre from being the political language used by slaves to give authority figures parallels for their own misguided actions into a representation of royalist solidarity in defeat. Although Ogilby's fables may still be viewed as tales of protest that are voiced from a position of weakness, the genre is destabilised because fabulist aesthetics (and the underlying politics of these aesthetics) were appropriated by both royalists and parliamentarians.[27] Since the fable served a political function, changes within the body politic affected the nuances of the work. As the political nuances are closely tied to the fable's allegory (and ways in which the allegory is interpreted), fabulist aesthetics are also affected. The same is true of the court masque.

In *Cupid and Death* we are therefore presented with a work that has inherited political and aesthetic tensions, partly from its source material, partly from generic instability and partly from the impact of contemporary events. Considering the negative view of non-monarchical rule offered by Ogilby's text, the fact that Shirley's masque was produced in a quasi-republican court setting seems all the more remarkable. Why would the commonwealth permit that which could potentially be seen as royalist propaganda to be performed for the Portuguese ambassador at a time when they were negotiating a treaty? If we read *Cupid and Death* through Ogilby's text, we could make assumptions about its agenda that are not substantiated by the masque. This may in part be due to the fairly neutral tone of the two tales that have been conflated by Shirley in comparison to some of the more robust pieces in Ogilby's translation. For all the ideological moralising of Ogilby's work, Shirley's masque is politically ambivalent.

Chaos, the grotesque and the comic figure heavily in the masque, which opens with the Host and a Chamberlain preparing an inn for the arrival of two notable guests and their respective entourages. After spending the night at the inn, Cupid and Death embark on their separate journeys, unaware that the Chamberlain (disgruntled in his choice of wife) has switched their arrows. Cupid thus becomes the slaughterer of youth, while Death causes havoc through inspiring amorous sensations in the old. Order is restored when the gods, hearing Nature's pleas, send Mercury to give Cupid sight. The accidental murderer thus aborts his killing spree and youth may once more enjoy the pangs of love. However, a caveat is inserted at the end of the narrative: although the young are free to fall in love again, Venus's child is now banished from the courts of princes.

One could assume that the masque advocates a return to monarchical rule through invoking the gods to restore order. As Lois Potter comments, the authority figure within the court masque is silent: his or her attributes (and by extension, the monarch's idealised qualities) are discussed through personification or metaphorical imagery.[28] In sending his messenger, one could argue that the absent Jupiter fulfils this role: the god's lack of physical representation may allude to the fact that the erstwhile king's heir is now in exile. However, this sense of resolution is complicated by overt criticism of Stuart government:

HO[ST]: Love has two
   Gentlemen, that wait on him in his Chamber,
   Of speciall trust, he cannot act without them.
CH[AMBERLAIN]: Their Names sir, I beseech you?
HO: *Folly* and *Madness.*
CH: A pair of precious entertainments, and fit
   To be o'th' privy counsel.

(sig. B1v)

In 1649, the king's privy council was abolished and, in its stead, the commonwealth established a council of state.[29] Folly and madness therefore become the personified qualities associated with monarchy. This kind of exchange was commonly used in Jacobean and Caroline drama and therefore does not necessarily represent a republican bias. However, the removal of these lines from a 1659 reprint suggest that this banter may have become unpalatable in the twilight years of the commonwealth: with the imminent restoration of monarchy, there may have been a need to sanitise the masque of any lines that might have been judged as a critique of monarchical rule. Alternatively, such lines may have ceased to have any comical or topical significance ten years after the abolition of the privy council.[30]

The banishment of Cupid from the courts of princes adds further weight to the idea that *Cupid and Death* may reinvent the masque for a court that (paradoxically) lacks a monarch. Wiseman observes that love, which she reads as the bond between a king and his subjects, has forsaken the court.[31] When this metaphysical bond has been severed, civil unrest may ensue. Such a reading frames the narrative within Hobbesian philosophy. In *Leviathan* (1651), Thomas Hobbes's notoriously complex text asserts that the natural state of humanity is one of war. The Sovereign, in whatever form it may take, has authority only as long as the populace over which it governs is willing to forsake some of their freedoms, and when government breaks down humanity reverts to its natural state of war.[32]

While implicitly alluding to Hobbesian principles of government, Wiseman also acknowledges that mutual love between monarch and subject was a feature of the court masque. The right of the sovereign to govern has been forfeited because the love of the subjects (and their willingness to be governed) has forsaken the court. However, another trait of Jacobean and Caroline government is present in the narrative. Under James I and initially under Charles I, the royal favourite was an influential (and disliked) figure at court. After the Duke of Buckingham's assassination in 1628, Henrietta Maria replaced the duke as her husband's confidante and adviser.[33] By banishing Cupid from the courts, Mercury alludes to the negative consequences that may occur through the influence of loved ones. A dichotomy between the public and the private is established:

> *Cupid*, the Gods do banish thee
> From every Palace, thou must be
> Confin'd to Cottages, to poor
> And humble Cells, *Love* must no more
> Appear in Princes Courts, their heart
> Impenetrable by thy Dart,
> And from softer influence free
> By their own wills must guided be.
>
> (sig. D2v)

By endeavouring to reject domestic love in the context of the court, the masque suggests that it is necessary to separate the public and the private spheres. The perception of Charles I as being in thrall to his wife was so great that, four years after the regicide, *Cupid and Death* continues to remember and reinvent Henrietta Maria's perceived dominance of her husband. In banishing love from the court, Shirley refers not only to the conjugal love between monarch and spouse but also to the cult of Neoplatonic courtly love that Henrietta Maria had fostered within her circle.[34] While a private man may be allowed to experience love, a prince ought not to allow domestic bonds to affect policy. Courtship and courtiership may bear some similarities, but the anointed monarch should not become uxorious to their favourite or their spouse.

Although the allegory of *Cupid and Death* can thus be interpreted in divergent ways, there are many threads within the text that could make it fit for a republican audience. The printer's claim that Shirley owned the text but refused to admit involvement in the performance of the masque is equally open to interpretation. A noted playwright before the beginnings of civil unrest, Shirley returned to his previous profession of schoolmaster at the outbreak of civil war.[35] This represents not so much a retirement from the stage as the need to find another profession as a consequence of theatre closure. The printer may declare that Shirley denies participation in the staging of the masque and is reluctantly acquiescing to the publication of an authorial text, but by authorising the printing of the masque the performance is made publicly known.

The meanings of the text and the paratext are therefore open to multiple interpretations, partly due to the instability of the textual reproduction but also because of the curious circumstances of its performance before the Portuguese ambassador. Shirley's Caroline masques are equally ambiguous. His 1634 masque, *The Triumph of Peace*, was performed at Whitehall by the Inns of Court. Celebrating Charles as the ultimate peacemaker, the masque is laden with textual and contextual ironies.[36] *The Triumph of Peace* is represented as a sign of loyalty to the Crown after one of the Inns' lawyers, William Prynne, had angered the court.[37] The fact that the Inns of Court responded to the fining and mutilation of one of their members by expelling Prynne and putting on a masque in honour of the monarch is not without its ironies. One of the threads in *The Triumph of Peace* is concerned with masquing culture. Confidence, Phansie, Opinion, Novelty, Admiration, Jollity and Laughter open the entertainment with a metatheatrical discussion regarding masques. A further anti-masque continues this thread, where interlopers, including a property-maker's wife, interrupt the masque:

> My husband is somewhere in the workes; I'me sure I helpt to make him an Owle and a Hobbihorse, and I see no reason but his Wife may bee admitted in *Forma paperis*, to see as good a maske as this.[38]

The property-maker's wife thus asserts a right to watch the masque. Although citizens would expect to be barred from experiencing courtly entertainments, the intruders claim a creative right in the production. In so doing, the property-maker's wife alludes to the translation of properties from the office of the works to the masquing stage.[39] However, this comment also overlooks the possibility that 'worn' properties may have been hired out or sold by the revels office to acting companies, and instead points to the role of women as producers and not just keepers of commodities.[40] 'Women', Natasha Korda writes, 'worked actively in a number of trades that would have had commerce with the theatres'.[41] Although Korda's study focuses upon the playhouse and specifically domestic properties or household stuff in Shakespeare, the statement by the property-maker's wife runs parallel to Korda's argument. Both propose arguments regarding the manufacturing of properties, and the writing of a property-maker's wife into the masque relocates women from being consumers or spectators of theatre to participants in the production of drama.[42]

For the property-maker's wife, this engagement with theatrical production invests a certain degree of ownership: since she has assisted her husband in making properties, she claims a right to watch the masque, and this right is given further weight by her husband's heavy involvement in masque production. Elements from the anti-masque threaten to invade the masque proper, an idea that is also apparent in *Cupid and Death*. This emphasises the theatricality of the masque and provides an alternative to the apotheosis of monarchy. Shirley writes the mundane into *The Triumph of Peace* (and the Inn setting of *Cupid and Death* demonstrates a return to the ordinary, despite the extraordinary guests). Through this, Shirley discusses the artificiality of masques and the impossibility that the dramatic form could ever succeed in rendering the monarch absolute. The use of allegory can only disclose transient representations that never permanently and thoroughly honour the monarch. This reflection upon drama was to be imitated in the 1650s by Davenant when he produced dramas for a paying audience. As we will see, the legacy of the Caroline court masque is present in these entertainments. This is partly due to Davenant's own career before the civil war.

A courtier playwright during the reign of Charles I, Davenant successfully negotiated the commonwealth period and was granted one of only two patents when theatres reopened at the Restoration.[43] However, during the protectorate, Davenant was also permitted to stage entertainments for a paying audience, initially at his home, then at the Cockpit theatre in

Drury Lane.[44] Having written the last Caroline masque, *Salmacida Spolia* (1640), Davenant now turned his pen and directorial skills to producing short scripts padded out with instrumental music and dance. The first of these interludes, *The First Days Entertainment at Rutland House* (1656), is split into two sections. The second part deals with the relative merits of Paris and London, while the first is concerned with the idea of drama. A debate is staged between Diogenes, who is introduced by a 'consort of instrumental musick, adapted to ... [his] sullen disposition',[45] and Aristophanes, presented by 'musick, befitting ... [his] pleasant disposition' (sig. B8r). Rhetoric and music conjoin to lead the audience to agree with Aristophanes's assertion that public representations can be morally good. The first legal public performance of the protectorate is concerned with asserting the moral benefit of reformed plays.[46]

What were these reformed plays that Davenant produced from 1656 until 1659? As early as 1639, Charles I granted Davenant a patent to produce theatrical entertainments involving music, drama and dance.[47] Theatre closure and the outbreak of civil war meant that this patent was never put to use. Some have suggested that Davenant wanted to introduce opera to England but was thwarted in this plan by civil unrest, and critics have also assumed that Davenant used the paradoxical situation of being permitted to perform plays while theatres were banned as a means to produce opera.[48] Music never received the same level of scrutiny as the playhouses and was not judged to be as objectionable as drama. This hints that music could be used as a means to reform drama and thus offer a new form of performance to that experienced in the early seventeenth century.[49] As we will see, however, the use of music does not represent a significant shift from masquing culture towards opera. Rather, the use of music in Davenant's dramas creates some continuity between court masques and protectorate entertainments.

That Davenant had knowledge of operas from his European travels should not lead us to assume that the dramas he produced during the protectorate were operas. Davenant was an admirer of the operatic form, as is clear from the discussion of recitative music in his Restoration medley, *The Playhouse to be Let* (1673):

> Recitative Musick is not compos'd
> Of matter so familiar, as may serve
> For every low occasion of discourse.
> In Tragedy, the language of the Stage
> Is rais'd above the common dialect;

Our passions rising with the height of Verse;
And Vocal Musick adds new wings to all
The flights of poetry.[50]

This quotation neatly encapsulates some of the thoughts that are known to have influenced the Florentine Camerata in their development of opera, as does Davenant's claim on the title page to *The First Days Entertainment at Rutland House* that the production was performed 'After the manner of the Ancients'. Opera had originated in Italy at the end of the sixteenth century. The idea of setting words entirely to music came from Girolamo Mei's reading of Greek tragedies and humanist ideas regarding the unification of classical art. Mei concluded that classical tragedies were composed throughout, and so a new style of composition known as recitative – a form of declamatory singing which drew from recent developments in tonality, rhythm and harmonisation – emerged as composers found ways to set an entire play to music.[51] In masques, music is presented as a necessary element of the form. This is distinct from opera, where music is significant to the drama's aesthetic composition.

This brief description of the emergence of opera is inevitably reductive; the harmonic features of recitative were a consequence of early modern tonal developments and therefore do not mark a return to Greek concepts of tonality.[52] However, it is useful to have some understanding of how early Italian opera works in order to assess the extent to which Davenant's protectorate entertainments can be considered as 'opera'. Since opera is founded upon aesthetic principles regarding the performance of Greek tragedy, the relationship between the aesthetic and the political (and music) is very different from that found in court masques, where political iconography or covert iconoclasm is fundamental to the aesthetic form. With this knowledge of the different ways in which politics and aesthetics are connected, we can assess whether or not it might be more fruitful to consider Davenant's 'operas' as being another type of entertainment that involves music.

Opera developed in different ways in different European countries. In France, the strong tradition of dance (and especially ballet) meant that dancing became a more dominant feature of French opera than of its Italian counterpart.[53] That English opera would not be identical to Italian opera is therefore not surprising. Despite this, to assume that Davenant produced an embryonic form of opera, 'semi-opera' or even 'heroic musical drama' is misleading. The music for Davenant's entertainments is now lost; consequently, analysis of the music scores is impossible. However, there is enough evidence in the printed texts of these entertainments to gain an idea of how music might have been used in performance.

The publication and circulation of the text of Davenant's entertainments copied the continental practice of printing the libretto to operas prior to performance.[54] This does not necessarily mean that they are operas. Instead, it is an indication of commercial concerns. Where most Stuart court masques were printed in retrospect to reach a wider audience, Davenant's text was printed to entice an audience. The title page tells the audience where and when viewers could watch the performance, not when and where the masque was performed. The text was printed no longer as a material memory of the entertainment but as a taster of the spectacle that those wealthy enough to buy a ticket could observe at Drury Lane. The pragmatism of mounting commercial theatre rather than a desire to emulate the operatic model may therefore explain why these texts appeared in print before performance. Furthermore, as already noted, there are a few examples of the text of a court masque being printed before the entertainment was performed; this demonstrates some fluidity in the practice of printing masques.

The title page of *The Siege of Rhodes* (1656) advertises it as being 'sung in Recitative music'.[55] The letter to the reader boasts that the 'music was composed, and both the vocal and instrumental is exercised, by the most transcendent of England in the Art, and perhaps not unequal to the best masters abroad; but being recitative and therefore unpractised here, though of great reputation amongst other nations, the very attempt of it is an obligation of our own'.[56] Recitative music is presented as something foreign and exotic. We are led to believe that the text was set entirely to music, but (if this was the case) evidence from the later entertainments suggests that this experiment was abandoned. Significantly, *The Siege of Rhodes* would be revived at the Restoration as a spoken play. This emphasises that, unlike opera, music was not integral to the production of Davenant's dramas.

Although Davenant claims recitative music was not practised in England until it was introduced by his production, in England in the early seventeenth century, a type of declamatory singing developed as the result of the need to project sound in large spaces such as the Banqueting House while performing masques. Furthermore, travellers to Europe would have been familiar with recitative. English declamatory singing may have been influenced by Italian developments, though evidence is scarce, and that other development of the Italian Baroque – figured bass (a method of using numbers to indicate harmony in music notation) – did not feature in English music until the 1630s.[57] Nevertheless, transnational encounters meant that ideas and influences were shared across Europe. The English composer (and painter) Nicholas Lanier had experimented with a declamatory style that paralleled recitative, as did William and Henry Lawes.[58] An account of Jonson's 1617 masque, *Lovers Made Men*, states that 'the whole masque was sung (after the Italian manner) *Stylo recitative*, by Master *Nicholas Lanier*; who ordered and made both the Scene, and the Musicke'.[59] While this might be a reference to English declamatory music rather than Italian, it is presented to the reading public as being derived from Italian music. By the 1650s, it is not the idea of recitative music that is novel but the fact that it is being listened to in England by a paying audience.

From this digression we can draw some important conclusions. In producing these musical extravaganzas, Davenant flirted with the possibilities of opera and reinvented the Stuart court masque for the playhouse. Davenant had been involved in the production of masques at court and therefore knew how to mount them. Although Davenant would have had knowledge of opera through his continental travels and the people with whom he consorted, he never visited Italy.[60] Consequently, we can only conjecture whether Davenant ever experienced an Italian opera. On 5 May 1659, John Evelyn wrote that he saw 'a new Opera after the Italian way in Recitative Music and Sceanes, much inferior to the Italian composure and magnificence'.[61] Evelyn, who had travelled extensively in Italy, recognised an attempt by Davenant to follow operatic conventions, but Evelyn did not acknowledge Davenant's entertainment to be of the same quality as Italian opera. Perhaps the type of declamatory singing had more affinity with the music performed in Stuart court masques than in the Italian opera houses: since the former Caroline courtier-playwright, Davenant, and his collaborators had experience of mounting Stuart court masques, it seems inevitable that Stuart court masque conventions would influence these protectorate productions. This borrowing from the masque form might explain Evelyn's dissatisfaction with the entertainment as 'opera'. Furthermore, *The Siege of Rhodes* was entered in the Stationers' Register and Kirkman's catalogue as a masque.[62] This not only demonstrates that at least one contemporary perceived the work to be in the manner of the English entertainment and not the Italian spectacle but also officially labels Davenant's work as a masque.

In Italy, opera transferred from the courts of noblemen and princes to the public theatre in the early seventeenth century.[63] By the late seventeenth century, the masque had migrated from the Caroline court to the English stage. The entertainments that Davenant produced between 1656 and 1659 work at the margins of court drama and the public theatre, and some public stage spectacles such as rope dancing were brought into these masques.[64] For a fee, wealthy Londoners could experience the performance rather than having knowledge of the spectacle only through the printed text. Once we place these productions in the context of court masques, we can understand more fully how they might have operated and why they were performed despite theatre closure. In the rest of this chapter, I examine two of Davenant's masques in more detail: *The Cruelty of the Spaniards in Peru* (1658) and *The History of Sir Francis Drake* (1659). I will reserve further discussion of *The Siege of Rhodes*, the other masque that Davenant produced under the protectorate, until Chapter 4, as it had an interesting afterlife on the Restoration stage.

New modelled masques and the politics of protectorate drama

How did Davenant succeed in mounting masques in the playhouse while a ban on stage plays was still in place? Although *The First Days Entertainment at Rutland House* presents arguments for a reformed drama, it seems unlikely that the entertainment alone swayed parliament. That Cromwell and many other parliamentarians enjoyed music and did not share William Prynne's disapproval of stage plays is now well known.[65] It is therefore not so much the fact that Davenant was allowed to stage a public masque that is striking, rather the fact that the act for theatre closure was not repealed until the Restoration.

Despite this, Davenant is a curious person to have been permitted to mount these productions. Appointed poet laureate in 1638 and knighted by the monarch in 1643, Davenant was a notable supporter of Charles I. He served under William Cavendish, Duke of Newcastle, and had passed messages between Charles and Henrietta Maria during the civil wars.[66] While travelling to Virginia in 1650, Davenant was intercepted by the commonwealth, arrested, imprisoned and sentenced to death.[67] Within five years of his arrest, Davenant was freed and could be found proposing reformed entertainments to be performed for his erstwhile captors. Davenant successfully created a new role for himself under the protectorate.

The new writer (and producer) of the protectorate masque was careful in his choice of subject matter. While negotiating with the secretary of state, John Thurloe, Davenant talks of his proposed entertainments as providing moral representations. He also cites more pragmatic reasons

Reinventing the masque 95

for the performances: the people, Davenant argues, 'require continuall divertissements being otherwise naturally inclin'd to that Melancholy that breeds Sedition'.[68] Drama is figured in this way as a form of political didacticism and is also a medicinal necessity to keep the humours balanced in the body politic. Such a view echoes the advocacy of holiday pastime found in the Stuart *Declaration of Sports* (1617, reprinted 1633), where James I argued that permitting sport on Sundays and holy days was necessary to prevent idleness and discontent while also maintaining a stock of healthy cannon fodder in the event of war.[69] However, Davenant goes on to argue that performances are not only beneficial as a way to appease boredom (and thereby prevent revolution) but may also be a tool for political manipulation:

> If morall representations may be allow'd (being without obscenenesse, profaneness, and scandall) the first argument may consist of the Spaniards barbarous Conquests in the West Indies and of their several cruelties there exercis'd upon the subjects of this Nation:[70]

Davenant's desire to dramatise sadistic Spaniards was not arbitrary. Cromwell actively pursued an anti-Spanish foreign policy. Dramatic representations of cruelty committed by Spanish conquerors could therefore only aid in resurrecting the anti-Spanish sentiment that, in the 1620s, had so strongly opposed the possibility of a betrothal between the then Prince Charles and the Spanish Infanta. In a manuscript written in the same hand as the letter to Thurloe, Davenant makes a more frank and pragmatic plea for dramatic representation.[71] Davenant proposes that these entertainments will promote a nationalist agenda through depicting heroic English actions in contrast to those of foreign foes:

> chiefly of those famous Battails at Land and Sea by which this Nation is renowned; representing the Generalls and other meritorious Leaders, in their Dangers Successes and Triumphs; and our Enemies in such acts of Cruelty (like that in Amboyna) as shall breed in the Spectators courage and animosity against them; diverting the people from Vices and Mischeife; and instructing them (as in a Schoole of Morality) to Vertu, and to a quiet and cheerefull behaviour towards the present Government.
>
> In order to which, tis humbly desired, that the Councill of State would please to give a Licence for publick Representations; and that they would authorize those to whom the Grant is directed, to suppresse all other publick Presentments; least scandalous arguments may be againe introduced.[72]

The extract quoted above appeals to concerns regarding civil unrest, but finishes upon a mercantile note. Drama can assist the body politic by being of moral benefit to the public, but only if Davenant has exclusive rights to perform plays. Commercial concerns come into focus through the suggestion that the producer be granted a monopoly as a way of guaranteeing 'respectable' theatre. Drama becomes a means to educate the audience into allegiance to a new style of government while simultaneously reminding the public who their established enemies are. In some respects, Cromwell's anti-Spanish foreign policy was out of date. By the 1650s, Spain's power was on the wane and France (England's ally against Spain) was to become the leading Counter-Reformation power.[73] However, the policy spoke to popular sentiments and established Cromwell as the inheritor of the Elizabethan anti-Spanish mantle.

Although Davenant desired to produce anti-Spanish drama as an astute response to Cromwellian foreign policy, his first two productions had different subject material.[74] Spain's 'Conquest in the West Indies' would not have been a palatable topic in 1655/56 because of the initial expedition to Hispaniola proving disastrous for the protectorate. Contemporary events made a dramatic representation of English soldiers liberating Incas from Spanish oppressors impossibly ironic, and celebratory images of Spain were unlikely to have been countenanced by state or spectator.[75] However, following an alliance with France, what came to be known as the 'western design' (the attacking of Spain through its colonies) began to bear some fruit, as did the successful invasion of the Spanish Netherlands.[76] With the changing times came the premiere of *The Cruelty of the Spaniards in Peru*. In this work, Elizabethan anti-Spanish foreign policy is reinvented to become synonymous with the anti-Habsburg policy adopted by Cromwell.

Set in the West Indies, *The Cruelty of the Spaniards in Peru* celebrates the idea of Cromwell's government as the liberator of the peoples oppressed by Spanish colonial rule. Beginning with the Spanish discovery and conquest of Peru in the sixteenth century, the episodic narrative skips a century to prophesy that Cromwell's red-coated New Model Army will relieve the Incas from their Hispanic foes. Both temporal and historical realities are thus suspended as the play moves from sixteenth-century colonialism to enact a prophetic future where Spanish occupation is ended. The brutality of Spanish policy in the New World was a prominent idea in the 1650s. Cromwell justified his war on Spain through alluding to the country's violent colonisation of the New World and the perceived violation of English colonialist rights.[77] John Milton wrote pamphlets advocating a tough stance on Spain, invoking the memory of the 1588 Armada, Spanish oppression in the colonies and ways in which Spain tampered with English commerce.[78] Despite the obvious political reasons for publishing these tracts, the ferocity with which the Spanish carried out their expansionist policies was well known in sixteenth- and seventeenth-century Europe. A translation of Fr Bartolomé de Las Casas's (1474–1566) *Brevassima Relación de la Destrucción de las Indias*, entitled *The Spanish Colony: or a Brief Chronicle of the Acts and Gestes of the Spaniards in the West Indies* appeared in English in 1583. This text fuelled Elizabethan anti-Spanish sentiment. Seventy years later, Casas's text was to be resurrected in a nationalistic translation by John Philips. The seventeenth-century text affirmed its (dubious) historical accuracy under the emotive (and less pithy) title, *The Tears of the Indians: Being an Historical and True Account of the Cruel Massacres and Slaughters of Above Twenty Millions of Innocent People; committed by the Spanish in the Islands of Hispaniola, Cuba, Kamaica [sic], &c. As Also, in the Continent of Mexico, Peru and Other Places of the West Indies to the Total Destruction of Those Countries* (1656).[79] Davenant therefore had a plethora of anti-Spanish material from which to construct his masque, and lurid details of Spanish violence are provided in the text of *The Cruelty of the Spaniards in Peru*. The description of the action at the start of the fifth entry focuses upon the skilfully produced properties that set the scene:

> farther to the view are discern'd Racks, and other Engines of torment, with which the Spaniards are tormenting the Natives and English Mariners ... Two Spaniards are likewise discover'd, ... with Rapiers and Daggers by their sides; the one turning a Spit, whilst the other is basting an *Indian* Prince, which is rosted at an artificiall fire.[80]

The prospective audience is assured that the fire is a property, emphasising the grotesque theatricality of the spectacle. Artifice, so central to the masque form, is used as a means through which difference is demarcated. However, the torturing of both Incas and English mariners also represents how the fate of English colonialist ambitions and the plight of Native Americans become intricately linked within the masque's narrative. By representing Cromwell's western design as liberating an oppressed nation, Davenant makes a moral claim regarding expansionist aspirations. The New Model Army is not content to rescue English mariners, but must also save the Incas from torture. In depicting the Spaniards as roasting an Inca prince upon a spit, Davenant invokes cannibalistic imagery: this ironically pre-empts the numerous scatological tracts and ballads depicting the demise of the Rump Parliament that appeared in the months leading up to Restoration.[81] Spanish colonisation is aligned with a grotesque form of regicide, where special tortures are afforded to Inca rulers. However, it does not necessarily follow that the English will allow the Incas to return to their pre-colonised state. Instead, Spanish Catholic conquest is replaced by English Protestant colonialism.

Wiseman has argued that the pre-colonised state of the Incas represented an Edenic innocence, echoing one thread of Renaissance thought that gestures to ideas connected to the 'noble savage' which was perhaps most famously propounded in Michel de Montaigne's *Of the Cannibals*.[82] The first song certainly seems to support this idea of a prelapsarian existence:

> Whilst yet our world was new,
> When not discovere'd by the old,
> E're begger'd Slaves we grew,
> For having Silver hills, and Strands of Gold.
> CHORUS: We danc'd and we sung,
> And lookt ever young,
> And from restraints were free,
> As waves and winds at Sea.
>
> (sigs A4v–B1r)

The song details the carefree existence of the Incas in their pre-Hispanic naked innocence. However, other passages contradict the image presented here. Later in the entertainment, we learn that the last Inca king made an unfortunate choice of wife, a 'foraign Beauty' who 'so far prevail'd on his passion, that she made him on his age assign a considerable part of his Dominion to a younger son … This youth … invaded his elder Brother at the unfortunate time when the Spaniards … landed, and made a prodigious use of the division between the two Brethren' (sigs B4r–B4v). Although the masque endeavours to erase memory of Stuart monarchy by splicing together a past Elizabethan and a future Cromwellian existence, allusions to Henrietta Maria's uxorious husband cannot be laid to rest. *Cupid and Death* restored order through banishing love from the courts of princes, and *The Cruelty of the Spaniards in Peru* offers a cautionary tale against mixing affection and government. Because the Edenic existence of the Incas has been contaminated by the arrival of a foreign queen, the idea of the Incas as representing humanity in its state of innocence is

Reinventing the masque 99

radically rewritten to resemble the Hobbesian view of the natural state of humankind to be one of war:[83]

> Twelve *Incas* have successivly
> Our spatious Empire sway'd;
> Whose power whilst we obey'd,
> We liv'd so happy and so free.
> As if we were not kept in awe
>   By any Law,
> Which martiall Kings aloud proclaim.
> Soft conscience, Nature's whisp'ring Oratour,
> Did teach us what to love or to abhor;
> And all our punishment was shame.
>
> (sig. C1v)

These lines merge Hobbesian politics with ideas of Edenic innocence. The Incas lived in a state of natural innocence before they learned disobedience to their king. However, these lines also emphasise that the Incas were happy *as if* the 'martiall Kings' did not keep peace through governing by the sword. Hobbesian politics are both affirmed and inverted by showing the Incas returning to a state of war as a consequence of government breaking down, yet the state of war also supplants natural innocence. Echoing one argument that reads the biblical narrative of eating of the tree of knowledge as representing the commencement of Adam and Eve's sexual relationship,[84] Davenant's masque conflates the idea of misplaced love with civil unrest. Natural obedience to the Inca king meant that laws did not need to be consciously followed: Incas naturally felt the difference between good and evil, love and abhorrence. When the king entrusts his love to a 'foraign Beauty', however, the connection between the Incas and 'Nature's whisp'ring Oratour' is severed and the natural inference of what good and evil embody is replaced by knowledge of good and evil. The masque thus warns against disobedience to the (and of the) monarch and offers a cautionary tale regarding the perils of wifely influence in government through replacing prelaspsarian narratives with a more pragmatic view of government.

As much as the masque endeavours to forget monarchy by emphasising protectorate policy and supporting the western design, it cannot refrain from remembering and reinventing the civil war and the perceived relationship between Charles I and Henrietta Maria. Janet Clare rightly identifies tensions within the masque stemming from a republican agenda that paradoxically recalls a pre-civil-war royalist idyll.[85] In June 1637, Charles was to boast that he was the happiest king in Christendom, unaware that parliamentary discontents were to culminate in civil war and regicide.[86] However, since the masque is concerned with creating a connection between Elizabethan and Cromwellian anti-Spanish policy, the pre-civil-war nostalgia is not necessarily as paradoxical as it may appear. The idyllic royalist past to which the entertainment might refer could equally be interpreted as being Elizabethan rather than Caroline. When we consider that some parliamentarians rewrote the Elizabethan era as a period where monarch and parliament governed cohesively (and some who would learn to support republicanism admired Elizabeth), it is possible for the masque to have multiple interpretations.[87] Republicans and royalists alike could therefore interpret the pre-civil-war Inca existence in accordance with conflicting ideologies.

The prophetic depiction of the New Model Army offering a Protestant salvation from Catholic tyranny alters the nuances of the masque. The ending offers the type of reconciliation common to the chaotic and sometimes grotesque anti-masques that the appearance of the monarch afforded the Stuart court masque.[88] The Spanish eagle is forced to acknowledge the might of the English lion and the final dance celebrates a special relationship between Incas and English:

> an Ayre, consisting of three Tunes, prepares the grand Dance, three *Indians* entring first, afterwards to them three *English* Souldiers, distinguisht by their Red-Coats, and to them a *Spaniard*, who mingling in the measures with the rest, does in his gestures and expresse pride and sullennesse towards the *Indians*, and payes a lowly homage to the *English*, who often salute him with their feet ... whilst the *English* and the *Indians*, as they encounter, salute and shake hands, in signe of future amity.(sig. D4r)

The masque thus asserts a new order between the Old and New World, where Inca and English colonist may coexist amicably. It also shifts the focus from being a tale of an Eden lost by love, war and foreign invasion to a post-apocalyptic assertion of rebirth and renewal. Although the masque seeks to establish a link between Elizabethan and commonwealth policies, these apocalyptic notions have more similarities with pre-Elizabethan ideas. These parallels are not deliberate, but still invoke ideas of Tudor expansion. Under Henry VIII and Edward VI, England had trifled with apocalyptic notions of empire. Universal reform of the church could and would be achieved towards the end of time with the overthrow of the (satanic) papal monarchy. Such visions had a European rather than a New World context and were held less coherently by the end of the 1540s. The notion of an empire of liberty appears to have been abandoned entirely by Marian and Elizabethan governments, while in Scotland Buchanan wrote verses for the future James VI (and James I of England) advising against empire building.[89] In reality, the construction of Cromwellian foreign policy within this masque does not so much establish a link with Elizabethan ambitions, but unconsciously turns earlier Edwardian principles of Protestant empire into a coherent agenda.

Ironically, it was notions of apocalyptic spirituality that fuelled Habsburg colonialist ambitions. Columbus's expeditions were aligned with the conquest of Granada (and the overthrow of Islam in Spanish territories), while Portuguese and Spanish expansion was perceived as a way to convert heretics to Catholicism rather than purely an exercise in land acquisition.[90] Although Cromwell certainly appears to have been more tolerant of religious diversity than his Habsburg counterparts, some protectorate thoughts regarding the New World were rationalised by similar apocalyptic rhetoric.[91]

Of course, mercantile considerations also fuelled Cromwellian ventures in the New World. Knowledge of the wealth the Americas had to offer undoubtedly influenced Cromwellian desires to expand settlements there. Although the English had been journeying to (and claiming land in) the New World under Elizabeth and her Stuart successors, none of these monarchs appears to have followed an apocalyptic agenda in the Americas.[92] Francis Drake's mercantile New World exploits were recorded by his contemporaries, but were also commented upon in the protectorate. Writing in 1587, Lopez Vaz gave the following account of an encounter between Spanish settlers and Francis Drake. Later writers would revise this encounter in the seventeenth century:

> [Drake] was informed that at the very same time many mules were coming from Panama to Nombre de Dios laden with gold and silver. Upon this news Francis Drake taking with him an hundred shot, and the negroes stayed in the way till the treasure came by, accompanied and guarded only by those that drove the mules, who mistrusted nothing at all. When Captain Drake met with them, he took away their gold
> ...
> Captain Drake carried from the coast of Peru, of silver eight hundred sixty six quintals, at 100 pound weight the quintal all which sum amounteth to a

million and thirty eight thousand and two hundred ducats. He carried away a hundred thousand pesos of gold, that is ten quintals, which last sum amounteth to an hundred and fifty thousand ducats: over and besides the treasure consisting of pearl, precious stones, reals of plate and other things of great worth.[93]

The passage quoted above was written by a Portuguese, so inevitably is biased against Drake. Its translation into English as one of the vast compendia of narratives relating to English seafaring and exploration compiled by Richard Hakluyt, however, complicates the account. A negative view of English pirateering is appropriated to celebrate English exploration. The wealth Drake stole may well be an exaggeration, but this suits multiple perceptions of Drake: he can be considered as a plundering thief, but also as a latter-day Robin Hood. It also emphasises the mercantile nature of Elizabethan involvement in the New World. The Americas offered a way of increasing Elizabethan wealth: the apocalyptic ideas that were floated under the early Tudors had been abandoned.

In focusing his final protectorate masque upon Drake's exploits in the New World, Davenant alludes to the mercantile nature of both Elizabethan and Cromwellian colonialist aspirations. Davenant's main source material was a text that may have been designed to curry favour at the Jacobean court. *Sir Francis Drake Revived* (1623) does not appear to have been put to this use, but a 1652 reprint (designed to inspire 'this Dull and Effeminate age')[94] means it had some topicality during the commonwealth. Drake's role as adventurer meant he was the ideal vehicle through which to celebrate English military victory, and there is no allusion to his status as hero of the defeat of the Armada.

In some respects, the defeat of the Spanish Armada in 1588 would appear to be the ideal means of both celebrating English maritime might and negating the expansionist ambitions of Counter-Reformation Spain. However, the defeat of the Armada was also a triumph for English monarchy: the bodily presence of Elizabeth at Tilbury to rally the troops before a possible invasion has been questioned, but this event has been afforded cultural verification.[95] History has been reinvented to write the queen's heroism into the Armada narrative and thereby give the story monarchical authority. Time alters the nuances of a work: in the 1650s, Drake's story was revised to celebrate commonwealth values and not to construct the apotheosis of a monarch.

By following the lead of *Sir Francis Drake Revived* and locating Drake's adventures in the New World, Davenant avoids defining military success through allusions to monarchy. The Americas thus become a useful space

Reinventing the masque 103

to celebrate English seafaring military conquests: with the Atlantic Ocean separating the colonies from the monarch, the idea of monarchy can be removed from the narrative. Despite this, Davenant's decision to return to the New World for his 1659 masque, *The History of Sir Francis Drake*, may also have been influenced by financial concerns. The description of the frontispiece to the physical performance emphasises the continuity between *The History of Sir Francis Drake* and the previous masque:

> This Frontispiece [i.e., the proscenium arch] was the same which belong'd to the late Representation; and it was convenient to continue it, our Argument being in the same country.[96]

The Cruelty of the Spaniards in Peru and *The History of Sir Francis Drake* are connected, but are variations upon a theme rather than a sequence. Davenant argues that, because both masques are set in the same country, it is 'convenient' to recycle the frontispiece. This argument can be inverted: it is also convenient to set both masques in the same country because the scenery may be recycled.

English military success is displaced in *The Cruelty of the Spaniards in Peru*, where liberation will happen in a Cromwellian future. An idyllic image of warfare is presented through the depiction of this prophecy. Likewise, *The History of Sir Francis Drake* smooths over some of the more unpleasant elements of soldiering and New World living found in the source material. Instead, we are presented with an image of heroic Elizabethan valour. Marking a modulation in the development of the masque, the piece has a speaking, eponymous hero and not a personification of abstract virtues. Iconography is still a feature of the masque, but here the icon is given a voice.

As with *The Cruelty of the Spaniards in Peru*, *The History of Sir Francis Drake* aligns the English colonisers with a group who are oppressed under the Spanish.[97] This time, the focus shifts from the Incas to the Symerons: slaves whom the Spanish brought over from Morocco to mine for gold.[98] Once more, civil unrest is alluded to: the Symerons revolted and established their own mini-kingdom. The 'brave Warriors of Wapping' (sig. B3r) immediately strike up an alliance with these 'Moorish People' (sig. B1v) against their mutual foe. During the discussion, the Symeron king grants Drake freedom of his territory:

> KIN[G]: Welcom! and in my Land be free,
> And pow'rfull as thou art at Sea.

> DRAK[E] SEN[IOR]: Monarch of much! and stil deserving more
> Then I have coasted in the Western shore!
> Slave to my Queen! to whom thy virtue showes
> How low thou canst to virtue be;
> And, since declar'd a Foe to all her Foes
> Thou mak'st them lower bow to thee.
>
> (sig. B3r)

In granting Drake freedom, the Symeron king offers a form of government different from the one experienced by the Elizabethan sailors. However, this is quickly taken back into the Elizabethan narrative. The Symeron king gains greatness through aligning himself with English policies. Drake may be enslaved to his queen, but the alliance co-opts the emancipated Symerons to English colonialist ambitions. By bowing to Elizabeth, the Symeron king acknowledges the greater virtue and authority of the absent English monarch. This affords the king greater honour, but also brings the freed Symerons back into a colonial framework. The emancipated Symerons have voluntarily subordinated themselves to a Protestant European power. The possibility that the New World may offer a different type of government is therefore negated. Despite this, there are ambiguities in the lines quoted above. Territorial boundaries mediate slavery to the Old World. Drake is a slave to Elizabeth while at sea. Once he has docked and disembarked from the western coast of the Americas, Elizabeth's power becomes a matter of negotiation precipitated by her lack of territorial jurisdiction. An element of choice therefore governs Drake's New World exploits and subordination to the monarch becomes contractual.

Once an alliance is formed, the allies set about plundering Spanish gold. Chiming with Lopez Vaz's description of Drake's looting, the group successfully accumulate a hoard for English coffers. In negotiating the plan of operation, the Symeron king and Drake discuss how to thwart the Spanish:

> KIN: Instruct me how my *Symerons* and I
> May help thee to afflict the Enemy.
> DRAK. SEN: Afford guides to lead my bold
> Victorious Sea_men to their Gold,
> For nothing can afflict them more,
> Then to deprive them of that store
> With which from hence they furnished are
> T'afflict the peacefulll [sic] world with war.
>
> (sig. B3v)

Ransacking is thus turned into a virtue. Spanish imports of gold in both the sixteenth and the seventeenth century are presented as a way through which Spain may fund the Counter-Reformation. Spain can no longer wage war because Drake has 'appropriated' Spanish gold. Historical reality is reinvented in order to create a moral agenda for Drake's mercantile expeditions, and English pirates gain honour by raiding Spanish coffers. Drake's honour increases through a prophetic vision that he will circumnavigate the globe. In turn, English nautical might is celebrated through Drake's adventures: 'This Prophesie will rise / To higher Enterprise. / The English Lion's walk shall reach as far / As prosp'rous Valour dares adventure War' (sig. C4r). Spanish conquest is depicted as an affliction, but English warfare is valiant. The Symeron prophecy thus anticipates future English – possibly Cromwellian – maritime might. This offers an extension to the Inca prophecy in *The Cruelty of the Spaniards in Peru*, which looks to the New Model Army to establish an empire of liberty.

The sense of honour is carried through to the end of the masque, to the point that even the Spanish may be freed from oppression. We are presented with a tableau of a Spanish bride, tied to a tree. Demanding an explanation, Drake is given the following account:

> ROUSE: A party of your SYMERONS ...
>   Did e're the early dawning rise,
>   And closse by VENTA-CRUZ surprise
>   A Bride and Bridegroom at their Nuptial Feast,
>   To whom the SYM'RONS now
>   Much more then fury show;
>   For they have all those cruelties exprest
>   That Spanish pride could e're provoke from them
>   Or Moorish Malice can revenge esteem.
> DRAK. SEN: Arm! Arm! the honour of my nation turns
>   To shame, when an afflicted Beauty mourns.
>
> (sigs D3r–D3v)

English honour cannot permit a damsel to remain distressed, and Drake rescues the Spanish couple. Later in the narrative, the Symerons account for their actions by claiming they have learned barbarous behaviour from Spanish attitudes towards them. By following a code of revenge, rather than looking to personal honour, the Symerons have mimicked Hispanic deeds. Strains within the Anglo-Symeron alliance are exposed: whereas amity between the unknown Incas may be portrayed in *The Cruelty of the*

Spaniards in Peru, Old World tensions between Symerons, Spaniards and English come into focus in *The History of Sir Francis Drake*.

Revenge and reciprocal cruelty between Symeron and Spaniard is thus replaced by English equitable justice: the bride and her groom are not responsible for Spanish colonial policy and may therefore be released from their punishment. Drake thus liberates the innocent, echoing the prophecy in *The Cruelty of the Spaniards in Peru* that the New Model Army will free the Incas. Once more, Protestant English colonialist aspirations are depicted as offering an alternative to Catholic Spanish colonising.

In the sixth entry, Drake's adventures culminate in the seizing of gold. Unlike Vaz's description of the affair, the mules laden with gold are guarded by 'Five hundred foot' and 'sixty horses' (sig. E2v). Within seventy years, 560 Spanish troops have been added to the narrative, upping the stakes and affording Drake greater valour in his acquisition of the lucre. While these figures appear an absurd exaggeration, their inflation emphasises English military achievement and Drake applauds abstract notions of English valour:

> If English courage could at all be rais'd,
> By being well perswaded, or much prais'd,
> Speech were of use: but Valour born, not bred,
>   Cannot by Art (since being so,
>   It does as far as Nature goe)
> Be higher lifted, or be farther led.
> All I would speak, should tell you, I despise
> That treasure which I now would make your Prize:
> Unworthy 'tis to be your chiefest aime.
> For this attempt is not for Gold, but Fame.
>
>   (sig. E1v)

Drake locates courage as an innate quality of the English. Pre-empting nature/nurture debates, the pre-battle rallying of the troops is discarded as unnecessary. In its place stands a cautionary tale regarding prizing gold too highly. Acquiring gold is a means to an end and not an end in itself. Elizabethan narratives of colonialism as profitable and a way to gain honour have been modified. Drake's exploits are now celebrated as affording honour through material glory.

In some respects, Drake was the ideal Elizabethan hero.[99] Unlike his fellow explorer, Walter Ralegh, Drake's fame (and notoriety) was limited to the Elizabethan period. Drake therefore had no embarrassing connections with the Stuart court, although Ralegh was also reworked after his execution in 1618 to represent the true Protestant hero.[100] In establishing a link between Elizabethan heroes and the protectorate, these masques endeavour to erase not so much the memory of monarchy but the idea of Stuart monarchy. However, through discussing honour and glory as English virtues, *The History of Sir Francis Drake* presents an alternative to a conflation of Elizabethan and Cromwellian colonialism.

By replacing profit with glory, *The History of Sir Francis Drake* follows an agenda that is not Elizabethan. Instead, the masque harks back to Jacobean colonialist ideas. The first permanent English settlement in America was Jamestown, named after the monarch who granted the 1606 patent. The initial plan for the settlement and for the Virginia Company was to gain financial benefit from New World enterprises. However, it quickly became clear that the dividends Spain had reaped in Peru would not be forthcoming in Virginia. Tracts were printed from 1609 that made a virtue of necessity. Gold was no longer the glory that the folk of Jamestown searched for, but was replaced by martial might and courage. Andrew Fitzmaurice has identified this as representing a shift in thought from the classical humanism that had influenced Elizabethan colonialist aspirations to a classical Roman civic tradition. Founded upon republican civic principles, this tradition was hostile to commercial concerns. Preempting utilitarian notions relating to the greatest good for the greatest number, honourable deaths were promoted as an occurrence that could be necessary for the common good.[101] The apocalyptic narratives of *The Cruelty of the Spaniards in Peru* and (though less so) of *The History of Sir Francis Drake* thus have little affinity with Elizabethan policy.

Taking into account these different views of colonialism, the agenda of Davenant's masques becomes opaque. They seem to be a hybridisation of pre-Marian thoughts on England as a possible empire for liberty, Jacobean colonialist rewriting of Roman civic philosophies and (most ironically of all) Spanish Counter-Reformation apocalyptic empire building. This curious mixture encapsulates Cromwellian anti-Spanish foreign policy, although it is highly doubtful that Cromwell actively drew from these influences. Instead, it offers an example of how, over time, thoughts that were once ascribed to a specific occurrence became generally accepted maxims. Ideas may have been transmitted and appropriated without the appropriator necessarily having knowledge of the genesis of the ideas or how others may have used these concepts. These vague ideas became received opinion and shaped attitudes and assumptions regarding the past and its connection with the present. Rather than being representative of what the Marxist critic Georg Lukács defines as the ultimate ideal of historical fiction, to represent 'the concrete prehistory of the destiny of the people', these often ironically contradictory and complex engagements with the past came to be representative of the fluid way in which abstract notions can be disseminated and understood.[102]

Tensions between the endeavour to erase the memory of Stuart monarchy abound in the two masques by Davenant discussed above. *The Cruelty of the Spaniards in Peru* and *The History of Sir Francis Drake* attempt to promote Cromwell's anti-Spanish foreign policy through claiming it as the child of Elizabethan anti-Spanish sentiment. However, the narratives cannot avoid alluding to Stuart administration. This contradiction is further emphasised when we consider the personnel involved in the production of Davenant's masques. John Webb, the nephew, son-in-law and assistant of Inigo Jones, designed the scenery for Davenant's productions, while musicians who had enjoyed patronage at the Caroline court were responsible for the music.[103] These masques operate at the margins of court drama and the playhouse, Caroline court culture and protectorate entertainment. Certainly, scenery was not commonly used in the Jacobean and Caroline playhouse – such a practice tended to be reserved for court entertainments.[104] Both the performances and the textual productions of Davenant's masques are thus as ambiguous as the enacting and printing of Shirley's one documented foray into commonwealth masquing culture.

Davenant's masques for the playhouse thus replace the focal image of the order-restoring monarch with a celebration of English liberating valour. Londoners could pay to experience the theatricality of a protectorate masque, which is in contrast to the purchasing of a souvenir brochure for the Stuart masque. This does not so much represent a democratisation of the masque (they would still have been costly to watch and therefore would have attracted a wealthy audience),[105] rather it is an indication of what can happen to these entertainments when there is no monarch. The generic conventions of the masque are pushed to their extreme, reducing the dance elements and altering the nuances of the performance. This generic instability mirrors political uncertainty, where notions of government and 'court' are radically remodelled. Shirley's masque was performed in an ambiguous courtly space, and Davenant's productions are suspended between the court stage and the playhouse. At the Restoration, the process of producing drama for the playhouse would be very different to the way in which plays were performed before theatre closure. This is partly due to continental influences being brought back by those who went into exile during the commonwealth (in particular, women actors and scenery were commonplace in European theatres).[106] However, the significance of Davenant's protectorate masques should not be overlooked. These entertainments allowed a London audience to grow accustomed to the types of performance that were to follow at the Restoration. After Shirley paved the way to a radicalisation of the masque through appropriating it for the protectorate, Davenant reinvented the Stuart court masque to make it fit for a paying audience. In so doing, Davenant established a connection between Caroline court entertainments and the revived Restoration stage.

At the Restoration, Anthony Sadler printed *The Subjects Joy for the Kings Restoration, Cheerfully Made Known in a Sacred Masque Gratefully Made Publique for His Sacred Majesty*, a panegyric which sought to restore the monarch to his or her place at the centre of the masque form. In celebrating the Restoration in this masque, recent history is reinvented to narrate the return to monarchical government.[107] However, the heyday of the Stuart court masque had gone, and Sadler's piece represents not so much a restoration of the masque as a nostalgic coda to its courtly manifestation. Davenant had made the form suitable for the playhouse and it could never satisfactorily return to being a courtly entertainment. The masque underwent a major transformation, and so too did Davenant: at the Restoration, Davenant's role altered once more. Appointed manager of one of the two new theatre companies, Davenant had greater scope for producing different types of plays compared to the restrictions under which he had worked in the 1650s. One of the enterprises that Davenant embarked upon was to rewrite his 1656 masque, *The Siege of Rhodes*, into an epic, ten-act heroic spoken drama. This entertainment and its afterlife upon the Restoration stage will be the starting point of my next chapter.

Notes

1 See Laura Lunger Knoppers, *Constructing Cromwell: Ceremony, Portrait and Print, 1645–1661* (Cambridge: Cambridge University Press, 2000); Roy Sherwood, *The Court of Oliver Cromwell* (London: Croom Helm Ltd, 1977).

2 See, for example, Susan Wiseman, *Drama and Politics in the English Civil War* (Cambridge: Cambridge University Press, 1998), pp. 137–64; Eric Walter White, *The Rise of English Opera* (London: John Lehmann Ltd, 1951); Janet Clare has been the most radical by hinting that these entertainments have more affinity with masques (*Drama of the English Republic: 1649–1660* (Manchester: Manchester University Press, 2002), pp. 186–7)). In another article, Clare has labelled these entertainments 'pseudo masques'

('The production and reception of Davenant's *Cruelty of the Spaniards in Peru*', *MLR*, 89 (1994), 832–41), a term adopted by Ayanna Thompson in *Performing Race and Torture on the Early Modern Stage* (New York and London: Routledge: 2008); Roger North dismisses late seventeenth-century English opera as not being true opera in his musical treatises. See 'Of opera' in *Roger North's Cursory Notes of Musicke (c. 1698–1703) Physical, Psychological and Critical Theory*, ed. Mary Chan and Jamie C. Kassler (Kensington, New South Wales: Unisearch Ltd, 1986), pp. 227–34. See also *Roger North's 'The Musical Grammarian 1728'*, ed. Mary Chan and Jamie C. Kassler (Cambridge: Cambridge University Press, 1990), esp. pp. 215–16, pp. 260–1.

3 Lauren Shohet, *Reading Masques: The English Masque and Public Culture in the Seventeenth-Century* (Oxford: Oxford University Press, 2010).

4 R. Malcolm Smuts, *Court Culture and the Origins of a Royalist Tradition in Early Stuart England* (Pennsylvania: University of Philadelphia Press, 1987).

5 John H. Astington, *English Court Theatre, 1558–1642* (Cambridge: Cambridge University Press, 1999), pp. 171–2.

6 Lauren Shohet has highlighted the importance of addressing the masque as a bi-medial form that reaches a wider audience upon the paper stage (The masque in/as print, in Marta Straznicky (ed.), *The Book of the Play: Playwrights, Stationers, and Readers in Early Modern England* (Amhurst and Boston: University of Massachusetts Press, 2006), pp. 176–202).

7 Peter Walls, *Music in the English Courtly Masque* (Oxford: Oxford University Press, 1996), pp. 17–22.

8 Wiseman, *Politics*, p. 182; Clare, *Drama*, p. 153. *Cupid His Coronation* was never printed and only one manuscript exists in the Bodleian Library, Oxford (MS Rawlinson B.165 fols 107r–113v).

9 Matthew Locke and Christopher Gibbons, *Cupid and Death*, ed. Edward J. Dent, 2nd rev. edn (London: Stainter and Bell, 1974).

10 Walls, *Music in the English Courtly Masque*, pp. 23–33.

11 A great number of Inigo Jones's costume designs still exist, and are preserved at Chatsworth House. For reproductions of these designs, see Stephen Orgel and Roy Strong, *Inigo Jones and the Theatre of the Stuart Court*, 2 vols (Berkeley and Los Angeles: University of California Press, 1973).

12 See, for example, David Lindley's introduction to his edition of Stuart masques: *Court Masques*, ed. David Lindley (Oxford: Oxford University Press, 1995).

13 For a discussion of the chaotic ending of the revels, see, for example, Astington, *English Court Theatre*, pp. 175–8.

14 For example, Campion tended to provide more detail about the music, whereas some earlier Jonsonian masques focus upon set and costume design

and occasionally music (Walls, *Music in the English Courtly Masque*, esp. pp. 22–4, 33).
15 James, Shirley, *Cupid and Death* (London, 1653), title page.
16 Clare, *Drama*, p. 153; Wiseman, *Politics*, p. 122.
17 Clare McManus, *Women on the Renaissance Stage: Anna of Denmark and Female Masquing Culture in the Stuart Court (1590–1619)* (Manchester: Manchester University Press, 2002), pp. 164–201 and 210; Melinda J. Gough, 'Courtly *comédiantes*: Henrietta Maria and amateur women's stage plays in France and England', in Pamella Allen Brown and Peter Parolin (eds.), *Women Players in England, 1500–1660* (Aldershot: Ashgate, 2005), pp. 193–215 (p. 205).
18 Murray Lefkowitz, 'Masque: Commonwealth (1649–60)', *Grove Music Online* www.grovemusic.com/shared/views/article.html?section=music.17996.4 (accessed 14 September 2006).
19 Clare, *Drama*, p. 153; conversely, Wiseman, *Politics*, states that it was sponsored by the government (*Politics*, p. 114).
20 Potter asserts that the performance space was Whitehall (*Revels*, 4:296), though evidence is scarce.
21 In Lindley's select edition of court masques, only Samuel Daniel's *Tethys' Festival* (1610) includes a preface to the reader, while some other masques contain commendatory epistles to members of the nobility. Daniel's preface claims the text was printed at the behest of Anna of Denmark and Prince Henry, who wished to 'preserve the memory' of the occasion and not out of any desire by the author to see his text in print (*Tethys' Festival* in *Court Masques*, pp. 54–65 (p. 54)).
22 Wiseman, *Politics*, p. 122.
23 See, for example, Stephen Orgel, *The Illusion of Power: Political Theatre in the English Renaissance* (Berkeley: University of California Press, 1975).
24 In discussing fables, Annabel Patterson succinctly refers to Hegel: '*because* the fabulist "dare not speak his teaching openly", he can "only make it intelligible in a kind of riddle which is at the same time always being solved"' (Patterson, *Fables of Power: Aesopian Writing and Political History* (Durham, NC, and London: Duke University Press, 1991), p. 105).
25 Clare, *Drama*, p. 154.
26 Patterson, *Fables of Power*, p. 87–8.
27 Patterson discusses (though does not limit her study to) parliamentarian and royalist appropriations during the civil wars. See *Fables of Power*, chapters 3–4, and *passim*.
28 Lois Potter, *Secret Rites and Secret Writings: Royalist Literature, 1641–1660* (Cambridge: Cambridge University Press, 1989), p. 157.

29 Austin Woolrych, *Britain in Revolution, 1625–1660* (Oxford: Oxford University Press, 2002), pp. 434–9.
30 See the 1659 edition, which, unlike the 1653 text, advertises itself as a 'private entertainment' on the title page. *Cupid and Death* (London, 1659).
31 Wiseman, *Politics*, p. 123.
32 See Thomas Hobbes, *Leviathan*, ed. J. C. A. Gaskin (Oxford: Oxford University Press, 1996).
33 Potter, *Secret Rites*, pp. 77–80; Woolrych, *Britain in Revolution*, pp. 56–8.
34 Karen Britland, *Drama at the Courts of Queen Henrietta Maria* (Cambridge: Cambridge University Press, 2006).
35 Wiseman, *Politics*, p. 122; Clare, *Drama*, p. 153.
36 For a discussion, see Wiseman, *Politics*, pp. 115–24.
37 See my Introduction, p. 7.
38 James Shirley, *The Triumph of Peace* (London, 1633), sig. D2v.
39 The Office of the Works had a wide-ranging portfolio, ranging from the design, maintenance and upkeep of buildings through to erecting seating and temporary structures for court entertainments (Astington, *English Court Theatre*, pp. 14–15).
40 Natasha Korda, *Shakespeare's Domestic Economies: Gender and Property in Early Modern England* (Philadelphia: University of Pennsylvannia Press, 2002), pp. 200–7.
41 Korda, *Shakespeare's Domestic Economies*, p. 210.
42 Korda, *Shakespeare's Domestic Economies*, pp. 194–5.
43 Robert Hume, *The Development of English Drama in the Late 17th Century* (Oxford: Clarendon Press, 1976), pp. 19–22.
44 Clare, *Drama*, p. 30, Wiseman, *Politics*, p. 139.
45 William Davenant, *The First Days Entertainment at Rutland-House* (London, 1656), sig. A6r.
46 See also Wiseman, *Politics*, pp. 142–5.
47 Claude V. Palisca, *Baroque Music*, 3rd edn (Englewood Cliffs, NJ: Prentice Hall, 1991), p. 33.
48 Wiseman, *Politics*, pp. 137–9; White, *English Opera*, suggests that this patent would have led to a 'popularisation of the masque' by having it performed in an opera house. Such slippage in terminology demonstrates the emphasis that mid-twentieth-century musicologists place upon opera. The title of White's book, which points to Davenant's productions as tentative steps in the development of English opera, also directs the reader to assume a connection between Davenant's productions and opera. See White, pp. 28–30.
49 Potter, *Revels*, 4:296.

50 William Davenant, *The Play House to be Let*, in *The Works of Sr William Davenant*, (London: 1673), sigs I4r–Q1r (sig. K1v).
51 Palisca, *Baroque Music*, pp. 30–1.
52 Palisca, *Baroque Music*, p. 30.
53 Palisca, *Baroque Music*, pp. 221–31.
54 Clare, *Drama*, p. 185.
55 William Davenant, *The Siege of Rhodes* (London, 1656), title page.
56 Davenant, *The Siege of Rhodes*, sig. A3r.
57 Ian Spink, *English Song: Dowland to Purcell* (London: B. T. Bastford, 1974), pp. 40–6; Spink, *Henry Lawes: Cavalier Songwriter* (Oxford: Oxford University Press, 2000), pp. 7–8.
58 Palisca, *Baroque Music*, p. 249.
59 Ben Jonson, 'A Masque Presented in the House of the Right Honorable the Lord Haye', in *The Works of Benjamin Jonson. The Second Volume* (London, 1640), sig. C2r. See also White, *English Opera*, p. 28.
60 Mary Edmond, *Rare Sir William Davenant: Poet Laureate, Playwright, Civil War General, Restoration Theatre Man* (Manchester: Manchester University Press, 1987), p. 129.
61 *The Diary of John Evelyn*, ed. Guy de la Bédoyère (Woodbridge: Boydell Press, 1995), p. 110.
62 E. Arber (ed.), *A Transcript of the Registers of the Worshipful Company of Stationers, 1640–1708 AD*, 3 vols (London, 1913), 2 (27 August 1656).
63 White, *English Opera*, p. 24.
64 For example, rope dancing features in *The Cruelty of the Spaniards in Peru* ([London]: 1658), sig. B1v.
65 Percy A. Scholes thoroughly and energetically dispels this myth (*The Puritans and Music in England and New England: A Contribution to the Cultural History of Two Nations* (Oxford: Oxford University Press, 1934)). See also Martin Butler, *Theatre and Crisis, 1632–1642* (Cambridge: Cambridge University Press, 1984); Margot Heinemann, *Puritanism and Theatre: Thomas Middleton and Opposition Drama Under the Early Stuarts* (Cambridge: Cambridge University Press, 1980).
66 Edmond, *Rare Sir William Davenant*, pp. 74, 93; 99–100.
67 Wiseman, *Politics*, p. 139; Edmond, *Rare Sir William Davenant*, pp. 117–19.
68 Cited in Wiseman, *Politics*, p. 141. The entire text of Davenant's proposal is transcribed by C. H. Firth, 'Sir William Davenant and the revival of drama during the protectorate', *English Historical Review*, 18 (1903), 319–21.
69 See *The Kings Majesties His Declaration to His Subjects, Concerning Lawfull Sports to be Used* (London, 1618). Bull baiting and 'Interludes' were still forbidden on Sundays and holy days. James I was not solely responsible

for the authorship of *A Declaration of Sports* (Jane Rickard, *Authorship and Authority: The Writings of James VI and I* (Manchester: Manchester University Press, 2007), p. 174, n. 3).

70 Cited in Wiseman, *Politics*, p. 142; Firth, 'Sir William Davenant', p. 321.
71 James R. Jacob and Timothy Raylor, 'Opera and obedience: Thomas Hobbes and "a proposition for advancement of morality" by Sir William Davenant', *The Seventeenth Century*, 6 (1991), 205–50.
72 Sheffield University Library, Hartlib Papers, 50H 53/1/1a—2b. Transcribed and reproduced in Jacob and Raylor, pp. 249–50 (p. 249).
73 Woolrych, *Britain in Revolution*, pp. 631–7.
74 These two entertainments are *The First Day's Entertainment at Rutland House* and *The Siege of Rhodes*.
75 Wiseman, *Politics*, p. 143; Clare, *Drama*, pp. 236–7.
76 Woolrych, *Britain in Revolution*, pp. 676–80.
77 See *A Declaration of His Highness, by the Advice of His Council; Setting Forth, on Behalf of the Commonwealth, the Justice of their Cause Against Spain, 26 October 1655* (London, 1655).
78 Clare, *Drama*, pp. 135–6.
79 Clare, *Drama*, pp. 135–6.
80 William Davenant, *The Cruelty of the Spaniards in Peru* (London, 1658), sig. C4r.
81 For a discussion of these Restoration pamphlets, see Mark Jenner, 'The roasting of the rump: scatology and the body politic in Restoration England', *Past and Present*, 177 (2002), pp. 84–120.
82 Wiseman, *Politics*, pp. 147–8. See also Michel de Montaigne, 'Of the cannibals' in *The Complete Essays*, trans. M. A. Screech (London: Penguin, 1987). Montaigne specifically refers to the Incas in his essay.
83 Jacob and Raylor's article discusses the similarities/differences between Hobbesian politics and the aesthetic and political judgements behind Davenant's entertainments ('Opera and obedience').
84 See James Grantham Turner, *One Flesh: Paradisal Marriage and Sexual Relations in the Age of Milton* (Oxford: Oxford University Press, 1987), pp. 124–73.
85 Clare, *Drama*, pp. 238–9.
86 C. V. Wedgwood, *The King's Peace* (London: Collins, 1955), p. 21.
87 For discussions of the nostalgia cult for Elizabeth, see Michael Dobson and Nicola J. Watson, *England's Elizabeth: An Afterlife in Fame and Fantasy* (Oxford: Oxford University Press, 2002); John Watkins, *Representing Elizabeth in Stuart England: Literature, History, Sovereignty* (Cambridge: Cambridge University Press, 2002). Lucy Hutchinson, a republican and wife

of a regicide, compares Elizabeth's perceived qualities to Henrietta Maria's negative attributes (Hutchinson, *Memoirs of the life of Colonel Hutchinson*, ed. N. H. Keeble (London: Phoenix Press, 2000), p. 70).
88 Clare, *Drama*, p. 155. Clare makes these observations in relation to the similarities between Stuart court masques and *Cupid and Death*.
89 Arthur H. Williamson, 'An empire to end empire: the dynamic of early modern British expansion', in Paulina Kewes (ed.), *The Uses of History in Early Modern England* (San Marino: Huntington Library, 2006), pp. 223–52 (pp. 230–3).
90 Williamson, 'An empire to end empires', p. 224.
91 Williamson, 'An empire to end empires', pp. 245–6.
92 Williamson, 'An empire to end empires', p. 234.
93 'A discourse of the West Indies and South Sea written by Lopez Vaz a Portuguese, continued unto the year 1587. Wherein, certain voyages of our Englishmen are truly reported', in Richard Hakluyt *Voyages and Discoveries* ed. Jack Beeching (Harmondsworth: Penguin, 1972), pp. 307–9 (pp. 308–9).
94 *Sir Francis Drake Revivd* (London, 1653), sig. B1r.
95 Dobson and Watson, *England's Elizabeth*, pp. 9–10.
96 William Davenant, *The History of Sir Francis Drake* (London: 1659), sig. A2r.
97 Clare, *Drama*, p. 263.
98 Following Clare, I will adopt the spelling used by Davenant and not the Spanish spelling. This is because I am dealing exclusively with the dramatic reconstruction and not the historical *cimarrónes* (*Drama*, p. 270, textual note).
99 Clare, *Drama*, p. 266.
100 Mark Nicholls and Penry Williams, 'Ralegh, Sir Walter (1554–1618)', *Oxford Dictionary of National Biography* (Oxford: Oxford University Press, 2004) www.oxforddnb.com/view/article/23039 (accessed 13 December 2007).
101 Andrew Fitzmaurice, 'The civic solution to the crisis of English colonization, 1609–1625', *The Historical Journal*, 42 (1999), pp. 25–51 (pp. 30–9).
102 Georg Lukács, *The Historical Novel*, trans. Hannah and Stanley Mitchell (London: Merlin Press, 1962, repr. 1989), p. 337.
103 John Orrell, *The Theatres of Inigo Jones and John Webb* (Cambridge: Cambridge University Press, 1985), p. 18.
104 Astington, *English Court Theatre*, esp. pp. 119, 125–6, 212; Orrell, *Theatres of Inigo Jones*, pp. 4–5.

105 Jacob and Raylor, 'Opera and obedience', p. 210.
106 Hume, *Development of English Drama*, pp. 236–7.
107 Anthony Sadler, *The Subjects Joy for the Kings Restoration* (London, 1660).

4
Heroic drama on the commonwealth and Restoration stage

Davenant's final protectorate masques offered his audience a romanticised image of the successes of western adventures, but his second masque, *The Siege of Rhodes* (1656), looked east. Recent scholarship on the Ottoman Empire and encounters between Islam and Christianity in the early modern period demonstrate that Davenant was not alone in producing fictional renderings of the Turk.[1] Many of these 'Turk' plays are concerned with empire, but also displace English anxieties from the geographical location of England to a foreign land. *The Siege of Rhodes* is no exception. Pre-empting the fashion for heroic drama that was to dominate the 1660s, *The Siege of Rhodes* (despite its exotic location) rewrites the civil wars. Unlike much of the heroic drama performed during the 1660s, however, *The Siege of Rhodes* is not preoccupied with ideas of restoration.[2] Events had not progressed far enough for royalists or parliamentarians to anticipate the return of the king.

That Davenant was permitted to mount productions while there was still a general ban on theatrical productions is an anomaly. It suggests that, had historical events not intervened, the third measure for theatre closure that the more radical parliament of 1648 had implemented might have been revoked or mediated. Such speculation cannot further our understanding of the drama, but it can help lay to rest some assumptions regarding the connection between the stage and royalism. At the Restoration, Charles II reinstated the Stuart tradition that only members of the royal family could be patrons of acting companies.[3] With this move, the position of the theatres became annexed to wider concerns regarding loyalty to the Crown.[4] Whether or not the theatres promoted royalism, the legacy of civil war coinciding with theatre closure means it is inevitable that a royalist bias will be identified in early Restoration drama, which would in turn influence readings of Davenant's protectorate masques. However,

Davenant was to revise *The Siege of Rhodes* at the Restoration. This suggests that, for the author at least, the drama needed some modification to fit the changing times.

This chapter seeks to identify some of the changing political ideologies that led to the alterations to *The Siege of Rhodes* at the Restoration. In so doing, I will also address its aesthetic legacy, which is perhaps the most important aspect of the masque's afterlife. I will do this through analysing John Dryden's epic *The Conquest of Granada* (part 1, 1670; part 2, 1671) and George Villiers's burlesque of heroic drama, *The Rehearsal* (1672). These later plays indicate *The Siege of Rhodes*'s cultural significance upon the Restoration stage. First, however, I will examine the problem of allegorical interpretation presented by *The Siege of Rhodes* and how this masque altered theatrical practice.

Ambiguity on stage and page: allegorical uncertainty in *The Siege of Rhodes*

In theatrical terms, *The Siege of Rhodes* marks a transferral from public performances happening in the private space of Davenant's home in Rutland House to the public realm of the Cockpit theatre in Drury Lane. This change in performance space marks a subtle but important movement towards the reopening of the theatres. Within four years, monarchy would be restored and actors would be allowed to perform once more. However, during the late 1650s, only Davenant was permitted to mount and print new forms of public theatrical entertainment.

The Siege of Rhodes has a rather confusing publication and licensing history. Part one was entered in the Stationers' Register, performed and first printed in 1656, and the second part was entered in the Stationers' Register on 30 May 1659.[5] In 1658, the first part was reprinted with some minor alterations, but the second part did not appear in print until 1663, with a dedicatory epistle addressed to Edward Hyde, the Earl of Clarendon. Parts one and two were reprinted in 1670, together with the dedication to Clarendon. This letter inserts the masque into royalist culture (since Clarendon was Charles II's chief adviser while in exile and during the first decade of the Restoration). By 1670, however, Clarendon had fallen from grace and gone into exile, rendering the reprint of the epistle obsolete.[6] Although Clarendon's impeachment and hasty exile makes the letter's praise of his eminence ironic in the context of the 1670 reprint, in 1663 the paratext had different nuances. Davenant claims the play requires protection from persecution:

Heroic drama

> Yet when I consider how many and how violent they are who persecute Dramatick Poetry, I will then rather call this a *Dedication* than a *Present*; as not intending by it to pass any kind of obligation, but to resceive a great benefit; since I cannot be safe unless I am shelter'd behind your Lordship.
>
> ...
>
> Dramatick Poetry meets with the same persecution now, from such who esteem themselves the most refin'd and civil, as it ever did from the Barbarous. And yet whilst those virtuous Enemies denie *Heroique Plays* to the Gentry, they entertain the People with a Seditious *Farce* of their own counterfeit Gravity. But I hope you will not be unwilling to receive (in this Poetical dress) neither the Besig'd nor the Besiegers, since they come without their vices: for as others have purg'd the Stage from corruptions of the Art of the Drama, so have I endeavour'd to cleanse it from the corruption of manners; nor have I wanted care to render the *Ideas* of Greatness and Vertue pleasing and familiar.[7]

Davenant's arguments for staging reformed drama as laid out in his letter to Thurloe (see pp. 94–5) in the 1650s are reappropriated for the Restoration. In the 1650s and the 1660s, drama is presented as a refined form that has been purified of vice and deformity in structure. Despite Davenant's improvements to theatre productions, his drama still requires protection from disapproving voices. Owing to the official reopening of the theatres at the Restoration, the context implicitly points to these disapproving, persecuting figures being parliamentarians. According to Davenant, these parliamentarians perform farce when conducting state affairs, but will not permit the performance of morally beneficial drama. In 1663, Davenant seeks the archetypal royalist, Clarendon, to protect his work. He does so by subscribing to (and forming) the stereotypical caricature of the precise parliamentarian puritan.[8]

Such a reading of the dedication is not without its textual and contextual ironies. When Henry Herbert came to resume his role as Master of the Revels at the Restoration, he was disgruntled by the rights afforded to Davenant as manager of one of the two acting companies that were permitted to perform plays in London. Davenant and Thomas Killigrew were effectively given the rights to license the plays that they produced, thereby usurping the Master of the Revels's role. Herbert was especially angered by Davenant being awarded management of the Duke of York's Company. He believed that Davenant had turned coat and 'obtained Leave of Oliver and Richard Cromwell to vent his Operas in a time when … [Herbert] owned not theire Authority'.[9] Herbert remained loyal to the Crown, whereas Davenant had compounded with the protectorate as a means of establishing himself as a playwright and impresario. Herbert's protest focuses attention on the fact that Davenant had been permitted to mount productions by those whom, at the Restoration, Davenant sought to accuse of persecuting him and his work: had Davenant's work truly been condemned in the commonwealth, he would not have been allowed to 'vent' his masques.

A further textual irony is added by the very entertainments that the epistle introduces. Those who had watched Davenant's masque in 1656 would be aware that the 1663 text was a Restoration revision of the first part of *The Siege of Rhodes*. This, coupled with the circulation of the printed text of the 1656 edition, emphasises the fact that Davenant's work was permitted in the 1650s. Furthermore, the second part may not even have been modified: we may be presented with the 1659 text of part two under the auspices of the Restoration and the text might have been written during the time of the allegedly disapproving protectorate. The dedication therefore exposes metatheatrical tensions within the textual production of the entertainments.

Both versions of Davenant's drama are ambivalent in terms of the morality of the siege: as he states in the dedication, both besiegers and besieged possess virtues worthy of praise. There is no tragicomic restoration at the end of the second part. Since the play functions through displacing topical allusions to a foreign land, this lack of a restoration might suggest that the play was performed before the Restoration.[10] Consequently, the fact that the second part of *The Siege of Rhodes* does not end in jubilant restoration might be explained through the uncertainty of the conditions under which it was written and first acted. If we read *The Siege of Rhodes* as echoing (and displacing) topical events, the hesitant ending could be a response to hesitant times.

While this possible performance history may offer an explanation regarding the ambiguous ending of *The Siege of Rhodes*, like the first part, the second part could also have been redesigned to accommodate the Restoration. As the earliest printed edition of the second part dates to 1663, we do not know if some modifications were made to the text between its entry in the Stationers' Register and its publication. However, the title pages to the 1663 editions of both texts offer some clues as to how part two might have been conceived in 1659. Unlike commonwealth editions of Davenant's masques, the printed text was published after performance. This suspends the commonwealth procedure of using the text to advertise the masque. The Restoration edition of part one states that modifications have been made to the piece, whereas part two makes no mention of

Heroic drama

alterations to the text.[11] This suggests that part two might not have been amended. Since no 1659 text survives, it is tempting to assume that part two of *The Siege of Rhodes* was not performed until the Restoration despite being penned and licensed in the last year of the commonwealth: no text was printed to advertise the production because no production took place. Whatever the lost writing and performance history of the masque, a resolution that is sympathetic to ideas of royalist restoration is not provided in the drama.

Despite this, there are episodes within both the commonwealth entertainment and the Restoration modification of part one which may have met an appreciative reception from a royalist. The central characters, Alphonso (a Sicilian nobleman) and his wife, Ianthe, are strongly reminiscent of an idealised view of Charles I and Henrietta Maria. Providence has led Alphonso to become entangled in the siege that is being inflicted upon the beleaguered Rhodes, and Ianthe (as a supportive wife) seeks to offer Alphonso some relief. Direct parallels with Henrietta Maria are found in Ianthe's decision to sell her jewels: in 1642 Henrietta Maria had sold some of the crown jewels to fund Charles's war effort, bought munitions in the Netherlands, raised a troop and also sought assistance from foreign monarchs. These actions led to accusations of treason from some parliamentarians.[12] In contrast, in the 1656 version of part one, Ianthe's actions are afforded muted praise from the Ottomans, who have intercepted her before she can reach Rhodes:

> MUST[APHA]: This is *Ianthe*, the *Cicilian* Flower,
>   Sweeter then Buds Unfolding in a Shower;
>   Bride to *Alphonso*, who in *Rhodes* so long
>   The Theam has been of each Heroick Song;
>   And she for his relief those Gallies fraught;
>   Both stow'd with what her Dow'r and Jewels brought
> SOLY[MAN]: O wond'rous vertue of a Christian wife!
>   Advent'ring lifes support and then her Life
>   To save her ruin'd Lord![13]

The sale of jewels to assist the Rhodians against their Ottoman conquerors is recognised as a virtuous use of property. Through the fictional construction of Ianthe, Henrietta Maria's actions, which were believed by some parliamentarians to affect the sovereignty and stability of the three kingdoms, are stripped of their treasonable connotations. The political implications of selling Crown property to fund a war against the sovereign's subjects are rewritten to depict a wife selling personal commodities for her husband's benefit.[14]

Such direct and romanticised parallels between the play's characters and the royal couple echo the Neoplatonic courtly love that Henrietta Maria encouraged amongst her circle at court. Since Davenant had been one of the principal masque writers in the 1630s and had assisted in the fostering of this Neoplatonist ideal, it seems inevitable that Neoplatonism would feed into his commonwealth entertainments.[15] Despite this, it is striking that a commonwealth government would sanction potentially positive references to the former king and his controversial queen. Davenant had pre-circulated the masque to Bulstrode Whitelock, and the text does not appear to have been seen as contentious.[16] However, since the masque claims to represent abstract virtues rather than specific individuals and affords all antagonists and protagonists some heroic deeds, the specific resonances of Ianthe's support of her husband become muted by wider concerns.

The supportive and conjugal love depicted between Ianthe and Alphonso feeds into discussions regarding the place and function of marital relationships. In the 1640s, John Milton published several divorce tracts, and marriage tracts went into multiple editions throughout the seventeenth century.[17] Furthermore, the marriage laws had been revised in 1653, which demonstrates that marriage was a topic of serious debate in the mid-seventeenth century. This context means that the marital relationships in *The Siege of Rhodes* could be responding to the various discourses of conjugal love that were current in the period and not to state affairs, neutralising the aspects of Charles and Henrietta Maria's relationship that were judged by some parliamentarians to be dangerous. Allegorical representations of the royal couple were made fit for a protectorate audience. Not only is the private life of the monarch thus remodelled to suit a commonwealth, but the nature of kingship is (re)defined as a form of government that is non-absolute. Lamenting that the European powers are not sweeping to the rescue of the besieged Rhodes, Alphonso learns about statecraft:

> Thou see's not, whilst so young and guiltlesse too,
> That King's mean seldom what their States-men do;
> Who measure not the compass of a Crown
> To fit the Head that wears it but their own;
> Still hind'ring peace, because they Stewards are,
> Without accompt, to that wild spender, War.

> Still Christian Wars they will pursue, and boast
> Unjust successes gain'd, whilst *Rhodes* is lost;
> Whilst we build Monuments of Death, to shame
> Those who forsook us in the chase of Fame.
>
> (1656 edn, sig. B3r)

Rhodes is forsaken, while war is waged elsewhere by the island's reluctant liberators. The lines are ambiguous but seem to offer a cynical view of government. The body politic may have a monarch at its head, but the head has little control over the actions of councillors. Kings do not act alone, and, while they may strive for peace, their advisers encourage war amongst their fellow Christian states. The lack of denominational toleration leads to expensive wars and an inability to realise that the true foes to Christian Europe are the Turks.[18] This passage might appear to be an implicit attack upon protectorate foreign policy but may also indicate a recognition and celebration of Cromwellian toleration. In 1656, Cromwell and his government permitted Jews to return to England.[19] This reversed King Edward I's banishment of the Jews in 1290 and demonstrated a greater degree of religious toleration than was practised by many other European states.[20] The decision to readmit the Jews to England might have been based upon a need to make use of the network of financiers that the Jewish community would bring, though Fifth Monarchists encouraged the return of the Jews as a way to convert them to Christianity and thereby bring about the second coming of Christ.[21] Mercantilism or radical religiosity may have therefore fuelled this decision. However, tolerance was extended to some other forms of Protestant Christianity. Cromwell even permitted Catholics to practise their faith in Dunkirk when the commonwealth acquired the region in 1658, though toleration of Catholicism on a broader scale (and of Islam) was not encouraged.[22]

Similarly, Islamic states had complicated relationships with European countries. Interdependent through trade yet culturally different, Islamic territories (and perhaps the Ottoman Empire in particular) had uneasy connections with Europe in the seventeenth century.[23] As Albert Hourani has noted, 'Christians and Muslims presented a religious and intellectual challenge to each other'.[24] While the Qur'an had been available in Latin translation from the twelfth century and some French and Dutch universities were teaching Arabic by the early seventeenth century, an English version did not appear until 1649 and most Western Europeans had little understanding of the faith. Even countries such as Spain that had been (temporarily) conquered by Islamic nations lacked a neutral understanding of Islam because of animosity between the Visigoths and Morocco.[25] From the Middle Ages onwards, some Christians believed Islam to be a particularly heretical form of Christianity. However, many were not that generous. If early modern Christians considered Islam at all, they often viewed the faith as a false religion that was conceived by violent, lustful and intemperate men who fostered their faith through warfare.[26] As Matthew Dimmock has recently demonstrated, the figure of 'Mahomet' was constantly recalibrated by the English, but these mythologies suggest more about English sensibilities and their sense of the world than an 'authentic' representation of Islam.[27]

Although travel and commerce between East and West permitted a greater understanding of both cultural exchange and cultural difference, fear of the military might of the Ottoman Empire continued until the eighteenth century.[28] The view of oppressive conquering Muslims besieging Christian Rhodes presented in the drama is therefore sympathetic to some of the common perceptions of Islam and Islamic rulers in the seventeenth century. While Christian Western Europe wages internecine war, Rhodes is left to the will of Solyman and his minions. Thus exposed, it is inevitable that the island will fall despite the endeavours of Alphonso and Ianthe.

Solyman is thus figured as the conquering antagonist. Despite this, he is not devoid of honour. Clare identifies parallels between the first part of *The Siege of Rhodes* and Thomas Kyd's Elizabethan play *The Tragedye of Solyman and Perseda* (printed in 1599), but she also notes major differences in the characterisation of Solyman in each drama.[29] Unlike Davenant, Kyd fosters the notion of the unjust, intemperate Turk. Kyd does this by depicting Solyman's desire for Perseda overcoming his friendship for Erastus (whom Solyman had freed). Solyman reneges upon his decision to allow the couple to enjoy connubial love, and, after Erastus has been strangled, Solyman repents that his lust for Perseda overcame his friendship to Erastus and the tragedy ends with multiple carnage. The Turks self-destruct and Rhodes is recovered from its Ottoman invaders.

With its bloody end, Kyd's tragedy concludes very differently to Davenant's text. Unlike *The Siege of Rhodes*, there is no lament in Kyd's play that Western European states are late in providing assistance against the Turkish invasion. The island has not been temporarily forsaken and, from the start, England and France assist Erastus in defending Rhodes. In both plays, Solyman adores an unattainable woman, but whereas Kyd's Solyman self-destructs through seeking to satiate his desire for Perseda, Davenant's Turk can control his appetite. Davenant's Solyman may represent an alien culture, but this culture subscribes to an honour code, which obfuscates allegorical interpretations of the play.

Despite being allowed to leave Rhodes unmolested, Alphonso chooses to assist in the defence of the island and he rejects Solyman's offer of friendship. It is Alphonso and not Solyman who breaks the honour code, negating the idea of the 'lustful Turk' prevalent in Western constructions of Ottomans.[30] This development clouds the allegorical readings of Charles I as Alphonso. If Alphonso is a representation of Charles, he has broken his agreement with Solyman, which can be taken as mirroring Charles I's prevarication and insincere negotiations with parliament.

This reading of Charles's behaviour during his reign helps to demonstrate how Davenant made allegorical readings of monarchy fit for a protectorate audience. In the context of the modified political allegory of protectorate masques, such an interpretation is appealing, but it is not wholly satisfactory. By extension, Solyman should represent Cromwell. While some parallels can be found in Solyman's military skill, further parallels are ultimately unsubstantiated by the text. Ultimately, the drama is ambivalent in terms of its political outlook. This has led Clare to argue that it is at once a royalist and a parliamentarian play.[31] As paradoxical as this may appear, this statement neatly encapsulates this transitional text, where ideas that were once ascribed to monarchy are being made suitable for a non-monarchical state and then modified at the Restoration.

Writing about the unfinished heroic poem *Gondibert*, which Davenant penned c. 1650 (first while in exile and then when he was imprisoned and awaiting execution), Lois Potter commented that the poem 'examines not so much public actions, but private motives'.[32] The narrative of the poem is elucidated by topical contexts; however, topical events are not narrated by the poem.[33] Rather than the poem reinventing civil war and regicide, themes within the poem are clarified through knowledge of its cultural and political context. Elements of the poem have an affinity with current affairs, but in no way does the poem seek to explicate the historical moment.

Potter's observation is interesting in light of Davenant's preface to *Gondibert* and the poem's fretful publication, which is infused with post-regicide uncertainty. Book three of the poem abruptly ends with a valedictory letter as, in October 1650, Davenant expected imminent execution, and did not complete the poem prior to publication. The preface was first printed (without the poem) in 1650, and the poem was printed in 1651.[34] The author's preface endeavours to explicate the narrative.

Echoing Philip Sidney's *Defense of Poesy* (1595), Davenant argues that the poet has greater flexibility than the historian:

> why should a Poet doubt in Story to mend the intrigues of Fortune by more delightfull conveyances of probable fictions because austere Historians have enter'd into a bond to truth? ... by this I would imply, that Truth narrative, and past, is the Idoll of Historians (who worship a dead thing) and truth operative, and by effects continually alive, is the Mistresse of Poets who hath not her existence in matter, but in reason.[35]

'Truth operative' is the realm of the poet, whereas the historian is required to document the narrative truth of events. Under the guidance of the poet, historical events are fluid and pliable. The Poet can project a corrected version of historical events. Mapping fiction on to history means the poet can 'mend' or justify events. A historian's role is archaeological, whereas a poet's is anthropological. For Davenant, there is a universality to human action which can instruct contemporaries in their own modes of behaviour.

A poet must not be chained to historical accuracy, as historical truth can dim the valiant actions of the past. The reader wants these heroic deeds to shine more brightly. By contrast, the achievements of contemporaries can breed resentment, sedition and jealousy amongst their peers. The valour of the deeds of ancestors can be thoroughly acknowledged and emphasised through poetry. In the process, these heroic dead can offer idealised images of how one ought to act:

> It may be objected that the education of the Peoples mindes ... by the severall kindes of Poesy ... is opposite to the receav'd opinion, that the People ought to be continu'd in ignorance; a Maxime sounding like the little subtilty of one that is a Statesman only by Birth or Beard, and merits not his place by much thinking: For Ignorance is rude, censorious jealous, obstinate, and proud; these being exactly the ingredients of which Disobedience is made; and Obedience proceeds from ample consideration, of which knowledge consists; and knowledge will soone put into one Scale the weight of oppression, and in the other, the heavy burden which Disobedience lays on us in the effects of civill Warr: and then even Tyranny will seem much lighter[36]

Addressed to Thomas Hobbes, the preface argues that subjects should be educated into submission to their rulers. Through education and poetry, ignorance can be mediated, and idleness (something that many early modern statesmen argued bred discontent) could be prevented. Davenant

Heroic drama

therefore presents heroic poetry as a vehicle through which readers may encounter topical allusions and purified images of valiant heroes as a way to educate the reading public into obedience.

This view of heroic poetry is complicated by the poem that it prefaces. Incomplete, episodic and bursting with contradictions, *Gondibert* fails to present its readers with a clear example of virtue. Through this failure, the arguments presented in the author's preface unravel. By 1656, Davenant appears to have abandoned the experiment of using heroic poetry to depict virtue: the dedicatory epistle to *The Siege of Rhodes* argues for a different form of characterisation, which leads to a more ambiguous interpretation of historical events by the poet. However, both the poem and the drama are informed by their political contexts and are ambivalent about heroic valour, despite the desire to project the heroic. Davenant may have argued in the preface to *Gondibert* that using the past in the poem allowed him to present more thoroughly instances of valour and virtue, but it ultimately fails in these objectives. The temporal and geographic displacement of both play and poem confuses and muffles the significance of any topical allusions they may seek to explicate.

In *The Siege of Rhodes*, private love and public honour dictate the narrative of the piece and overt allegorical representation is avoided. At the Restoration, this dynamic was mediated by a substantive revision of part one and the possible addition of part two of *The Siege of Rhodes*, but ambiguities still cloud allegorical readings. In the Restoration version, Solyman takes a wife. Here, Alphonso's jealousy is mirrored by Roxolana's fears that Ianthe may have supplanted her in her husband's affections. Reconciliation is achieved in the play when Alphonso and Roxolana overcome their respective jealousies. The narrative does not revert back to Kyd's depiction of Rhodes being restored, but instead restores order in familial relations. Disturbances within the body politic are mirrored by connubial unrest. Marital discord proves easier to harmonise than siege warfare.

The Restoration revision of part one elaborates upon Ianthe's decision to sell her jewels to offer some relief to the Rhodians by inserting a discussion between Ianthe and her waiting women:

IANTH: If by their sale my Lord may be redeem'd
    Why should they more than trifles be esteem'd
...
MAD[INA]: All, Madam, all? Will you from all depart?
IANTH: Love, a consumption learns from Chymists Art.

> Saphyrs, and harder Di'monds must be sold
> And turn'd to softer and more current Gold.
> With Gold we cursed Powder may prepare
> Which must consume in smoak and thinner Air.
> MELO[SILE]: Thou Idol-Love, I'l worship thee no more
> Since thou dost make us sorrowfull and poor.
>
> (1663 edn, sig. B1r)

The addition of two waiting women to the narrative means Davenant may elaborate upon the sale of Ianthe's jewels. This insertion may fulfil the purely practical role of providing more female voices. With the reopening of the theatre came the continental practice of putting women actors upon the stage. However, the first known English woman actor to have performed on the commercial English stage was Catherine Coleman, who sang the part of Ianthe in the (pre-Restoration) production in 1656.[37] The full significance of the woman actor upon the seventeenth-century stage has, until very recently, been largely overlooked. Elizabeth Howe explicitly links the phenomenon of the female actor to royalism, claiming that the exiled court must have accepted the woman actor in the public playhouse because they had experience of her on the continent.[38] Howe also observes that women performed on the Caroline court stage, yet notes that a troupe of French women actors met a poor reception at Blackfriars in 1629. Caroline London playgoers appear to have been morally repulsed by the concept of women players.[39]

Performances by Henrietta Maria and her maids in waiting demonstrate that courtiers were familiar with women actors long before some courtiers were exiled in the 1650s. At the Restoration, Charles II and many members of the royal circle attended the public theatre to an extent that was unprecedented. Consequently, the distinction between court theatre and public theatre was tenuous in the first few decades of the Restoration.[40] With this migration of the court came a partial transferral of the courtly conventions of performance that courtiers had experienced at the English court and in Europe. Furthermore, in the protectorate, Davenant pre-empted this trend through introducing London citizens to the idea of the woman actor. It is Davenant's transferral of the woman actor from the court stage to the public playhouse that heralds her appearance upon the Restoration stage. Sophie Tomlinson acknowledges the significance of the role of Ianthe as a transition in female performance.[41] This transition is emphasised through costume. Tomlinson notes that Ianthe's first entry states that she is veiled, then moves on to discuss the heroic significance of Ianthe rather than her physical representation.[42] In the context of the theatrical performance, the use of the veil is noteworthy. Initially, Ianthe is hidden. Before being presented with the female form, the protectorate audience is introduced to the female voice. Davenant slowly unveils Ianthe before the audience, and, in so doing, establishes the notion that women could perform in the public playhouse. To an extent, Davenant's commonwealth entertainment may be considered as progressive both aesthetically and sociologically. This reordering of English theatrical practice continued at the Restoration: instead of one female actor in *The Siege of Rhodes*, we are now presented with multiple manifestations of femininity upon the Restoration stage.

By 1663, Ianthe is presented as performing tasks beyond the comprehension of her female attendants. War is not an art in which women ought to participate, yet love has given her the ability to turn her jewels into weaponry. This echoes not just Henrietta Maria's actions but the actions of other women during the civil wars. As the example of Brilliana, Lady Harley, demonstrates, women defended their estates while their husbands were fighting away from home. Although Harley's estate was eventually taken by the royalist forces, her resourcefulness did not go unnoted. Harley was not unique in defending her land, household and household stuff: many other noble women protected their families while their husbands fought in the civil wars.[43] Furthermore, in 1662, Margaret Cavendish published *Bell in Campo*, a play that celebrates women coming to the rescue of their beleaguered husbands through forming an Amazonian army.[44] Although a fictional work that radically asserts military equality between men and women, before celebrating the heroic and just command of Victoria, Cavendish's play hints at the need for women to engage in warfare to protect their husbands and property. Cavendish's army of 'heroickesses' support the 'Army of Reformation' against the 'Army of Faction'. This martial personification of ideas frequently addressed throughout the later seventeenth century implicitly engages with civil war discourse and invokes the recent past.

From the context of the civil wars, then, Ianthe's (and by extension, Henrietta Maria's) desire to support her husband is not an isolated example, though the comments of Ianthe's waiting maids suggest it is exceptional. It was not so much the sale of private goods by Henrietta Maria or her support of her husband that was contentious, rather the fact that she had dispersed Crown property and sought assistance from foreign powers. In the character of Ianthe, the more controversial aspects of Henrietta Maria's actions may be discreetly overlooked while her role as supportive wife can be celebrated. In the play, such virtue is beyond the comprehension of the waiting women, but is applauded by men. The enlargements made in the Restoration version of part one of *The Siege of Rhodes* do not further the plot, but place greater emphasis on the virtuous actions of Ianthe.

If the Restoration additions to the first part of *The Siege of Rhodes* do little to further the action of the drama, part two does not help in reconciling the ambivalence of part one. As Susan Wiseman has commented, the first part ends with Alphonso and the European coalition heroically fending off Solyman's troops. Their valour is mediated by Alphonso's jealousy.[45] The second part inverts this scenario. Alphonso overcomes his jealousy and Solyman relinquishes his victory to Ianthe. It does not necessarily follow that the play's ending is one of resolution. Solyman retains Rhodes, but permits Ianthe to determine the treaty on his behalf: since platonic love has vanquished him, he is relinquishing the fate of Rhodes to the woman whom he respectfully loves. Ultimately, parts one and two of *The Siege of Rhodes* each celebrate abstract notions of love and honour. The ability of the lovers to overcome their jealousy elevates them above the conventions of siege warfare. As we have seen, some parliamentarians criticised the influence Henrietta Maria held over Charles and condemned her meddling in affairs of state. The perception of Charles as governed by his wife weakened his position as a monarch and helped to foster the belief that he made a poor ruler. Here, Davenant depicts the victor relinquishing the terms of the conquest to the woman who represents the defeated Rhodians, thereby celebrating the power a woman can hold over a leader. The passing of the terms of treaty to Ianthe is a more generous suggestion than Alphonso's offer to return to the defeated island and be Solyman's 'Suppliant, not ... [his] Foe' (sig. I2v). Love thus turns Solyman into an uxorious victor. Distinctions between Christian and Muslim or Rhodian/ European and Turk cease to be of significance. The purpose of the siege, and who the (male) victor is, becomes ambiguous.

Whether the Restoration audience perceived the ending differently is difficult to assess from the one contemporary account by an audience member that survives. The first recorded performance of the second part of *The Siege of Rhodes* was on 2 July 1661. Judging by Pepys's diary entry, the play was well executed but of little note:

> Today was acted the second part of *The Siege of Rhodes*. We stayed a very great while for the King, and the Queen of Bohemia. And by the breaking of a board over our heads, we had a great deal of dust fell into the ladies' necks and the

Heroic drama   131

men's haire, which made good sport. The King being come, the Scene opened; which endeed is very fine and magnificent, and well acted, all but the Eunuches, who was so much out that he was hissed off the stage.[46]

Since Davenant had used the same designs for *The Cruelty of the Spaniard in Peru* and *The History of Sir Francis Drake*, it is logical to conclude that he also reused scenery for both parts of *The Siege of Rhodes*. John Webb's set designs proved as magnificent in 1661 as they had done in 1656 and, with the exception of the part of Haly, the play was (according to Pepys) well performed. Observations upon the content of the play appear immaterial: of greater significance or comic value are the structural problems experienced in the theatre. If Ianthe had once been an allegorical manifestation of Henrietta Maria, the significance of this allegory was not commented upon by Pepys. By 1661, the dowager queen was less politically contentious, but the observation that Elizabeth of Bohemia was in attendance is significant. Charles I's elder sister came to represent the Protestant cause in Europe through her marriage to Frederick, Elector of the Palatinate, and her subsequent support of Frederick's election to the throne of Bohemia.[47] Frederick's acceptance of the kingdom of Bohemia led to the Thirty Years War, and Elizabeth's continental detractors accused her of causing strife to further her own ambitions to be a queen.[48] However, in England Elizabeth became emblematic of suffering Protestantism on the continent. Her iconography was appropriated by both royalists and parliamentarians as representative of how a monarch should behave.[49] Her image as a Protestant queen is ironic in light of the designs of the gunpowder conspirators who, in 1605, planned to replace James with Elizabeth.[50] However, for parliamentarians from the 1640s, Elizabeth acted as a foil to her sister-in-law. As the following passage indicates, some were of the mind that Prince Rupert of the Rhine had been encouraged to enter the war on his uncle's side by Henrietta Maria:

> some are of opinion, that it was infused into ... [Rupert's] braine by the Queene after he went over from hence, which was much against his Mothers (the good Lady Elizabeth) mind. And although she could not perswade him from coming againe into England, with a purpose to increase the division between the King and Parliament, yet she did refuse to give him her blessing, who went about so wicked a designe.[51]

Henrietta Maria becomes the cause of her husband's downfall by increasing faction and influences Elizabeth's son to behave against his mother's wishes. Allusion to Henrietta Maria in *The Siege of Rhodes* is clouded by counter-narratives that criticise her behaviour during the civil wars. The attendance of Elizabeth of Bohemia at this one documented performance means that those who observed her watching the play were also presented with the embodiment of this counter-narrative. Although, by 1661, Elizabeth's iconographic status was also on the wane, any attempts to decipher the allegorical meanings of the play are problematised by Elizabeth's presence. Instead, notions of love and honour are elevated above the political allegory present in the drama.

In addition to love and honour, a concern of both parts of *The Siege of Rhodes* is providence. Alphonso finds himself in Rhodes and, since providence has led him there, it is his duty to come to the beleaguered island's defence. Equally, it is Solyman's belief that providence spurs the Turks on in battle. Significantly, providence also fuelled the narratives of Charles and Cromwell. Ideas taken from the recent past permeate the narrative of the drama, but the entertainments are ambivalent over what these topical allusions may signify.

Recreating heroic drama: debating kingship in the Restoration

Davenant's entertainments predate the fashion for heroic drama that was to grace the Restoration. During his exile, Charles II had developed French tastes in art and requested that Roger Boyle, Earl of Orrery, produce heroic drama for the Restoration stage. Charles II's active involvement in suggesting that this type of drama ought to be performed seems to point to the conclusion that royalist narratives permeate Restoration heroic drama. Recognition of Orrery's political pragmatism can support this view, though, as John Kerrigan has argued, Orrery's astuteness might not necessarily render his literary writings royalist.[52] Textual ambiguities can affect the political interpretations of allegorical works. Furthermore, a monarch's aesthetic interest does not necessarily stem from a political agenda, though a politically controversial play would lead those involved in its production to be punished.[53] While many of the plays undoubtedly reflect upon the current political and cultural moment, few are explicitly about recent events: Orrery's *The Black Prince* (1669) reads more as half inaccurate chronicle play, half Mills and Boon, than as a reflection upon contemporary anxieties. Yet beneath the baffling love hexagon at the centre of the play, we can identify contemporary ideas relating to nationhood.[54]

Orrery, as Charles's chosen writer of heroic drama, was a master of the genre, but other writers experimented with the form.[55] Heroic drama flourished in France, whereas it enjoyed only a brief popularity in England. Derek Attridge suggests this divergence in theatrical practice in the two countries may be due to linguistic differences: inflections and stresses in English are very different to those in French. Whereas the stresses and rhymes in French emphasise the rhythmic cadences of the language, in English the rhyming couplets sound forced and unconvincing.[56] Nevertheless, heroic drama was to be one of the dominant modes of dramatic representation in the first two decades of the Restoration.

Davenant's occasional collaborator and successor as poet laureate, John Dryden, followed Davenant in writing critical essays about drama and in producing heroic drama. The printed edition of parts one and two of *The Conquest of Granada* (1672) is prefaced with Dryden's *Of Heroique Playes. An Essay* and ends with his *Defence of the Epilogue. Or, An Essay on the Dramatique Poetry of the Last Age*. Each follows a similar line of argument. The postscript asserts that English drama and language have become more refined since the time of the three playwrights believed to have dominated the early seventeenth century, Shakespeare, Jonson and Fletcher (regarded from the later seventeenth century and into the eighteenth century as the triumvirate of wit).[57] Dryden thus echoes Davenant's critique in the preface to *Gondibert* of Edmund Spenser's use of English. Such discussions feed into criticisms that were debated in many contemporary paratexts. Dryden's brother-in-law, Robert Howard, responded to the belief that heroic couplets were a superior form of versification in his tragedy *The Great Favourite, or the Duke of Lerma* (1668). Here, Howard claims that 'nothing may seeme something by the help of a Verse'.[58] He goes on to assert the right of a poet to write as he or she chooses:

> I would have all attempts of this nature be submitted to the fancy of others, and bear the name of Propositions, not of Confident Lawes, or Rules made by Demonstration; and then I shall not discommend any Poet that dresses his Play in such a fashion as his fancy best approves; and fairly leave it for others to follow, if it appears to them most convenient, and fullest of ornament.[59]

Howard thus asserts the right of the poet to choose whatever form he or she thinks is best. Future writers may then decide whether they want to continue writing in a similar vein. The refined language that Dryden and Davenant believe to have evolved since the triumvirate of wit is, for Howard, a fallacy. This indicates the multiple perceptions of heroic verse and literary composition that were current in the Restoration and highlights the fact that there was by no means a consensus over how literature ought to be presented. This is emphasised in Dryden's prefatory essay to *The Conquest of Granada*. Here, Dryden offers an appraisal not of versification but of Davenant's dalliance with the heroic form. Acknowledging his deceased friend's work, Dryden proceeds to point out the deficiencies in the erstwhile laureate's writings:

> For Heroick Plays, ... the first light we had of them on the *English* Theatre was from the late Sir *William D'Avenant*: It being forbidden him in the Rebellious times to act Tragedies and Comedies, because they contain'd some matter of Scandal to those good people, who could more easily dispossess their lawful Sovereign than endure a wanton jeast; he was forc'd to turn his thoughts another way: and to introduce the examples of moral vertue, writ in verse, and perform'd in Recitative Musique.[60]

Perpetuating the myth that governments in the 1650s were opposed to all forms of entertainment, Dryden claims that Davenant used heroic drama as a means to negotiate theatre closure. Tragedies and comedies are specifically selected as the genres that were forbidden. In emphasising the negative approach to these dramatic forms in comparison to the introduction of heroic drama, Dryden presents a prehistory to the type of drama that was to become popular on the Restoration stage. Rather than celebrating heroic drama as a poetic form that is introduced to England by its newly restored king, Dryden locates its genesis in the complicated attitudes to theatrical production in the 1650s.

Davenant is thus credited with introducing English theatre audiences to heroic drama. However, it is in need of refinement to make it fit for the Restoration stage:

> In this Condition did this part of Poetry remain at his Majesties return: When growing bolder, as being now own'd by a publick Authority, he review'd his *Siege of Rhodes*, and caus'd it to be acted as a just Drama; but as few men have the happiness to begin and finish any new project, so neither did he live to make his design perfect: There wanted the fulness of a Plot, and the variety of Characters to form it as it ought: and, perhaps, something might have been added to the beauty of the stile:[61]

This reinforces the often-repeated maxim that 'puritan' regimes in the 1650s were intolerant of performances in comparison to Charles II's belief that drama 'might serve as Innocent and Harmlesse divertisements for many of our Subjects'.[62] However, the very fact that Davenant could mediate the ban on theatrical production undermines Dryden's argument: had the commonwealth been against the staging of plays, Davenant would not have been allowed to perform his masques publicly. Furthermore, the patent granting Davenant and Killigrew management of the two theatre companies at the Restoration emphasises that control of performances is necessary. According to the patent, some plays 'Containe much Matter of Prophanation and Scurrility ... [and] for the most part tende to the Debauchinge of the Manner of Such as are present at them'.[63] Plays *might* serve as harmless and morally beneficial entertainments, but only when cleansed of scandal. According to Dryden, Davenant used the opportunity of the Restoration to revise his drama as he was now permitted to include 'a wanton jeast'. The patent, however, suggests that Davenant and Killigrew have been entrusted to stage orderly drama. The charges that Dryden lays against commonwealth governments could be applied to the restored regime's attitudes to drama.

Dryden glosses over the complexities of Restoration attitudes to drama, and in so doing helps to consolidate the myth that royalists took a more generous view of the theatre than their parliamentarian counterparts. His comments entwine the political with the aesthetic merit of Davenant's text. Dryden judged *The Siege of Rhodes* to be inferior to the drama that superseded it at the Restoration. What is interesting about Dryden's criticism of *The Siege of Rhodes* is that he blames the political circumstances under which it was originally produced (and the subsequent untimely death of the author) for the drama's deficiencies. This, however, only highlights the fact that the production had been mounted while the theatres were closed. In 1663, the dedicatory epistle to Clarendon which Davenant had written to preface *The Siege of Rhodes* highlighted textual and contextual tensions between the commonwealth production of the drama and the Restoration revision. The arguments propounded by Dryden a decade later consolidate this tension by reminding the reader of the circumstances surrounding the production of Davenant's dramas.

Since Charles II encouraged the production of heroic drama, it is absolved of its connection with Davenant's protectorate masques and the political circumstances of the commonwealth. French influences reinvented the genre as a form that had migrated to England with the royalists returning from exile. Davenant's *The Siege of Rhodes* became, for Dryden, a crude prelude to the works that would follow in the Restoration. Dryden acknowledges Davenant's experiments with the form, but proposes his own definition of what heroic drama ought to embody. For Dryden, love and valour replace love and virtue as the principal tenets of heroic poetry. He argues that Davenant's tentative explorations into the new form failed because Davenant was unable to desist from the conventional practices of 'common Drama'.[64] Unable to progress from established dramatic modes, Davenant's entertainments fail as heroic drama and are also unsuccessful as unrefined drama. Davenant's commonwealth masques thus sit uneasily between the heroic and the mundane: it becomes the duty of Dryden and other Restoration playwrights to rectify Davenant's mistakes.

Although Dryden is interested in the aesthetic legacy of Davenant's experiments with heroic poetry, this is not the main focus of his essay. Much of Dryden's critique is concerned with justifying the play that it prefaces.[65] Consequently, the essay is interested not so much in defining what heroic poetry is but in promoting *The Conquest of Granada*. As with *The Siege of Rhodes*, *The Conquest of Granada* deals with encounters between East and West. While the subject matter and source material are very different, Dryden establishes a connection between the two through juxtaposing the two works.

As with the Restoration *Siege of Rhodes*, *The Conquest of Granada* is an epic, two-part drama. The ten acts provide the rich, complex and multiple narratives that Dryden argues are necessary to heroic drama. Chaste, virtuous and constant women are represented by Almahide, Queen of Granada, and Benzayda, a Zegry. Echoes of the allegorical referencing of Henrietta Maria are virtually non-existent in these two roles: direct parallels to Henrietta Maria cannot be drawn, despite both characters proving supportive and stoical wives (in contrast to Lyndaraxa who uses her feminine wiles to ensnare any man willing to set her upon the throne). By the time of each part's first performance in 1670 and 1671 respectively, such allegorical referencing had ceased to be topical. In the depiction of chaste, constant women, however, there are resonances of the cult of Neoplatonism that Henrietta Maria had encouraged amongst her courtly circle. Through the tropes of heroic drama, distant cultural memories of the Caroline court are evoked.

It is likely that many contemporaries would have been unaware of these resonances, and it is doubtful that Dryden was conscious of these connections. An association that would have been more significant to a contemporary audience is that Almahide was originally played by Nell Gwyn.[66] Six months before the premier of *The Conquest of Granada*, Gwyn had scandalously given birth to an illegitimate child, fathered by Charles II.[67] The audience's knowledge of Gwyn's sexual exploits adds a metatheatrical twist to the narrative that is not without its ironies, which negates representations of chaste virtue and the idea that heroic drama ought to embody love and valour. Almahide eventually marries Almanzor. Valiant he may be, but it is difficult to describe Almanzor's actions as honourable. As king maker, Almanzor is the ultimate mercenary. Loyalty is of little significance as he casually conquers kingdoms at the behest of prospective usurpers. When those to whom Almanzor awards the crown fail to show gratitude, his pride is injured and impatience spurs him to restore the erstwhile king. Through the actions of Almanzor, the fate of Mahomet Boabdelin, last Islamic king of Granada, becomes one of deposition, restoration and (eventually) regicide. Thus the memory of civil war and regicide is tentatively invoked. The right to rule ceases to be located in Stuart notions of primogeniture or absolutism and instead becomes attached to warfare.

'Kingship' within *The Conquest of Granada* is depicted as both providential and contractual. In discussing heroic drama, Anne Barbeau identifies this sense of divine justice as being prevalent in Dryden's theories and creations of the genre.[68] Barbeau goes on to assert that Dryden uses historical narrative within his heroic plays as a means through which to demonstrate instances of divine justice.[69] For Barbeau, internal or natural law (or conscience) is often at odds with external (parental and/or civil) law.[70] The normative characters experience conflict between internal and external laws, yet learn to exercise restraint. Conversely, those who abjure their conscience and fail to recognise parental and civil responsibilities get their comeuppance: divine intervention affords justice, echoing some Restoration panegyric that celebrated the providential return of monarchy.[71] However, these 'normative' characters may also be accused of the intemperance Barbeau ascribes to the other characters: Almanzor actively intervenes in the body politic. Although he does not do this to instate himself as ruler, he is willing to become the instrument of Lyndaraxa and the men whom she seduces. When Abdella (suitor to Lyndaraxa and brother to Boabdelin) proves ungrateful, Almanzor decides to restore his brother to the throne of Granada:

> ALMANZ[OR]: I am, but while I please a private man;
> I have that Soul which Empires first began:
> From the dull crowd which every King does lead,
> I will pick out whom I will choose to head:
> The best and bravest Souls I can select,
> And on their Conquer'd Necks my Throne erect.
>
> (part 2, V:i, 474–9)

For Almanzor, kingship is a form of government over which he has control; he is not a normative character who patiently awaits divine justice. Whereas Almanzor appears to be content to be a powerful subject, Lyndaraxa has different notions of kingship. At the beginning of the play, we witness Lyndaraxa promising herself to whichever of her suitors is successful in usurping Boabdelin and thereby making her queen. Lyndaraxa does not stand by her man. When a counter-coup reinstates Boabdelin, the aspiring queen rejects the man whom she encouraged to rebel. For Lyndaraxa, a king is he who has authority, bears a crown and can command respect. Lyndaraxa will 'love a King but a poor Rebel hate' (part 1, V:i, 54). In this respect, Lyndaraxa could be perceived as subscribing to the civil laws Barbeau claims to have been rejected by the character: Lyndaraxa will honour the holder of office, demonstrating a respect for civil law. However, the fact Lyndaraxa is willing to offer allegiance to whoever holds the orb and sceptre (and encourages usurpation for her own personal and material advancement) undermines this gloss. Lyndaraxa chooses when to adhere to civil law and, when her intrigues fail, she encourages an uprising.

Lyndaraxa may share similar views with Almanzor about the essence of monarchy, but Almanzor claims that he chooses not to become a monarch himself. At the end of part two, we witness fate revoking this choice. Discovering that he is the product of a clandestine marriage between the King of Spain's aunt and the Duke of Arcos, Almanzor has little option but to embrace his royal blood and become assimilated to the religion and culture of Spain. Contractual government is replaced by primogeniture as Islamic Granada is conquered by Catholic Spain. Almanzor can anticipate being consort to Almahide once she has finished her period of mourning for her deceased husband. This will complete the conversion of Granada from Islamic to Spanish rule. As Granada is conquered, Queen Almahide converts to Christianity. The recent widow is renamed Isabella by Queen Isabel of Spain, and is thus adopted to Spanish government. Since Almahide has converted to Christianity and allowed herself to be assimilated to Spanish imperialism, she has little choice but to marry Almanzor:

> Q. ISAB[EL]: I am her Parent, now, and may command
>   So much of duty as to give her hand
> (*Gives him* [Almanzor] *Almahides hand*)
> ALMAH[IDE]: Madam, I never can dispute your pow'r,
>   Or, as a Parent, or a Conquerour:

> But, when my year of Widowhood expires,
> Shall yield to your Commands and his desires.
>
> (part 2, V.iii, 333–8)

Different notions about kingship are made possible as a consequence of the civil war and are here open to debate. Spain has a right to Granada through conquest, but this right is consolidated by marriage. The prospective marriage between Almahide and Almanzor merely solidifies the connection between Granada and Spain: since Almanzor is discovered to be cousin to the Spanish king, Spain is afforded tighter control over the newly conquered state. Marital contracts are dynastic pacts and cease to be founded upon abstract notions of love and honour. This marriage (and the conversion of Almahide to Christianity) at the end of the play represents the thorough conquest of Granada by the Spaniards and a discarding of Islamic culture in favour of Spanish expansionism.

A play by the English poet laureate that celebrates Spanish imperial success might seem a little curious. Less than fifteen years previously, the previous laureate was producing *The Cruelty of the Spaniards in Peru*. For centuries, Spain had been England's greatest foe and, as was noted in Chapter 3, anti-Spanish sentiment had been fostered throughout the commonwealth period. By the late 1660s, England had found other European powers with which to war: the Dutch were England's greatest trading rivals and, despite Charles II's admiration of all things French, French absolutist government was causing concern in England. France had succeeded Spain in the role of prime Counter-Reformation power; although still a potent country, the Hispanic nation had ceased to be viewed as a major threat.[72] Spanish conquest could therefore be a topic for partial celebration.[73]

The text is careful to focus upon Almahide's (and Granada's) conversion to Christianity. However, beneath this celebration of Spain's expansionist aspirations lies a problem not acknowledged in the play. The Christianity to which Granada is converted is that of Catholic Spain. The popish plot, exclusion crisis and 1688 revolution may have been future historical events, but in 1671 Catholicism was still troubling to Protestant England. In the late 1660s, Charles II's brother and heir apparent, James (and the person to whom *The Conquest of Granada* is dedicated), converted to Catholicism. When news of this broke, it sparked a major debate regarding the rights of succession.[74] This political crisis scandalised the nation seven years after the first performance of *The Conquest of Granada*, but knowledge of James's conversion caused disquiet long before the popish plot. Although Dryden's play may seek to celebrate love, valour and the bringing of Granada into the Christian fold, the very applauding of Christian conversion brings Catholicism into focus. Unofficially, the Restoration court was tolerant of Catholics: Charles's wife, advisers and (with the notable exception of Nell Gwyn) mistresses were all largely Catholic. Wary lest their power should weaken, Parliament increasingly took measures to curb Catholic influence.[75] The forced happy resolution within the body politic of the play therefore highlights divisions within the English body politic.

The play's celebration of Granada's conquest and conversion to Christianity is further complicated by the means through which the conquest succeeds. Spain gains control of Granada through rebellion and dissent amongst the various tribes who live in Granada, echoing the different national concerns within the three kingdoms that led to the civil wars, and foreshadowing allegations of a pan-British popish plot.[76] Strife in the body politic is mirrored by unrest in the family, where Benzayda and her husband Ozmyn are affected at the political and domestic level by civil unrest. Benzayda goes against paternal and tribal loyalties in marrying Ozmyn: he is an Aberacerrgo and was responsible for the manslaughter of her brother. Charged by her father with executing Ozmyn in revenge for the accidental murder of her brother, Benzayda cannot perform the deed and instead elopes with the captive.

Benzayda justifies paternal disobedience by asserting that her father was unjust and she resolves to die rather than allow Ozmyn to be executed. The scene is transformed from one that focuses upon the private vengeance of a father disposing of his son's murderer to one of wooing. For Alex Garganigo, these episodes reflect how the plot elevates an assertive woman who empowers her beau. This is in contrast to Lyndaraxa's emasculation of men through her desire for power.[77] The debauched court woman and the courtesan are managed by the play: contemporary sexual transgressions and the influence Charles's lovers were perceived to hold over him (most notably the Catholic Lady Castlemaine) are sanitised in Dryden's representation of Granada.[78]

The narrative not only contains these women and female transgressions, it also presents a courtly ideal. Gwyn's playing of the chaste Almahide highlights the inconsistencies between the Restoration reality and the platonic ideal of the play. Within the drama, the representation of the good woman is also not without its problems. Rejecting the paternal selection of her husband, Benzayda marries Ozmyn. Reconciliation between Selin and the couple is brought about when Ozmyn rescues his father-in-law from the murderous wrath of Abenamar, Ozmyn's father:

SELIN: *Benzayda*, I have been too much to blame;
But, let your goodness expiate for my shame;
You, *Ozmyn's* vertue did in chains adore;
And part of me was just to him before.
My Son!
OZMYN: My father!
SELIN: Since by you I live,
I, for your sake, your family forgive.
Let your hard father still my life pursue;
I hate not him, but for his hate to you:
Ev'n that hard father yet may one day be
By kindness vanquish'd as you vanquish'd me.
(part 2, II.i, 94–103)

The reconciliation is marred by the behaviour of Ozmyn's father. Unable to forgive Ozmyn for rescuing Selin, Abenamar resolves to execute his son. This deed is not committed, however, and eventually both fathers are reunited and reconciled with the couple. Parental and civil order is restored through the fathers forgiving and succumbing to the wishes of their children. Filial disobedience may cause short-term grief, but there is no long-term punishment. Parental control is mediated by the child exercising choice over which of the edicts to obey. Ultimately, the valour that Dryden purports to be at the heart of the heroic drama proves difficult to uphold. Honour and valour become flexible entities that alter to suit changing events.

The play plots the various episodes that lead to the conquest of Granada. In so doing, it presents many different responses to these transitions in the war. The conquering Spanish and the governing classes of Granada each observe and participate in these changing times. Each side claims a right to the territory:

ARCOS: The Monarchs of *Castile* and *Arragon*
Have sent me to you, to demand this Town:
To which their just, and rightful claim is known.
BOAB[DELIN]: Tell *Ferdinand* my right to it appears
By long possession of eight hundred years.
When first my Ancestors from *Affrique* sail'd.
In *Rodriques* death your *Gothique* titles fail'd.
ARCOS: The Sucessours of *Rodrique* still remain;
And ever since have held some part of *Spain*.

>   ...
>   You have no right, except you force allow;
>   And if yours then was just, so ours is now.
> BOAB: 'Tis true, from force the noblest title springs;
>   I therefore hold from that, which first made Kings.
> ARCOS: Since then by force you prove your title true,
>   Ours must be just; because we claim from you.
>
> (part 1, I.i, 292–300, 303–8)

And so the dialogue continues, with each argument being matched with a counter-argument. We are offered an ambivalent and contradictory discussion on the nature of kingship and the right to rule. The complicated familial relationships (as represented by Ozmyn, Benzayda and their fathers) have parallels within the body politic. Paternal and civil law are called to question and judged non-absolute. Unlike turbulent domestic relationships, however, trouble within the body politic cannot be resolved through parents acquiescing to their children. Only through Spanish conquest can Granada reconcile political discontent. Despite this, Benzayda and Ozmyn's relationship brings into focus the widespread repercussions of factional disputes. The couple come from different, warring, tribes and Almanzor warns Boabdelin of the trouble these two groups might provoke:

> BOAB: I do not want your Councel to direct,
>   Or aid to help me punish or protect.
> ALMANZ: Thou wantst 'em both, or better thou wouldst know
>   Then to let Factions in thy Kingdom grow.
>   Divided int'rests while thou thinkst to sway,
>   Draw like two brooks thy middle stream away:
>   For though they brand, and jar, yet both combine
>   To make their greatness by the fall of thine
>   Thus, like a buckler, thou art held in sight,
>   While they behind thee, with each other fight.
>
> (part 1, I.i, 222–31)

Arrogance and belief in his royal prerogative leads Boabdelin to initially reject Almanzor's advice. In so doing, he is ripe for deposition. For Alan Fisher, the ideal king is rendered foolish in Boabdelin's inability to control the factions and Almanzor is the *de facto* ruler of Granada long before he is appointed.[79] The allusion to faction also has topical and historical relevance in 1670.

Heroic drama

Charles II's reign was turbulent. His reliance upon cabals and favourites caused unease, as had his father's behaviour a quarter of a century earlier. However, while the discussions regarding kingship and faction are topical, the exotic location renders parallels with Restoration England ambiguous. The allegory in the play is more concerned with ambivalently discussing notions of kingship than presenting a moral representation of what kingship is.

The Conquest of Granada thus presents vague images of the heroic: there are no normative characters to be the true heroes of the piece. Instead, we are presented with a series of debates regarding the nature of kingship as well as civil and parental obedience. These ideas were relevant in 1670, but are also informed by the cultural memory of the previous thirty years. Civil war, regicide and Restoration are tentatively invoked as the play examines unrest and foreign invasion in another land. This depiction of the Spanish conquest calls into question the rights by which a monarch governs. In presenting Almahide and Almanzor with the regency of the town at the end of the play, both the right to rule by hereditary principles and the right to rule by military conquest are upheld. Almanzor, in discovering that he is cousin to the Spanish king, is given hereditary legitimacy to support his desire to marry Almahide. As the widow of the conquered king, Almahide is permitted to remain queen of Granada. This establishes continuity between old and new regimes. The balance between the hereditary right to rule and military conquest never fully favours one form of governance over another. Lyndaraxa's desire for power may never reach fruition and might be condemned, but, without her thirst for a crown, the Zegrys would not have revolted. This aids the Spaniards in gaining control of Granada.

Spain's arguments relating to their ownership of Granada lie in both hereditary right (via descendants of Rodrique, who was the last Visigoth king of Granada eight hundred years before the action of the play takes place)[80] and military victory. Arcos and Boabdelin question the legality of Spain's claim to Granada:

ARCOS: To gain your freedom you a Contract sign'd,
   By which your Crown you to my King resign'd;
   ...
BOAB: The force us'd on me, made that Contract voyd.
ARCOS: Why have you then its benefits enjoy'd?
                              (part 1, I.i, 317–18 and 325–6)

The Spaniards are claiming their contractual right, yet Boabdelin argues the contract is void owing to the agreement being forced from him, and the text seems to be preoccupied with broken oaths.[81] Throughout the seventeenth century, state oaths were sworn to both king and parliament, and, in the 1650s, royalists who had their lands sequestered were forced to compound for their estates and take the Solemn League and Covenant.[82] Rather than being a means of gaining perpetual allegiance to the ruling regime, oaths became connected to the current moment: they could be amended, made obsolete or replaced by new declarations of allegiance. Time voided the oath as political circumstances changed. Boabdelin makes similar arguments: since he was forced into the contract with the Spaniards, he can renege upon it. The Zegrys may have broken faith with Boabdelin through assisting the Spanish in their conquest, but Boabdelin has also broken contract. Since allegiances to the monarch and peace treaties may be annulled, civil and parental law are also subject to renegotiation. Adherence to civil and familial regulation can be made void when the monarch treats contractual obligations with contempt. Order is restored at the end of the play, but it is a new order under Spanish government. Unlike Boabdelin, Arcos subscribes to contractual obligation and seeks to impose it upon Granada: under direct Spanish governance, civil, parental and judicial law become more absolute.

Boabdelin's reasoning for wanting to void the contract complicates ideas of Spain restoring order to Granada. The promise to give Granada to Spain was forced from Boabdelin, which hints at the possibility of use of torture. In discussing representations of torture upon the Restoration stage, Ayanna Thompson argues that torture is depicted as a means of violence that is barbaric and un-English.[83] In *The Cruelty of the Spaniards in Peru*, members of the English New Model Army are tortured alongside the Incas, demonstrating solidarity between the English and Incas against the Spanish. Although *The Conquest of Granada* does not depict English suffering because of Spanish cruelty, the English audience can register these references to cruelty.[84] The depiction of the Spanish conquest of Granada is therefore not wholly celebratory of the victory. Almanzor concurs with Arcos over why Spain ought to be given to Granada, but the lines quoted above become ironic as Alamanzor elaborates upon why he agrees with his father:

For him you took, but for your selves you kept.
Thus, as some fawning usurer does feed

Heroic drama

> With present summs th' unwary Unthrifts need;
> You sold your kindness at a boundless rate,
> And then orepaid the debt from his Estate:
> Which, mouldring piecemeal, in your hands did fall;
> Till now at last you came to swoop it all.
>
> (part I, I.i, 336–42)

Spain might have legal title to Granada, but the terms of the settlement are far from honourable. Spain strips Granada's assets before taking the town by force. Legal, civil and parental law are restored at the end of the play, but the means through which they are restored renders the integrity of the new Spanish order ambiguous.

While the two parts of *The Conquest of Granada* explore ambiguous notions of kingship and conquest, the Prologue and Epilogue are concerned with theatrical culture. As I have already noted, the Epilogue to part two and the *Defence of the Epilogue* focus upon contemporary poetry in comparison to the triumvirate of wit. The Prologue to the first part, however, makes observations upon contemporary theatrical practices. Gwyn, wearing 'a broard-brim'd hat, and wastbelt' (p. 19) comments upon a comical exchange between the two theatre houses that is meant to amuse their shared audience:

> They thought you lik'd, what onely you forgave:
> And brought you more dull sence, dull sence much worse
> Than brisk, gay Non-sence; and the heavyer Curse.
> ...
> And may those drudges of the Stage, whose fate
> Is, damn'd dull farce more dully to translate,
> Fall under that excise the State thinks fit
> To set on all *French* wares, whose worst, is wit.
> *French* farce worn out at home, is sent abroad;
> And, patch'd up here, is made our *English* mode.
> ...
> Which makes you mourn, and makes the Vulgar laugh.
>
> (prologue to part 1, 24–6, 34–9 and 43, italics reversed)

Satirising French farce through Gwyn's costume and the prologue, Dryden conveniently overlooks that *The Conquest of Granada* is derived mainly from French sources, and English heroic drama stylistically imitates its continental cousin.[85]

The king's two bodies: dual kingship and heroic parody

The politics of Restoration heroic drama are therefore open to multiple interpretations as concepts of kingship are addressed through allegorical notions of love and honour. In addition to this, the aesthetic merits of heroic drama were questioned at the time. The prologue to *The Conquest of Granada* alludes to a metatheatrical dialogue taking place between the two theatre houses. Primarily responding to *The Conquest of Granada*, but also to the fashion for heroic drama, George Villiers, second Duke of Buckingham, wrote a play that challenged the types of productions that were mounted by both acting companies. *The Rehearsal* was played at the Theatre Royal in 1671. Focusing upon the trials and tribulations of the two kings of Brentford, Buckingham lampoons Dryden's construction of heroic drama. Serious discussion regarding kingship becomes subsidiary to the play as *The Rehearsal* focuses upon the absurdities of the heroic genre. *The Rehearsal* depicts a rehearsal of a piece of heroic drama by Bayes, and the fictional playwright comments upon the action throughout:

> BAYES: whereas every one makes five Acts to one Play, ... [I] make five Plays to one Plot: by which means the Auditors have every day a new thing.
> JOHN[SON]: Most admirably good, i'faith! and must
> certainly take, because it is not tedious.
> BAYES: I, Sir, I know that, there's the main point. And then, upon *Saturday*, to make a close of all, (for I ever begin upon a *Monday*) I make you, Sir, a sixth Play, that sums up the whole matter to 'em, and all that, for fear they should have forgot it.[86]

In addition to mocking heroic drama, Dryden's paratexts and forays into literary criticism are also ridiculed. *The Rehearsal* lampoons set pieces of the genre. Bayes's play is so confusing that the players give up and go to dinner: the unity and depiction of love and valour that Dryden seeks to present is judged unsustainable by Buckingham.

Bayes's play is thus incomprehensible, but allusions to civil war are present in the narrative. George McFadden reads *The Rehearsal* as political satire and argues that Bayes is intended to be a satiric representation not of Dryden but of Henry Bennet, Earl of Arlington.[87] McFadden's evidence that contemporaries read Bayes as such, and his discussion of the political rivalry between Buckingham and Arlington, are compelling, and he then goes on to speculate about how the role of Bayes came to be read as referring to Dryden. He suggests that 'the two kings of Brentford' could serve as a metaphor to describe how the multiple interpretations of the allegory within *The Rehearsal* means that there are two threads to the allegory. One is political and leads to Bayes being interpreted as a representation of Arlington, the other aesthetic and points to Bayes as being a comical depiction of Dryden. The political thread clearly represents faction through lampooning Arlington, whereas the aesthetic thread refers to the cultural legacy of Restoration and the presentation of the heroic drama genre.[88]

These two threads are tangled in the narrative of *The Rehearsal*, and the play-within-the-play is comically chaotic. As unstructured as the play that is being rehearsed in *The Rehearsal* may be, memory of civil war is not wholly absent from the text. In criticising faction, Buckingham is not only attacking Arlington but invoking the cultural memory of civil war. The two kings of Brentford are usurped, and then the play descends into a war as the usurpers lose control of the crown. The south-west of London is called to arms as the kingdom of Brentford experiences war throughout its dominions:

> LIEUT[ENANT] GEN[ERAL]: Advance from *Acton*, with the Musquetiers
> GEN[ERAL]: Draw down the *Chelsey* Curiasiers.
> LIEUT. GEN: The band you boast of, *Chelsey* Curiasiers,
>   Shall, in my *Putney* Pikes, now meet their Peers.
> GEN: *Chiswickians*, aged, and renown'd in fight,
>   Join with the *Hammersmith* Brigade.
> LIEUT. GEN: You'll find my *Mortlake* Boys will do them right,
>   Unless by *Fulham* numbers over-laid.
> GEN: Let the left-wing of *Twick'nam* Foot advance,
>   And line that Eastern hedge.
>
> (V.i, sig. G4v)

War is not displaced to an exotic, distant land, but is here relocated near to Westminster and London. In plotting the towns that are in the proximity of Brentford (and, as Bayes argues, could conceivably be in the kingdom of Brentford), war is mapped on to the landscape of southern England. The reference to '*Putney* Pikes' invokes the 1647 Putney Debates and the memory of one of the turning points of the civil war is therefore brought into focus in the Restoration satire. The stage becomes a micro-kingdom where war may be trivialised and terminated when the players want their dinner. The stage and the state become metaphysically connected through the allegorical discussion of politics. This connection is emphasised in the Epilogue:

> The Play is at an end, but where's the Plot?
> That circumstance our Poet *Bayes* forgot.
> And we can boast though 'tis a plotting Age,
> No place is freer from it than the Stage.
> ...
> If it be true, that Monstrous births presage
> The following mischiefs that afflict the Age,
> And sad disasters to the State proclaim;
> Plays, without head or tail, may do the same.
> Wherefore, for ours, and for the Kingdoms peace,
> May this prodigious way of writing cease.
> Let's have, at least, once in our lives, a time
> When we may hear some reason, not all Rhyme:
> We have these ten years felt its influence;
> Pray let this prove a year of Prose and Sence.
>
> (Epilogue, sig. H4r, italics inverted)

Buckingham proposes that plotting and scheming are endemic in society, though absent from drama. The reference to 'monstrous births' invokes the memory of civil war pamphlet culture, especially the *Mistress Parliament* pamphlets that depicted parliamentary faction and the prospective birth of the deformed republic.[89] Monstrous bodily deformity, in turn, alludes to one of Ogilby's translations of Aesop's *Fables*, which went into its third edition in 1673.[90] Here, Ogilby presents the tale of 'The Rebellion of the Hands and the Feet', where the body politic is translated into physical form. The woodcut presented with the fable figures a naked headless body brandishing a sword while the stomach is represented as devouring everything. The body has two faces: the one being the head that has been severed and is lying at the feet of its body, the other being a monstrous face attached to the body's chest. Drawing from grotesque imagery, the monstrous face and body remain animated while the symmetrical and orderly head languishes at the foot of the disorderly body (Figure 4). Once reason in the body politic has been removed, chaos ensues.[91]

Ogilby's allegory warns against faction and war as it is self-perpetuating: strife rarely leads to resolution. Buckingham argues that the fault lies in the love of faction and plotting: he suggests that plots have migrated from

Heroic drama 149

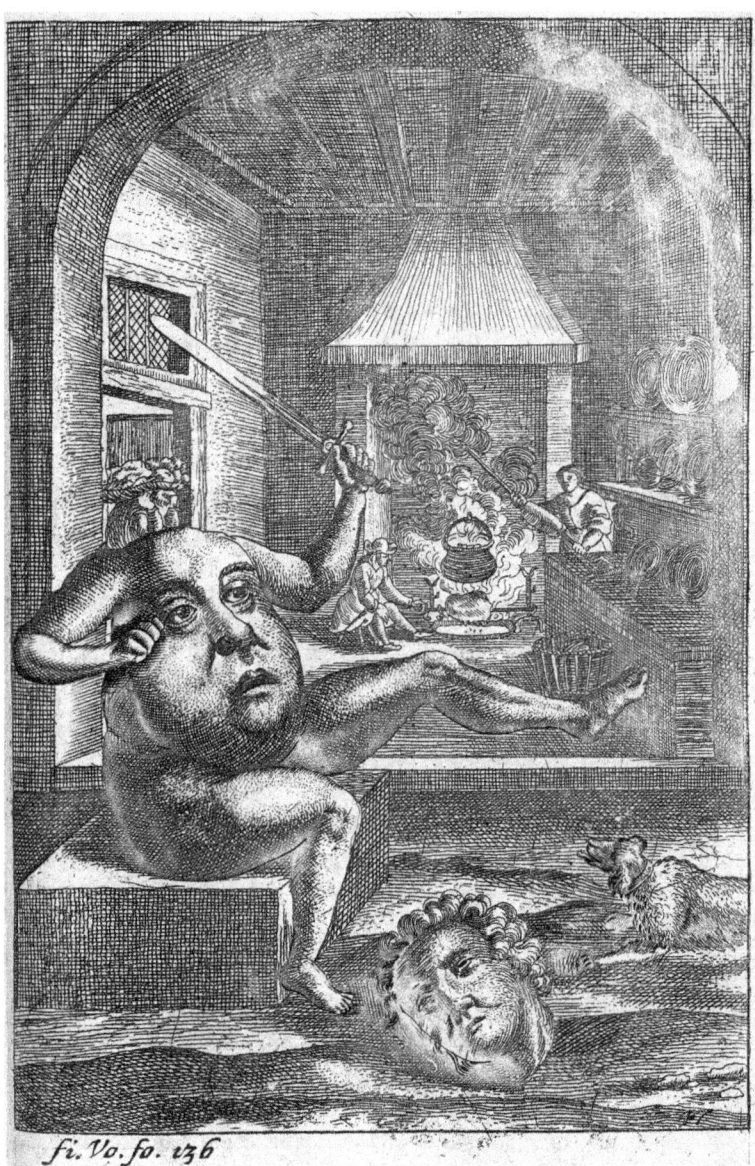

4 John Ogilby, 'Of the rebellion of the hands and the feet', in *The fables of Æsop paraphras'd in verse, and adorn'd with sculpture*, 3rd edn (London, 1673), Douce A. 694, Vol. 1 pp. 136–9 (p. 137)

the stage to the state, leaving the former aesthetically deprived of shape or form and the latter in a state of disorder. For Buckingham, the heroic couplet is to blame for the stage's perceived ills, as rhyme has usurped plot. Plots therefore go into exile and find a haven within the body politic. Only when plots are restored to the fictionalised space of the play's micro-kingdom can the macro-kingdom be fully restored. Ironically, the dramatic form that Charles II had encouraged to be produced is blamed for discontent in the country. Rather than connecting the reopening of the theatres with the restoration of monarchy and celebrating the triumphal return of both to the realm, Buckingham presents the restoration of drama as the dawn of ten years of decay. Only when the fashion for heroic drama declined could the stage properly flourish and order be restored in the body politic.

The Rehearsal did not mark the end of heroic drama, but this trend in theatrical production was short-lived. The 1670s saw more new plays produced in the genre than the 1660s, but it began to go out of vogue in the 1680s.[92] Buckingham's play is therefore representative not of a turning point in tastes but of the fact that a genre and its travesty may simultaneously be popular. Other playwrights such as Thomas Duffet would mock contemporary scripts and produce travesties of popular plays throughout the later seventeenth century, and Davenant's liberation of the woman actor on the public stage became a permanent aesthetic legacy.[93] Although Buckingham pleads for the performance of other dramatic forms, heroic drama was not the only type of play to grace the Restoration stage.

Davenant, Dryden and Buckingham all provide commentary upon the stage and the state. In making his commonwealth masque fit for a Restoration audience, Davenant presents stronger parallels between Ianthe and Henrietta Maria, yet remains ambivalent about issues of governance. Dryden's Granada is one of broken oaths and non-normative characters, echoing the previous thirty years of English history. The right to govern is called to question, but neither hereditary kingship nor the right to rule by conquest is fully supported. Although mainly a response to heroic drama, Buckingham's play also questions the essence of sovereignty: it does so through relocating these debates away from their displaced exotic locations and bringing them back to the playhouse and its fabled kingdom of Brentford. In restoring plots to the theatre, Buckingham satirises plotting within the body politic. Each of these plays is ambivalent about what monarchy may mean as both the stage and monarchical government sought to be re-established. Heroic drama and the mock heroic were adopted by these three playwrights as a way through which monarchy could be discussed. Other playwrights (and politicians) such as Orrery and Dryden's brother-in-law, Robert Howard, also appropriated the genre to explore ideas of monarchy and restoration.[94] Despite this, heroic drama did not have a monopoly upon representations of monarchy, government and the civil war period. Buckingham utilised the mock heroic to satirise heroic drama and make some allusions to kingship. Other writers would appropriate comedy as a means of directly addressing the civil wars and Restoration. Whether as heroic drama or comedy, the memory of the recent past found fictional constructions upon the Restoration stage.

Notes

1 See, for example, Bridget Orr, *Empire on the English Stage, 1660–1714* (Cambridge: Cambridge University Press, 2001); Gerald M. Maclean discusses English travel to the 'Ottoman Mediterranean' in *The Rise of Oriental Travel: English Visitors to the Ottoman Empire, 1580–1720* (Basingstoke: Palgrave Macmillan, 2004).
2 For a study into how Restoration culture was concerned with the Restoration, see Nicolas Jose, *Ideas of the Restoration in English Literature* (London and Basingstoke: Macmillan, 1984).
3 Andrew Gurr, *The Shakespearian Stage 1574–1642*, 3rd edn (Cambridge: Cambridge University Press, 1992), p. 28.
4 It has been taken as a given that the Restoration stage is an intensely political (and royalist) creation. See, for example, Nancy Klein Maguire, *Regicide and Restoration: English Tragicomedy, 1660–1671* (Cambridge: Cambridge University Press, 1992); Aparna Dharwadker, 'Class, authorship, and the social intertexture of genre in Restoration theater', *SEL*, 37 (1997), 461–82.
5 E. Arber, ed., *A Transcript of the Registers of the Worshipful Company of Stationers, 1640–1708 AD*, 3 vols (London, 1913), 2 (27 August 1656 and 30 May 1659).
6 See Tim Harris, *Restoration: Charles II and His Kingdom* (London: Allen Lane, 2005), p. 71.
7 William Davenant, *The Siege of Rhodes: the First and Second Parts* (London, 1663), sigs A2r–A3v. This quotation also seems to allude to genre as a socio-political construct. This suggests that there might be a prehistory to Aparna Dharwadker's thesis that class-based genres emerged at the Restoration and class and genre shape representations of authority and authorship. See Dharwadker, 'Class, authorship', esp. pp. 462–3.

8 Davenant was, to an extent, accustomed to having his work attacked. In 1629, his play *The Just Italian* had been poorly received at the Blackfriars theatre and he became embroiled in a quarrel with Philip Massinger that was played out in the prologues to plays (Peter Beal, 'Massinger at bay: unpublished verses in a war of the theatres', *YES*, 10 (1980), 190–203 (p. 190)).

9 N. W. Bawcutt (ed.), *The Control and Censorship of Caroline Drama: The Records of Sir Henry Herbert, Master of the Revels, 1623–73* (Oxford: Oxford University Press, 1996), p. 223. See also Lois Potter, ed., *The Revels History of Drama in English*, 8 vols (London: Methuen, 1981), 4:299.

10 Susan Wiseman states that it was performed in 1659 and 1661, and observes that it is possible that the 1659 and 1661 texts of part 2 are different (Wiseman, *Drama and Politics in the English Civil War* (Cambridge: Cambridge University Press, 1998), pp. 151–2).

11 Sonia Massai suggests that annotated manuscripts and textual alterations to later editions were generally used as a selling point by early modern publishers, and much paratextual material emphasises the desire to 'perfect' the copy (Massai, *Shakespeare and the Rise of the Editor* (Cambridge: Cambridge University Press, 2007), pp. 3–10).

12 Austin Woolrych, *Britain in Revolution, 1625–1660* (Oxford: Oxford University Press, 2002), esp. pp. 228, 260 and 289.

13 William Davenant, *The Siege of Rhodes* (London: J. M. for Henry Herringman, 1656), sig. C2r.

14 Jean Gagen argues that love and honour in Dryden's heroic plays stem from Renaissance humanist notions of honour and the platonic or Neoplatonic inheritance of notions of love. These ideas may similarly be applied to Davenant's pre- and post-civil-war masques (Gagen, 'Love and honor in Dryden's heroic plays', *PMLA*, 77 (1962), 208–20 (esp. 209–12)).

15 For a study that examines Davenant's early work in relation to the Caroline court, see Karen Britland, *Drama at the Courts of Queen Henrietta Maria* (Cambridge: Cambridge University Press, 2006), esp. pp. 131–49.

16 Janet Clare, *Drama of the English Republic: 1649–1660* (Manchester: Manchester University Press, 2002), pp. 185–6. Whitelock's response does not survive.

17 Throughout the seventeenth century, there was a proliferation of marriage tracts, some of which went through multiple editions. Although they differed in particulars, these tracts generally reached a consensus over the notion that the wife was subordinate to the husband. For an example of these marriage tracts, see William Gouge, *Of Domesticall Duties, Eight Treatises*, 3rd edn (London: George Miller, 1634); Matthew Griffith, *Bethal: Or a Forme For Families* (London: Jacob Bloom, 1633); William Whately, *A Bride-Bush*,

or a Direction for Married Persons (London: Bernard Alsop, 1623); and the Marquis of Halifax's pragmatic *The Lady's New Year Gift: or, Advice to a Daughter* (London: Randal Taylor, 1688).
18 This might be an implicit reference to the Thirty Years War (1618–48), partly a war of succession and partly a war of religion, in which most Western European powers were involved. It was widely commented upon at the time, and the English newsbook *The Moderate Intelligencier* published a series of articles about it in 1649 (*The Thirty Years' War*, ed. Geoffrey Parker, 2nd edn (London: Routledge, 1997), p. xii).
19 Woolrych, *Britain in Revolution*, pp. 638–40.
20 Robert M. Healy, 'The Jews in seventeenth-century Protestant thought', *Church History*, 46 (1977), 63–79 (66).
21 Healy, 'The Jews', pp. 70–6.
22 Woolrych, *Britain in Revolution*, esp. pp. 586–8, 641–8, 679–82.
23 Orr, *Empire on the English Stage*.
24 Albert Hourani, *Islam in European Thought* (Cambridge: Cambridge University Press, 1991), p. 8.
25 Hourani, *Islam*, pp. 8–9; 12–13.
26 Hourani, *Islam*, p. 10. See also C. A. Patrides, '"The bloody and cruel Turke": the background of a Renaissance commonplace', *Studies in the Renaissance*, 10 (1963), 126–35.
27 Matthew Dimmock, *Mythologies of the Prophet Muhammad in Early Modern English Culture* (Cambridge: Cambridge University Press, 2013).
28 Hourani, *Islam*, p. 10.
29 Clare, *Drama*, p. 182.
30 Orr provides a useful reading of an encounter between the Restoration English court and an embassy from Morocco. Rather than exposing any sexual intemperance in the Moroccan Ambassador and his entourage, the licentiousness of the English comes into focus (*Empire on the English Stage*, pp. 14–16).
31 Clare, *Drama*, pp. 184–5.
32 Lois Potter, *Secret Rites and Secret Writings: Royalist Literature, 1641–1660* (Cambridge: Cambridge University Press, 1989), p. 97.
33 Potter, *Secret Rites*, p. 94.
34 William Davenant, *Gondibert*, ed. David F. Gladish (Oxford: Oxford University Press, 1971), p. xi.
35 Davenant, *Gondibert*, pp. 10–11.
36 Davenant, *Gondibert*, p. 39.
37 *The Siege of Rhodes* (London, 1656), sig. G1r.
38 Elizabeth Howe, *The First English Actresses, 1660–1700* (Cambridge: Cambridge University Press, 1992), p. 23.

39　Howe, *The First English Actresses*, pp. 22–3.
40　Dharwadker, 'Class, authorship and social intertexture', p. 465.
41　See Sophie Tomlinson, *Women on Stage in Stuart Drama* (Cambridge: Cambridge University Press, 2005), pp. 156–62.
42　Tomlinson, *Women on Stage*, p. 150.
43　I use 'families' in the early modern sense of the word, encompassing all members of the household. For a fuller account of women's involvement in defending their households during the civil wars, see Antonia Fraser, *The Weaker Vessel: Woman's Lot in Seventeenth Century England* (London, Phoenix Press, 1984, repr. 2002), pp. 197–223.
44　Margaret Cavendish, 'Bell In Campo', in *Playes Written by the Thrice Noble Illustrious and Excellent Princess, the Lady Marchioness of Newcastle* (London, 1662).
45　Wiseman, *Politics*, pp. 157–68.
46　Robert Latham and William Matthews, eds, *The Diary of Samuel Pepys*, 11 vols (London: Harper Collins, 1995), 2:130–1 (2 July 1661).
47　Rosalind K. Marshall, *The Winter Queen: The Life of Elizabeth of Bohemia, 1596–1662* (Edinburgh: Scottish National Portrait Gallery, 1998), pp. 46–7.
48　Marshall, *The Winter Queen*, p. 46.
49　For an example of parliament appropriating Elizabeth to their cause, see *A Declaration of the Prince Paltsgrave to the High Court of Parliament, concerning the Cause of his Departure out of England in These Times of Distractions* (1642). Conversely, *Wortley's Lines Dedicated to Fame and Truth* (York: Stephen Bulkley, (1642) offers a royalist versification of Elizabeth's sufferings.
50　Marshall, *The Winter Queen*, pp. 25–6.
51　*A Declaration of the Prince Paltsgrav*, sigs A2v–A3r.
52　John Kerrigan, *Archipelagic English: Literature, History and Politics, 1603–1707* (Cambridge: Cambridge University Press, 2008), p. 255.
53　An example of this is John Lacy's adding of comic lines to his part in Edward Howard's *The Change of Crowns* (1667), discussed in my Introduction.
54　Kerrigan, *Archipelagic English*, p. 263.
55　For a discussion of Orrery's use of the heroic drama form in relation to Restoration politics, see Maguire, *Regicide and Restoration*, esp. chapter 6. See also Elaine McGirr, *Heroic Mode and Political Crisis, 1660–1745* (Newark: University of Delaware Press, 2009), pp. 41–5.
56　Derek Attridge, 'Dryden's dilemma, or, Racine refashioned: the problem of the English dramatic couplet', *YES*, 9 (1979), 55–77.
57　Paulina Kewes, *Authorship and Appropriation: Writing for the Stage in England, 1660–1710* (Oxford: Oxford University Press, 1998), p. 149.

58 Robert Howard, *The Great Favourite, or the Duke of Lerma* (London: printed for Henry Herringman, 1668), sig. A4r. The title page asserts that the play is a tragedy, though perhaps it ought to be considered as a tragicomedy. Howard's play was composed at the time of Clarendon's impeachment. Like many plays of this period, it is saturated with topical allusion and references.
59 Howard, *The Great Favourite*, sig. A5r.
60 *Of Heroique Plays. An Essay*, in H. T. Swedenberg *et al.* (eds), *The Works of John Dryden*, 20 vols (Berkeley, Los Angeles and London: University of California Press, 1961–2000), 11:8–18 (p. 9).
61 Dryden, *Of Heroique Plays*, 11:9.
62 Bawcutt, *The Control and Censorship of Caroline Drama*, p. 227.
63 Bawcutt, *Control and Censorship*, p. 227.
64 Dryden, *Of Heroique Plays*, p. 10.
65 William S. Clark, 'The sources of the Restoration heroic play', *RES*, 4 (1928), 49–63.
66 See the 'Persons Represented', *The Conquest of Granada by the Spaniards: In Two Parts* in H. T. Swedenberg *et al.* (eds), *The Works of John Dryden*, 20 vols (Berkeley, Los Angeles and London: University of California Press, 1961–2000), 11:21–2.
67 Maguire, *Regicide and Restoration*, pp. 211–12.
68 Anne T. Barbeau, *The Intellectual Design of John Dryden's Heroic Plays* (New Haven and London: Yale University Press, 1970), p. 70.
69 Barbeau, *Intellectual Design*, p. 10.
70 Barbeau, *Intellectual Design*, p. 6.
71 Dryden contributed to the panegyric that greeted the Restoration through publishing *Astraea Redux* (H. T. Swedenberg *et al.* (eds), *The Works of John Dryden*, 20 vols (Berkeley, Los Angeles and London: University of California Press, 1961–2000), 1:22–31).
72 Woolrych, *Britain in Revolution*, pp. 631–7.
73 Orr, *Empire on the English Stage*, p. 162.
74 Harris, *Restoration*, pp. 148–58.
75 Harris, *Restoration*, pp. 136–202.
76 Harris, *Restoration*, p. 137.
77 Alex Garganigo, 'The heroic drama's legend of good women', *Criticism*, 3 (2003), 483–505 (493).
78 Garganigo, 'The heroic drama's legend', pp. 498–99.
79 Alan S. Fisher, 'Daring to be absurd: the paradoxes of *The Conquest of Granada*', *Studies in Philology*, 73 (1976), 414–39 (419–23).
80 Washington Irving, *Chronicle of the Conquest of Granada* (1829), e-book, Project Gutenberg, www.gutenberg.org/etext/3293.

81 J. Douglas Canfield, 'The significance of the Restoration rhymed heroic play', *Eighteenth-Century Studies*, 13 (1979), 49–62.
82 For a study of seventeenth-century state oaths, see Edward Vallance, *Revolutionary England and the National Covenant: State Oaths, Protestantism and the Political Nation* (Woodbridge: Boydell Press, 2005).
83 See Ayanna Thompson, *Performing Race and Torture on the Early Modern Stage* (New York and London: Routledge, 2008).
84 Thompson in fact locates 'Englishness' in the Restoration audience who view the play and not the drama that she discusses.
85 The main source is Georges de Scudéy's *Almahide*, (Derek Hughes, *Dryden's Heroic Plays* (London and Basingstoke: Macmillan, 1981), pp. 3–4). For a discussion of the stylistic relationship between English and French heroic drama, see Attridge 'Dryden's dilemma'.
86 *The Rehearsal* (London, 1673), IV.i, sig. F1r.
87 George McFadden, 'Political satire in *The Rehearsal*', *YES*, 4 (1974), 120–8 (122).
88 McFadden, 'Political satire', 128.
89 See *Mistress Parliament Presented in her Bed* (1648).
90 John Ogilby, *The Fables of Æsop Paraphras'd in Verse, and Adorn'd with Sculpture*, 3rd edn, (London, 1673).
91 Ogilby, *The Fables*, 'Of the Rebellion of the Hands and the Feet', pp. 136–9.
92 Attridge, 'Dryden's dilemma', p. 56.
93 For an example of Restoration travesty, see T. Duffet, *The Mock-Tempest: Or the Enchanted Castle* (London, 1675), Duffet's even bawdier response to Dryden and Davenant's risqué adaptation of Shakespeare's *The Tempest* (performed 1667; published 1660; adapted by Thomas Shadwell, 1674).
94 See Jose, *Ideas of Restoration*, pp. 131–41.

5

Ideas of panegyric in early Restoration comedy

> Then to Westminster-hall where I heard how the Parliament had this day dissolved themselfs and did pass very cheerfully through the Hall and the Speaker without his Mace. The whole Hall was joyful thereat, as well as themselfs, and now they begin to talk loud of the king. Tonight I am told that yesterday, about 5 a-clock in the afternoon, one came with a ladder to the great Exchange and wiped with a brush the Inscripcion that was upon King Charles, and that there was a great bonefire made in the Exchange and people cried out 'God bless King Charles the Second'.[1]

The first few months of Pepys's diary for the year 1660 palpitate with uncertainty over whether Charles II would be restored to the throne. The declaration of Breda put an end to this, and the exiled king prepared to return to his loyal subjects. Universal joy was expressed, bonfires were lit and maypoles were erected. Old England became merry once more in anticipation of the arrival of its bonny king.

Such a reading of the restoration of the monarchy would seem to be supported by the extract from Pepys's diary that opens this chapter, which certainly reflects how much of the panegyric that surrounded the Restoration sought to define it. Pepys's diary anticipates Charles's return from exile with moderate pleasure, but this may have more to do with the novelty of the moment than a sudden burst of royalist fervour. The comments chime with royalist wishful thinking about providence leading to the return of the king rather than describing the ways in which the events surrounding the Restoration really unfolded. It may also reflect a desire to return to some form of political stability following the power vacuum caused by the death of Cromwell.

Pepys acknowledges that, in his youth, he was known for his roundhead leanings.[2] This illustrates the multiple and often contradictory attitudes to monarchy held by individuals, and there may not necessarily have been a deep-rooted sense of loyalty to monarchical rule. Since monarchy was the established form of government until the commonwealth and protectorate were imposed, for many, it would have been perceived as the natural choice for government. Not so much loyalty to the Crown but an unconscious assumption that monarchy would return may therefore have influenced some of the festivities.

In discussing public events, Pepys adopts a journalistic tone, which could lead the reader to infer that public opinion was more uniform that it actually was. In a previous entry, Pepys observes that 'Everybody now drinks the King's health without any fear, whereas before it was very private that a man dare do it'.[3] This suggests that there was genuine pleasure in anticipating Charles's return, but also a tendency by Pepys to generalise the mood of the public. Further examination of Pepys's diary entries demonstrates a more complex situation. His comments relating to the pleasure that was unanimously experienced in contemplating the restoration of Charles is undermined by a piece of gossip that precedes them:

> My Lord told me that there was great endeavours to bring in the Protector again; but he told me too, that he did believe it would not last long if he were brought in; no nor the King neither (though he seems to think that he will come in), unless he carry himself very soberly and well.[4]

Edward Montagu's speculation over whether Richard Cromwell or Charles Stuart would be reinstated as supreme ruler shows that there was uncertainty surrounding how the events that led to the restoration of the monarchy would unfold. It also reveals a sense of cynicism about the nature of leadership and government. Essentially, whoever was chosen to rule did not matter as long as the rulers behaved themselves. Such observations demonstrate the political expediency of Montagu, who had the ability to survive the transition between regimes.[5] It also suggests that the restoration of the monarchy came about in part as a result of exasperation with the lack of successful government following the death of Cromwell; the royalists achieved a restored monarchy because it seemed better than the constant coups and counter-coups that the country had experienced in the years between Cromwell's death and Charles's return.[6]

The euphoria that greeted Charles's return from exile and the lack of any attempt by parliament to limit the restored king's authority was a political coup and a successful public relations exercise for Charles. This

Ideas of panegyric

was partly due to the way in which the public joined in the festivities, both spontaneous and organised, which marked the return of the king. The irony of the overwhelming joy that greeted Charles was not lost on the monarch: he wryly rebuked his soon-to-be much-censured tardiness for staying away from his loyal subjects for so long.[7] Beneath this wave of public celebration, however, supporters of the objectives of the commonwealth were anxious. In contemplation of the anticipated Restoration, Mr Blackborne confided to Pepys that he was fearful as 'all good men and good things were now discouraged'.[8]

Overtly, the royalists had won a thorough and bloodless victory, but there were unresolved tensions caused by the abrupt Restoration. This meant that the Cavalier Parliament continued to work uneasily with the government more through fear of returning to the problems of the reign of Charles I and the period immediately succeeding Cromwell's death than through a genuine endorsement of policy.[9] The handling of the Restoration seemed designed to antagonise both the supporters of the 'good old cause' and royalists alike, and the newly restored stage utilised this tension by producing comedies that reinvented the recent past. This chapter will primarily address one late commonwealth and two early Restoration comedies that connect with the commonwealth: John Tatham's *The Rump* (published 1660), Robert Howard's *The Committee* (1663) and John Lacy's *The Old Troop* (1664). Each play offers very different images of recent history, and focuses upon different elements of the past.

These rewrites of the commonwealth were not uniform in approach. Some of the plays look back nostalgically to the period and panegyrise abstract cavalier virtues such as honour, whereas others question whether such virtues ever existed. Despite these ambiguous reflections upon the past, the dramas all share kinship with play pamphlets and the paper stage's use of satirical tropes through which to discuss contemporary concerns.[10] Not only do they draw from play pamphlets but they also feed into a tradition established throughout the civil war period and consolidated at the Restoration of remembering and reinventing the civil war and commonwealth. I shall start with Tatham, whose play addresses the twilight years of the commonwealth.

'True sons to the city':[11] London's restoration

Derek Hughes has commented that the immediate interest of Restoration drama was the Restoration.[12] While the heroic dramas discussed in

Chapter 4 ambiguously engage with ideas of restoration to discuss what kingship might mean, Tatham's *The Rump* emphatically enters into a discourse that is concerned with restored order and dramatises the events that led to the Restoration. His subtitle *Mirrour of the Late Times*, further emphasises the connection. Although the restoration of monarchy is not dramatised, Tatham historicises current affairs and brings us to the point of Restoration. Once the demise of the Rump and reinstatement of the Long Parliament has been portrayed, the audience is left to infer that the natural progression of events will lead to the re-establishment of monarchical rule. The post-Restoration audience's shared knowledge about how the events dramatised ultimately concluded therefore informs our multiple interpretations of the play.

The reason why the narrative does not take us right up to the Restoration might be the play's first performance occurring before this event took place. *The Rump*'s performance history is ambiguous. Following van Lennep, Susan Wiseman states that the play was performed in 1659.[13] Conversely, Hughes (after Harold Love) pinpoints the date of first performance to May/June1660.[14] More recently, Michael Cordner has suggested that the play was written around March 1660 to form part of London's anti-Rump festivities and is therefore too early to enter into discourse relating to the Restoration.[15] If we consider the play's relation to panegyric, Cordner's suggestion of a March 1660 compositional date appears logical. In making his comments about the Restoration stage's concern with the Restoration, Hughes cites Dryden's *Astraea Redux* and suggests that early Restoration drama feeds into the panegyrical tradition of the poem.[16] If *The Rump* was written directly after the Restoration and had a panegyrical intent, we would expect the play to culminate in hyperbolic joy that Charles had returned.[17]

Hughes may have identified a panegyrical intent in much early Restoration drama, but Tatham's play claims to reject the mode. 'Expect not here Language Three stories high; / Star-tearing Strains fit not a Comedy. / Here's no elaborate Scenes, for he [Tatham] confesses / He took no pains in't, Truth doth need no Dresses' (sig. A4v), declares the Prologue. The comic mode is incompatible with panegyrical and heroic hyperbole. Truth, however, can be grafted on to comedy. Despite asserting its role as a faithful account of current affairs, the play fails as a documentary. By 1659, it had become something of a London pastime to attack the beleaguered Rump.[18] Tatham's play relishes the comic potential that this lampoonery offers, and the satire cannot be described as a neutral rendering of recent occurrences.

Ideas of panegyric

Given its satirical edge, one could conclude that *The Rump* is the antithesis of panegyric. This would seem to support claims made in the Prologue that panegyrical constructs have been dismissed by Tatham. However, the play is intensely preoccupied by the idea of panegyric. In the opening scene, we are confronted with soldiers eulogising Bertlam (or John Lambert: Bertlam is an allegorical name so thinly veiled as to render it pointless). In many respects, the real Lambert[19] deserved some of the accolades bestowed upon him by the play's fictional soldiers; he was the army's 'rising sun' (I:i, sig. B3r) and an astute politician.[20] These qualities earned him the support of the army, which followed him to the point of mutiny towards the other commanding officers. On 12 October 1659, the Rump Parliament reordered the army under seven commissioners, but most of the regiments in the vicinity of London deferred to Lambert.[21] Tatham's play alludes to this by comparing Bertlam's abilities to those of the other Commissioners:

> *Leymore*[22] was a Stubborn Lad, yet *Bertlam* fitted him, and in his kind too, his Rhetorick silenc'd the Mouth of his Pistol; it had sent a bad Report else, and a home one. But *Bertlam*, brave *Bertlam*, that carries Charms on the Tip of his Tongue, acted the part both of a Souldier and a Courtier, an Enemy and a Friend, Exposing his Breast to danger, under the Canopy of Security; And all this for Us you knaves. He told 'um a fair Tale, but means to trust them no further than he can fling 'um. (I.i, sig. B1v)

Bertlam's qualities are applauded, but they are attributes that rest uneasily with the rhetoric of panegyric. The brave virtues that Bertlam boasts are those of political expediency. Notions of honour, valour and leadership have been marred by a sense of political pragmatism. For these soldiers, however, Bertlam's powers of deception are emblematic of his loyalty to the army.

History certainly seems to support this image of military loyalty. Following the suppression of the royalist uprising of August 1659, Lambert was awarded £1,000 with which to purchase a jewel. Instead, he divided the money amongst the troops who fought under him in Cheshire.[23] Such a move could be viewed as an act of benevolence in recognition of the support the army offered Lambert in gaining such a thorough victory. Equally, it could be perceived as a further example of the political expediency that Tatham's soldiers applaud: considering the major regime changes of the previous fifteen years had been instigated by the army, any sensible aspiring ruler would understand the benefits of maintaining a satisfied fighting force.

The image of Lambert with which the audience is initially presented in the opening scene is possibly closer to the later interpretations of the man than might have been planned. Immediately after the soldiers describe Bertlam as the ideal statesman (which is supported by the entry of the man himself), we are offered a view of his domestic affairs. The appearance of Lady Bertlam and her maid distorts the way in which Bertlam is perceived. In his conjugal relationship, he is not the alpha-male. This undermines the perception of him as alpha-statesman: as Charles I learned to his cost, a husband with an uxorious reputation was considered poor material for an early modern leader and could therefore be removed. Parliamentarian propaganda played upon an image of Henrietta Maria as meddling in the affairs of state, and Lady Bertlam seems to ape her monarchical predecessor.[24] For Lady Bertlam, the ultimate goal is status and public recognition. She hopes to gain this by actively furthering her husband's career:

> PRISS[ILLA]: She will be Protectoress whether he be Protector or not: If he had any Honour it must come from her, for ought I see; she is before hand with him, and hath Install'd her self already, I'm sure my Voyce was Herald to't (II.i, sig. D2r)

Here, we see Lady Bertlam gaining public honour for her husband while simultaneously earning him private dishonour. In a reversal of seventeenth-century notions of marriage and the representations of virtuous wives discussed in Chapter 4, Lady Bertlam commands Bertlam. Through her efforts, Bertlam received honour and favour, but this honour is gained through cuckoldry. Lady Bertlam's political aspirations are not limited to the bedroom. As a preliminary to the meeting of the Committee of Safety, we witness a parliament of women. This trope was not uncommon in anti-parliamentarian pamphlets as a means of satirically portraying a world turned upside-down.[25] The greatest concern of these women is that they are permitted to consort with virile cavaliers; while waiting, they bewail their fate in being married to cold-blooded parliamentarian men. The inability of parliamentarians to satisfy their women sexually is contrasted with the extremely capable royalists. Aphra Behn would elaborate upon this notion in her 1681/82 adaptation, *The Roundheads*.[26] In being 'a Man, every Inch of him' (II.i, sig, C4v), Cromwell becomes aligned with the cavaliers. His hot-bloodedness in comparison to the perceived impotence of the parliamentarian faction means those vying for the title of Protector lack the credentials to be his successor.[27] Yet these references to Cromwell's sexual virility also echo play pamphlets such as *A Bartholomew Fairing*, discussed in chapter 2.

Cromwell is a ghost that the play cannot forget. A Cassandra-like Mrs

Ideas of panegyric

Cromwell perceives the period succeeding Cromwell's death as one of decline and decay. She bitterly watches the demise of the political order established by her husband. In turning his back on Cromwell and his hereditary successors, Bertlam is represented as plotting his own political downfall, and ambition is ranked above loyalty by the dissembling parliamentarians. Lady Bertlam formally observes that Cromwell is 'of horrid memory' (II.i, sig. D4v), despite previously relishing his qualities. Cromwell, applauded in private by Lady Bertlam for his manliness, is publicly derided by her and his other erstwhile political bedfellows. For these ambitious parliamentarians, it is useful to consider Cromwell as the usurper of their right to rule.

The Rump's authority predated Cromwell as it had been the parliament that was sitting when Cromwell assumed power in 1653. Bertlam is perceived as reinstating the Rump Parliament as a means of distancing himself from the Cromwellian regime. The restored Rump functions as an attempt to erase the memory of Cromwell in order for Bertlam to assert his own authority over it. Lady Bertlam's insistence that the recollection of Cromwell is horrific to her, however, demonstrates that he is not a man to be easily forgotten.

With the support of the army, Lambert certainly seemed to be in a position to gain control, but he never realised this possibility. Tatham's play suggests that one reason for the failure is intricately linked with parliamentarian endeavours to forget Cromwell. Rather than building upon Cromwell's legacy, the Rump endeavours to assert its authority through forgetting him, but the intrigue required by the parliamentarians to distance their administration from Cromwell weakens the restored Rump's power. This desire to erase Cromwell is impossible since the parliamentarians are preoccupied with the deceased protector.

For Mrs Cromwell, the infamy with which the memory of Cromwell is greeted is worse than if the family name had been consigned to oblivion. Lady Bertlam may be concerned with furthering her husband's career as a means of her gaining personal prestige by association, but Mrs Cromwell has more familial preoccupations. The play argues that Marchamont Nedham may have devoted much of his considerable energy to maligning the Stuarts and thereby praising commonwealth governments (II.i, sig D1r),[28] but ultimately the Cromwell family suffers as a consequence of Cromwell's unorthodox rise to power:

MRS CROMWELL: Nothing Torments me more, then that ... [Cromwell], who whilst he liv'd, was call'd the most Serene, the most Illustrious and most

Puissant Prince; (whilst that the fawning Poets Panegyricks swell'd with Ambitious Epithetes) is now call'd th' fire-brand of Hell, Monster of Mankind, Regicide, Homicide, Murtherer of Piety, a Lump of flesh sok'd in a Sea of blood, Traytor to God and goodness, an Advancer of Fiends and Darkness; such as these and worse ... are daily cast in my Ears, by every idle fellow.

(II.i, sig. D3r)

This quotation emphasises the mutability of those who are endowed with 'three rare Qualities; Dissimulation, Equivocation and Mental reservation' (I.i, sig. C1r). It also censures the expediency of panegyrical constructs. Mrs Cromwell laments that, in death, Cromwell is depicted demonically. Through articulating these regrets, the play thus provides a direct commentary on the play pamphlets discussed in Chapter 2 that imagine Cromwell's ghost in hell. In so doing, *The Rump* both remembers and reinvents images of Cromwell through engaging with the recent past and alluding to the play pamphlets that were written in the wake of Cromwell's death.

Mrs Cromwell's lamentations negate the generally derisory comments that the play directs towards Cromwell. This in turn makes the suggestion that *The Rump* depicts foolish parliamentarians getting their comeuppance a little problematic.[29] It is true that members of the dissembling group are reduced to their humble beginnings by the end of the play – a fate that the Cromwell family also shares. Lady Bertlam bitterly bewails that the parliamentarians were seduced by Cromwell's 'Painted Titles that are so easily washt off' (V.i, sig. H4ᵛ). The fact that, while Cromwell lived, these titles had a semi-permanency complicates matters. In Tatham's interpretation of the protectorate, Cromwell's force of character meant that the inevitable failure of the republic was postponed until Richard Cromwell inherited the title of protector from his father. Ultimately, the protectorship was a prolonged masque: once the authority figure had departed, the painted titles were washed away and it seemed inevitable that the phoney noblemen would return to their humble origins.[30] Whatever the opinion held of Cromwell, the fact he could postpone what was perceived as the inevitable collapse of the commonwealth governments cannot be overlooked by the play.

Strong opinions are expressed in regards to Cromwell. Despite this, the text remains paradoxically neutral about the erstwhile protector. Since the parliamentarians are proven to be faithless, their judgements about Cromwell lack credibility and instead the mechanics of panegyric

Ideas of panegyric

are called to question. It may have been declared in the prologue that the tenets of panegyric have been dismissed, but the play cannot move away from notions of panegyric. The endeavours of the parliamentarians to distance themselves from Cromwell and his 'hateful' memory, as a means of carving out their new political order, merely emphasise the way in which panegyrical ideas were being debated. Lamenting their fall from grace, Prissilla (Lady Bertlam's maid) attacks panegyrical constructs:

> Hang your Dog Poetry, it made my Lord thrive so ill as he did: I think thou didst infect him he us'd to have a Serene brain, and Courage good enough (V.i, sig. I2r)

Whatever the reasons why the real Lambert failed to become protector, the fictional Bertlam's judgement is marred by the image that has been painted of him by fawning flatterers. Prissilla argues that panegyric has infected his brain: reading and hearing laudatory matter has a negative psychophysiological influence upon the body and the senses. Where Mrs Cromwell bemoans the mutability of panegyric, Prissilla offers a cautionary tale against placing faith in the truthfulness of panegyrical constructs as their transformative powers can lead the subject to become the opposite of how they are presented. Paying too much attention to valorisation can only lead to intellectual and physical weakness.

Prissilla's observations are sandwiched between episodes where the city celebrates the granting of a free parliament. Here, we see a restrained version of panegyrical rhetoric adopted:

> 1 PRENTICE: Oh noble *Philagathus*!
> 2 PRENTICE: Brave *Phylagathus*! [*sic*]
> 3 PRENTICE: Honourable *Philagatbus*! [*sic*]
> 4 PRENTICE: Renowned *Philagathus*!
> 1 PRENTICE: ... You that spoke even now you should be Coop'd up for Hawksmeat, shall be Cramm'd up for Capons; your Cellars shall become Warehouses, your Shops Exchanges, and your Mistresses persons of honor.
> OMNES: And what shall we be?
> 1 PRENTICE: Squires of the Body: Honor sufficient enough for men of our rank, Gentlemen.
> OMNES: Oh brave Champion!
> 1 PRENTICE: I tell you, I will have no more of that
>
> (V.i, sig. I1v)

The saviour of the city is given the appreciation he deserves. That is where the panegyric must end lest the Prentices become embroiled in their own rhetoric and suffer similar bodily and cerebral infection as Bertlam. 'Philagathus' means 'lover of the good'.[31] General Monck is the only person to be afforded allegorical praise as his efforts in bringing about a free parliament and rescuing London from the army are applauded. However, only moments before these accolades are bestowed upon Philagathus, the Prentices are seen bewailing the fact that their 'Champion' seems intent on carrying out the Rump's orders.

The play does not overlook the fact that Monck initially seemed to ally himself with the Rump and began to dismantle London's defences, neither does it offer any explanation as to why the fictitious Philagathus switched from aggressor to defender of London. In reality, General Monck's motives appear equally ambiguous. He left people guessing over what his intentions were until the moment that it seemed inevitable that the Rump would fall.[32] The Prentices may emphatically forgive Philagathus for initially following the Rump's orders, but the play cannot disregard the attempted 'rape' (V.i, sig. I1r) of the city by her champion.

Considering Tatham's status as writer of pageants for the lord mayor's shows, it comes as little surprise that the key points of Monck's dealings with London are critiqued. As Wiseman has observed, Tatham's career demonstrates a certain degree of 'political pragmatism'.[33] He successfully negotiated the transition from republican to monarchical government and continued to write pageants into the first decade of the Restoration.[34] Monck's actions feed into the mythologising of the city and therefore deserve to be minutely recorded by the city's playwright.

As a pageant-writer, Tatham would have been well aware of the workings of panegyric.[35] Shortly before the fall of the Rump, Lady Bertlam wonders 'that none of the Modern Poets have been ... [to visit] with their Encomiums since ... [Bertlam] Went!' (IV.i, sig. H1v). Sensing that a regime change might occur shortly, individuals are careful not to align themselves too closely to a failing political order, and, through this mutability, the play lampoons the perceived parliamentarian addiction to eulogies. Considering Tatham's employment, Lady Bertlam's comments regarding the changeability of those who write panegyric is exceptionally ironic.

The Rump has often been perceived as the start of a new form of comedy that would gain greater polish throughout the 1660s.[36] In particular, its role as a source play for Behn's exclusion crisis, cit-cuckolding comedy, *The Roundheads*, has been explored.[37] Its critique of panegyric, however, has been largely overlooked. Despite the prologue claiming to reject the rudiments of panegyrical constructs, the play is deeply concerned with how panegyric operates. It warns against believing in the image flatterers paint because the metaphorical mirror they use does not provide a true likeness of the subject. Ultimately, the panegyric of the play is unstable. There is no wholly right-minded individual who is deserving of hyperbolic praise, and if there were, the risk of bodily transformation caused by panegyric might render them unworthy. Perhaps the real focus of the valorisation is not a person but a personified space. London, saved from her metaphorical ravishing by Philagathus's timely shift of allegiance, can absorb and neutralise dissent. At the end of the play, we see the members of the erstwhile Rump reduced to their humble origins. London assimilates these wayward individuals while the Prentices, with a new-found sense of royalist fervour, roast rumps and drink to the healths of the king and (more readily) the general. The epilogue proceeds to reassure the audience that 'there's no Phanatick' (sig. K2v) amongst the audience's members. The process of watching the play restores all to innocence, and the purified public awaits the return of its king.

Although *The Rump* does not continue to the point of Restoration, the play concludes that everyone adjusts to their natural rank in the body politic. By the end of the play, we see that Lady Bertlam's political ambitions are resolutely thwarted. However, the role of the comically interfering wife continued to be played upon the Restoration stage. Behn elaborated upon Tatham's character to produce a more complicated figure. In so doing, Behn also drew from other early Restoration comedies. Cordner has proposed that Robert Howard's *The Committee* is another source play for Behn's *The Roundheads*.[38] As with *The Rump*, *The Committee* is governed by a strong parliamentarian wife seeking to secure her husband's good political fortune. She also endeavours to safeguard against the return of the monarchy. In his play, Howard satirises a perceived Presbyterian duplicity and panegyrises supposed cavalier virtues.

Plots and counter-plots: double-dealing in *The Committee*

Presbyterians were not wholly trusted by the restored regime because of the belief that their duplicity and self-interest caused the outbreak of war.[39] The religious tensions of the 1630s and 1640s fed through the Restoration and culminated in political crisis. The year 1678 is famous for being the year in which the renegade priest Titus Oates stirred up a political storm with his popish plot allegations.[40] It is also the year in which one James Mitchell, a radical Presbyterian minister, was executed, a case which illustrates, and helped to construct, popular attitudes to Presbyterians. The extent of Mitchell's torture prior to execution was deemed so harsh that he was pitied in some quarters.[41] However, amongst his critics, Mitchell's crime was judged so barbaric that it would make ideal light entertainment. As a consequence, the inevitable pamphlets were produced. One piece of literature briefly outlines Mitchell's death on the scaffold and gives details of his crime and character, before offering commentary on selected quotations from his letters. Mitchell had attempted to assassinate the Archbishop of St Andrews in July 1668.[42] To blacken Mitchell's image further, in the build up to the deed, we are given an account of his seduction of a gardener's wife:

> he ... [was] recommended to the *Laird of Dundass*, to be *Pedagogue* to his *Children*, and *Domestique Chaplain* for saying *extemporary Prayers*. He passed some time in his *Family* for a *gifted* and very *Holy Young Man*, till some of the Servants observed an *extraordinary* Familiarity betwixt *him* and the *young Woman* who was the *Old* Gardiners *Wife*. Being possest with this *Suspicion*, they observed him the more; and one Night, as they were watching, they saw his *Mistress* going to his *Chamber*[43]

After being discharged from service, Mitchell went to lodge in a widow's house in Edinburgh, 'with whom that *dishonour* of Mankind, *Major Weir* ... Boarded at the same time.'[44] Lest Mitchell's misdemeanours are insufficient to interest, titillate and warn the reader against being gulled by Presbyterianism, Weir's more earthly crimes were also brought into the narrative.

Weir, we are told, was brought up in the most fanatical part of the country, fought against the king, and, 'About the Year 1649. he had the *great trust* of the *Guards* ... committed unto *him* under the quality of *Major*, and from that time, to the day of his *Infamous Death*, was always called by the Name of *Major Weir*'.[45] Memory of civil war and the regicide is brought into the story about the attempted assassination, emphasising the perceived connection between fanaticism and disobedience to church and state. Weir shared a similar fate to Mitchell, but he was executed for bestiality, adultery and incest.[46] Although there appears little connection with this and the attempted murder of an episcopal grandee, its insertion into the narrative directs the reader to associate sexual freedom with Presbyterianism. The idea of the licentious friar, which had been current in pre-Reformation thought,[47] is mapped on to notions of the Presbyterian minister. Sexual licentiousness and political radicalism thus merge to portray Presbyterians as privately and publicly disreputable. The restored episcopal church and monarch were therefore to be upon their guard when dealing with the denomination. Nonconformists were equally sceptical of what motivated Presbyterians because of the handling of the Restoration settlement. Lucy Hutchinson, for example, wife of the regicide John Hutchinson, condemned 'the Presbyterian faction, who would obstruct any good rather than those they envied and hated should have the glory of procuring it; the sad effects of which pride grew at length to be the ruin of the most glorious cause that was ever contended for'.[48]

Seventeenth-century writers may have a sense of what they understand by Presbyterianism, but it is not a term that is easy to unpack. While it was used to describe one of the many denominations of Christianity, it also embodied some parliamentarian political views. This is due to one of the terms of the Solemn League and Covenant between parliament and the Scots being to establish Presbyterianism as the faith of England.[49] Austin Woolrych has attempted to describe the difference between religious Presbyterians and those who sympathised with Presbyterian political approaches. He does this by spelling 'Presbyterian' with a capital letter when discussing religious sentiments, and 'presbyterian' if he is referring to the political faction.[50] Previously, C. V. Wedgwood had adopted the oxymoronic phrase 'secular brand of Presbyterianism' as a means of achieving the same purpose.[51] As awkward as each term may seem, they demonstrate the complexity of perceptions of Presbyterianism in the seventeenth century. Hutchinson is not necessarily condemning those who practise Presbyterianism; instead, she could be deriding those turncoating, secular Presbyterians who did not remain faithful to the 'good old cause'. It is this 'presbyterian' double-dealing that we see satirised in *The Committee*. Mercenary parliamentarians are juxtaposed with principled cavaliers as a means of exposing the self-serving corruptibility of one faction compared to the integrity of the other.

We witness Mr Day, Chair of the Committee of Sequestration, endeavouring to curry favour with his fellow committee members. He does this by showing them a forged letter in which the exiled Charles supposedly tries to win Day to the royalist cause. This is meant to demonstrate Day's incorruptibility. However, the audience is aware that Mr Day is the puppet of his wife and (for this couple) political expediency takes precedence over loyalty to the commonwealth regime. The letter is a fabrication of Mrs Day's, and she minutely explains its purpose:

> In the first place (observe how I lay a design In politicks) d'ye mark, counterfeit me. A letter from the King, where he shall offer you great Matters to serve him, and his Interest under-hand Very good, and in it let him remember his kinde Love and service to me: This will make them look About 'um, and think you some body: then promise them If they'l be true friends to you, to live and dye with them[52]

The committeemen, as notable rogues themselves, realise that the letter is counterfeited. The purpose of the forgery, however, is interesting. It seeks to establish a connection between Mr Day and the exiled monarch. Parliamentarians may have desired to label all those who supported the Stuarts as malignants, but the counterfeited letter undermines this fictional committee's wish to be viewed as part of an alternative form of power. Under the new regime, Mrs Day is elevated from the ranks of kitchen maid to become a woman of consequence. Despite this, she perceives that true greatness can come only from the king and is aware of the need to manufacture loyalty.

While Mrs Day is busy defining a role for herself and her family on the public stage, her husband is attempting to conceal private guilt. Unlike the parliamentarian men of Tatham's play, Mr Day is perfectly capable of satisfying more than one woman. He also knows how to prevent any scandal that might result from his liaisons by acquiring abortions. The *Mistress Parliament* pamphlets that were produced in the late 1640s played with notions of monstrous births to describe the new political order metaphorically. Here, this idea is extended and inverted to present the termination of births that would undermine the tenuous political settlement. It is Mr Day's knowledge of how to induce miscarriages rather than the keeping of mistresses that horrifies the cavaliers. They are, however, willing to conceal his guilt if he returns their estates and allows them to forgo subscribing to the Solemn League and Covenant. Moral revulsion can be overlooked when the potential for blackmail can be realised. Although this moral plurality casts an ambiguous light on cavalier integrity, the play still celebrates cavalier loyalty to the Crown as the ultimate virtue. Howard's play suggests that, in usurping the king's authority, those who seek preferment under commonwealth governments consign themselves to begetting bad luck.

The final couplet of the play advises Mr Day that his ill-fortune in being uncovered as a cheat stems from supporting the wrong cause: 'if you will have good luck in every thing, / Turn Cavalier, and cry, God bless the King' (V.i, sig. S3r). The play advises that support of the Stuarts ultimately leads to good fortune despite initial hardship. The recommendation directed at Mr Day to become a turncoat is offered as a remedy for a guilty conscience and a means through which sin may be absolved. In portraying the chair of the Committee of Sequestration as publicly dishonourable and privately intemperate, Howard demonstrates the resentment held by cavaliers that they were forced to compound and subscribe to the Solemn League and Covenant. This was a military league and religious covenant initially made in 1643 between Scottish Covenanters and the English parliament for military assistance against the king in exchange for upholding Presbyterianism. If male royalists failed to subscribe to the Covenant and take the Oath of Engagement, they would lose the right to regain their estates.[53] In addition to dramatising this resentment, the play also suggests the process of compounding requires a degree of dissembling: all involved are acting their way through the procedure. Writing about the outright refusal of the Committee of Sequestration to allow her any money from her husband's estate, Margaret Cavendish laments that the opportunism of some placed women in an impossible situation:

> the Customes of England being changed, as well as the Laws, where Women become Pleaders, Atturneys Petitioners and the like, running about with their severall Causes, complaining of their severall grievances, exclaiming against their severall enemies, bragging of their severall favours they receive from the powerfull, thus Trafficking with idle words being in false reports ... if our Sex would but well consider, and rationally ponder, they will perceive and find that it is neither words nor place that can advance them, but worth and merit: nor can words or place disgrace them, but inconstancy and boldness: ... I mean not Noble, Vertuous, Discreet and worthy Persons, whom necessity did inforce to submit, comply and follow their own suites [i.e. suits], but such as had nothing to lose, but made it their trade to solicite[54]

Through the character of Mrs Day, Howard satirises some of the women whom Cavendish attacks for 'inconstancy and boldness' in seeking to gain from the misfortunes of others. The extract quoted above, however, also alludes to a more problematic issue for royalists: many did submit to the commonwealth and protectorate regimes. Post 1660, Cavendish endeavours to distance those who submitted out of necessity from those who submitted for financial gain. However, by the late 1650s, many royalists were returning from exile and it was by no means certain that monarchy would be restored. While contemporaries may have rewritten the narrative of the civil war to accommodate Restoration, Cavendish's account draws attention to tensions that she seeks to suppress. Publicly, there appears little distinction between the actions of women petitioning out of need and those petitioning out of greed. There is a distinction between private conscience and public representation that renders the interpretation of both opaque. Rather than ideological concerns governing action, the possession (or repossession) of wealth becomes the driving force.

Howard's fictional cavaliers do not need to trouble themselves with such practical concerns. Instead, Colonels Careless and Blunt can adhere to what are perceived to be royalist virtues. Loyalty to monarchical governance and a sense of honour are ordered above practicality, and the two cavaliers are unwilling to moderate their political views. For Mr Day, such abstract concerns are misplaced: he wonders that these cavaliers 'make an idol of that honour' (II.i, sig. N3r). However, Careless's and Blunt's idolatry ultimately means that each is rewarded with a like-minded fiancée. This would seem to chime with the representations of supportive unions discussed in the heroic dramas mentioned in Chapter 4. However, the wives-to-be can only 'hope' (V.i, sig. R3^v) that they will be loved by their gallants: the play may applaud cavalier honour, but it is deeply cynical of the marriage contract. It would appear that marriage oaths can be taken in the knowledge that they might be broken. State oaths, however, cannot be made and forsaken quite so easily.

In adhering to their royalist principles, Careless and Blunt refuse to take the Covenant and therefore fail to compound for their estates. This ideologically stubborn duo thus provide a dramatic rendering of a royalist's fears over what can happen to loyal cavaliers at the hands of a committee. The arbitrariness of the committee's judgements is highlighted by the fact that Arbella (as a woman) is not required to take the oath when compounding for her late father's estate. Instead she is given the ultimatum to either marry the Days' son Abel or lose everything. By attempting to force Arbella into marriage with Abel, the committee is inadvertently assisting Mrs Day in alleviating fears that a vengeful king may desire to punish those who usurped his authority.

If the king returns, the Days will need to reinvent themselves as royalists and marrying into a royalist family would help this transformation. By implementing contingency measures, the Days suggest that the processes of cause and effect mean that events will naturally lead to the Restoration: in reality, there was no teleological reason why civil war, regicide, commonwealth and Restoration should have happened.[55] In this reinterpreted historical space, the usurpers of monarchical government cannot rule out

Ideas of panegyric

the possible return of the king. A proposed marriage to a cavalier heiress could be mutually beneficial: Arbella can avoid heavy fines and the sequestration of her property, while the Days can safeguard themselves against royalist vengeance should monarchy be restored. Arbella's reluctance to acquiesce to the Days' plan is applauded as emblematic of the integrity and virtues to which a royalist ought to adhere. It also seems to allude to a lesser-known proviso in the Act of Indemnity and Oblivion:

> Except and always foreprized out of this Free and General Pardon, the detestable and abominable Vice of Buggery committed with Mankind or Beast: And Also Excepted all Rapes and carnal Ravishments of Women: And also Excepted all Ravishments with wilful taking away, or marrying of any Maid, Widow or Damse [*sic*]; against her will, or without the assent or agreement of her Parents, or of such as then had her in Custody; and also all Offences or aiding, comforting, procuring or abetting of any such Ravishment, Wilful taking, or Marrying, had, committed, or done[56]

This proviso suggests that forced marriages took place (or were perceived as taking place) during the 1650s. In refusing to pardon those who were complicit in such marriages, the Act highlights the occurrence as being of grave concern to the restored regime. Whether this concern was founded upon contemporary evidence of these types of marriages taking place or rumour that they might is open to speculation.[57] Even if forcible marriage did not occur, there was clearly an anxiety that they might have taken place and their potential as a dramatic construct was realised by playwrights.

The Committee condemns the political expediency of the Days' endeavours to marry Arbella to Abel and presents Mrs Day as lacking erudition in her schemes. This is in contrast to her adopted daughter, Ruth, whose plots are sanitised by her faithfulness to her royalist genealogy. Having been reared by this double-dealing couple, Ruth learns the art of dissembling. Because of Ruth's connivance, the committee is plunged into chaos, culminating in the secretary eagerly drinking the king's health. This parallels Margaret Cavendish's description of the way in which women behaved when compounding for their estates. Necessity taught some of Cavendish's counterparts to dissemble and submit to the demands of the committee and, for Cavendish, meant that they lost integrity. Howard turns this dissembling into a virtue: his female royalist needs to adopt underhand measures in order to maintain the integrity of her beau.

The royalists must gull the Committee as a way to maintain untainted ownership of their estates, but this deception is also a means by which they are rewarded in marriage. Blunt has difficulties contemplating marriage to Ruth until he learns that she is the daughter of a notable royalist. Committeemen's daughters may make ideal mistresses, but their genealogy prohibits a loyal cavalier from marrying them. Likewise, a committeeman's son ought not to aspire to a union with the daughter of a royalist.

The Days' desire for a union between their family and Arbella to safeguard against retribution should monarchy be restored offers an explanation as to what is perceived to cause a turncoat. By decapitating their king and expelling his heirs, parliament had dismantled conventional government. Governments in the 1650s had difficulty in justifying their rule of the country in the absence of a monarch.[58] Panegyrical writings and broadsheets in support of the various commonwealth rulers sought to establish a republican tradition, thereby legitimising a form of non-monarchical government. The fact that royalist panegyric continued to be produced and circulated throughout the commonwealth undermined this attempt to strengthen republican rule. Howard's play suggests that this production and dissemination of both monarchical and republican panegyric had a destabilising effect. Those who gained authority during Howard's fictionalised version of the commonwealth are consequently keen to curry favour with the erstwhile regime to safeguard against punishment if the Stuarts are restored. In reality, the declaration of Breda and the Act of Indemnity and Oblivion offered generous settlements. While Howard's play overtly satirises and emphasises the futility of presbyterian conniving, it may also offer implicit criticism of the lax punishments afforded to most individuals who gained from the commonwealth.

Howard's play was performed in full knowledge of the Restoration. Consequently, it is difficult to judge what drives the comedy. The satire could be a manifestation of resentment towards presbyterians due to their perceived self-serving behaviour during the commonwealth. Equally, it could be driven by royalist hostility to what they believed to be inappropriate land settlements at the Restoration.[59] In this context, the play can be read as reinventing the past as a means of turning royalist humiliation during the commonwealth and at the Restoration into comic retribution. The drive of the satire cannot be discerned with any certainty, but the handling of the Restoration settlement seems to have antagonised many royalists in its leniency towards those who had an active role in commonwealth politics.[60] Blunt imagines that 'The day may come, when those that suffer for their Consciences and honour may be rewarded' (II.i, sig. N3r). The comment can be interpreted as an implicit complaint that the Restoration did not punish republicans. It also reimagines the

Restoration. The prophesied Restoration in the play collides with the audience's knowledge of how the Restoration actually unfolded. This creates an ambiguous space; the mythical rewarding of the virtuous royalists in an imagined future is apocalyptic while simultaneously being anti-climatic. The audience is left to wonder whether they witnessed this day, or if it will ever come.

The criticism of presbyterian deviousness and valorisation of honourable cavaliers expounded in *The Committee* could therefore be as much an implicit criticism of Restoration negotiations as it is an explicit satire on commonwealth politics. Careless, Blunt, Arbella and Ruth personify the noble qualities expected of royalists. In rewarding these virtues, the play imagines that an untainted form of loyalty to the Crown could survive the commonwealth and ultimately prevail. Lacy's *The Old Troop* is under no such illusions. Rather than celebrating the noble royalist, *The Old Troop* questions whether such absolute loyalty ever existed.

Reforming old troops: the celebration of political expediency

In Lacy's play, self-interest is prized above adherence to a particular ideological conviction. This echoes Abraham Cowley's *Cutter of Coleman Street* (1663). A reworking of Cowley's 1642 play *The Guardian*, *Cutter* reflects upon commonwealth politics. *The Guardian* endeavours to circumvent discussion of contemporary events, whereas *Cutter* directly engages with current affairs. The courtly audience who saw *The Guardian* premiered in the relative safety and comfort of Cambridge, however, would have been well aware of the political crisis that was brewing. The prologue to the 1650 printed edition of the original play gives it a contemporary gloss by referencing the destruction of Cheapside Cross, eventually pulled down in 1643.[61] In reworking the play to incorporate the civil war legacy, however, *The Guardian*'s desire to suspend reality is subsumed by topicality: implicit hints at the impending troubles in the earlier play become the explicit setting of the later dramatic piece. Through absorbing and re-presenting *The Guardian*, city comedy plot devices present in the original play merge with the topical elements of the Restoration rewrite.

The Guardian contains a degree of moral ambiguity that is present in much city comedy. This feeds through to *Cutter*, where the eponymous parasite seeks a wealthy wife and so courts Tabitha. Cutter's betrothed is the daughter of a soap boiler who profited from the commonwealth. Unlike Colonels Blunt and Careless, Cutter has no moral qualms over making a pragmatic match with the godly. Cutter's courtship of Tabitha provides a means of satirising the perceived hypocrisies of puritanism. After deceiving Tabitha into believing it is God's will that they be married, Cutter shows his conversion to be short-lived: he promptly corrupts his new wife by introducing her to the pleasures of alcohol and marital debauchery. This not only exposes the hypocrisy of Tabitha's strict adherence to godly practices (she requires little cajoling to stray from the narrow way) but also supports parliamentarian propaganda that depicted the stereotypical cavalier as being a swaggering debauching drunkard.[62] The right-minded cavalier who was valorised in Howard's play is thus exposed to censure by Cowley. Despite this, Cutter also serves the function of displaying the hypocrisies of others: those whom he cheats lend themselves to the deception because of their gullibility and duplicity.

Cutter may expose the misdemeanours of others, but his status as a cavalier proves to be complex. He is a parasite to Colonel Jolly and therefore pretends to be a cavalier as a means of procuring favour. This ambiguity feeds into the reception of *Cutter* at its first performance in 1661, which was not wholly positive, though Pepys believed it to be 'a very good play'.[63] Some claimed the satiric humour to be anti-cavalier, citing the characterisation of Cutter and his underhand dealings as an example of this.[64] Cowley mediates criticism by asserting that Cutter and Worm were not intended to represent true cavaliers and thus the cavalier is redeemed from being implicated in the duo's behaviour.[65] Although Cowley can defend Cutter and Worm against charges of satirically representing cavaliers, criticism of Colonel Jolly cannot be dismissed with as much ease.

Colonel Jolly, in having his land sequestered as a consequence of supporting Charles I, is emblematic of the dispossessed cavalier. He seeks to regain his fortune through a downwardly mobile marriage to Tabitha's widowed mother. Not content with orchestrating his own marital bliss, he is complicit in duping his niece, Lucia, into marriage with the fop Puny. The plan is put in place to enable Jolly to acquire Lucia's fortune. Jolly also plans a match between his daughter, Aurelia, and Truman Junior (Lucia's lover).

The plot to disinherit Lucia does not reach fruition. Jolly, content to regain his property, allows Lucia to retain her fortune. In so doing, he negates accusations of dishonourable behaviour. The negotiations between Jolly and Truman Senior over the proposed marriages, however, demonstrate a darker agenda. Incensed that Truman Junior is held captive by Jolly, Truman Senior threatens to denounce the Colonel. On learning of Jolly's proposition to marry Truman Junior to Aurelia, Truman Senior takes a more congenial tone.

Ideas of panegyric 177

Angry threats subside at the prospect of a union between Truman Junior and Aurelia's anticipated wealth. In finding ways in which Lucia broke her father's will as a means of justifying the transferring of her portion to Aurelia, Jolly could be accused of the same underhand and arbitrary action that many royalists perceived the Committee of Sequestration to use. Truman Senior's acquiescence to the proposed marriage means that he is complicit in this sequestration of a dowry. Avarice and self-interest motivate the actions of these two patriarchs. Moral ambiguity takes precedence; there is no noble person who can epitomise royalist virtues. *Cutter* suggests that, in a post-civil-war period, individual interest takes precedence over the honour code and acting for the common good. When self-interest is the prime motivation for actions, royalist or parliamentarian ideological differences cease to be a major concern – unless the differences can be utilised as a way to attack one's enemies.

Cutter may have been a vehicle through which Lacy could display his credentials as one of the notable comic actors of the early Restoration.[66] If this were the case, Lacy would have had knowledge of *Cutter* when writing *The Old Troop*. As with *Cutter*, dissembling parliamentarians are attacked, and cavaliers are also subject to ridicule. Tell-troth's conversation with Flea-flint, Ferret-farm and the captain of the royalist troop highlights cavalier misdemeanours:

> TELL: I am a plain, honest-meaning man … that has div'd into the bottom of both your parties, and find that you have faults, but the other great wickedness.
> FLEA: I do not like this fellow, he had a sling against drink.
> FERRET: And plundering; but twenty to one he hath paid for't.
> FLEA: He had a plaguy jerk at flaying of flints too.[67]

Prior to this, we witness Ferret-farm, Flea-flint and Burndrop bribe the Lieutenant into overlooking the trio's crimes. As with the parasites of Cowley's play, we are given an image of people using the chaos that war brings to reap personal gain. This is emphasised by Tell-troth's observations over what motivates people to fight for their monarch:

> CORN[ET]: But wilt though fight for the King out of stark love and kindness.
> TELL: No, I'l fight for him as all men fight for Kings, partly for love, partly for my own ends. I'l fight bravely for a Battel or two then beg an old house to make a Garrison of, grow rich, consequently a coward, and then let the Dog bite the Bear, or the Bear bite the Dog (I.i, sig. B3v)

In stating this, Tell-troth is making allegations about the cavalier troop, allegations the captain of the troop seems willing to accept: 'in multitudes all are not virtuous, nor valiant' (I.i, sig. B4r). Since such observations are made following a successful bribe transaction, these value judgements are rendered ironic.

For Douglas Canfield the irony of these statements is carried through to the names of the characters. Tell-troth is not an honest figure but a dissembling turncoat.[68] Private motive and public action thus become fractured. However, this use of descriptive names may lead viewers into believing that characters personify certain virtues or vices in the same way that the characters whom Christian meets in John Bunyan's *Pilgrim's Progress* (part one, 1678; part two, 1684) represent their names.[69] Through this disjunction between the use of names and their reception, Lacy's play is addressing the rhetoric of praise that it seeks to reject.

Despite this appropriation of panegyric, the comedy of the drama directs us to read the way in which Lacy's play engages with panegyrical discourse differently. It dispels such mythology. Canfield's belief that Tell-troth represents the reverse of his name could be simplifying the complexity of the play and how allegory can be interpreted. Tell-troth is not an honest observer, but, since the events that he observes are governed by moral ambiguity, contradictions in his narrative are inevitable. When events are not transparent, it is difficult to respond in a transparent way.

Throughout the drama, there are a series of parallel episodes where members of the cavalier troop either commit misdeeds or respond to the misdemeanours of others. The play culminates in the marriage of Biddy to Tell-troth and Doll's betrothal to Raggou. Biddy, however, believes that she is conspiring to marry Doll to a woman. Although this has the appearance of comical absurdity, the discovery of the roundhead captain Tub-text in bed with two godly women renders the comic resolution politically ambiguous. Both roundheads and cavaliers behave dishonourably, but this does not prevent Tub-text being the subject of satire. Tub-text seduces the women by making them believe that, amongst the godly, actions that are perceived as sinful are permitted. The cavalier captain casts moral judgement upon this, condemning as blasphemous the nonconformist view that all actions are sinless amongst the elect:

> CAPT[AIN HONOR]: Blasphemous Rogue! how many poor fools hast thou deluded? Sirrah, it were just to make thee marry these two women, and hang thee for having two wives.
>
> (V.i, sig. I1r)

Indignation against nonconformist forms of religion spurs these comments. Tub-text's gulling of the two women is different to the duping of Biddy, but a reversal of moral norms is present in both instances. Biddy, the Lieutenant and the Cornet believe they are tricking Doll into marrying another woman out of a love of mischief. Although this does not take place, it still represents a breach of seventeenth-century moral and legal codes. The fact that the captain is privy to the knowledge that this marriage is an elaborate hoax does not diminish the tension between his desire to maintain propriety and his enjoyment of trickery; instead, the Captain's love of mischief leading to an advocacy of morally ambiguous behaviour is difficult to reconcile with his self-professed love of honour.

That Biddy is married to Tell-troth against her knowledge is hidden by the play's reconciliation. Having run away to accompany the troop, Biddy relinquishes autonomy over whom she marries. Her nuptials celebrate the idea that she is rescued from the possibility of becoming a fallen woman. Doll's role in providing universal succour to the troop before marrying Raggou, however, demonstrates that sexual licence amongst the cavaliers is also applauded. The moral ambiguity is further enhanced by the captain's condemnation of Tub-text. Here, the play flattens religious complexities around the nonconformist belief that inner grace means the elect can commit no sin. This is designed to expose the conviction to ridicule. In so doing, the play borrows from anti-parliamentarian rhetoric: sexual intemperance is combined with religious nonconformity as a means of attacking parliamentarians. Whereas sexual intemperance amongst the radicals is censured, cavaliers are allowed the occasional lapse of chastity. In celebrating Biddy as a symbol of chastity and Doll as the iconic cavaliering mistress, cavalier vices are also viewed congenially by their perpetrators. Captain Honor is more forgiving of his troop's misdemeanours than he is of roundhead vices.

The representation of the captain as the morally upright leader of a group of swaggering, morally ambiguous gallants is fully undermined in V.i. Taking Tell-troth's advice, the captain agrees to renege upon a deal that is to be made by his lieutenant with the parliamentarians. The captain believes his honour will appear untarnished by the occurrence (sig. H3v). Although Tell-troth condemns the roundhead captain for not enduring 'to plunder, but (in a godly manner) ... will take all he can lay his hands on' (I.i, sig B3v), he encourages Captain Honor to behave in a similar manner.

Ordering private advantage above a belief in the honour code is nowhere more apparent than in the case of the French cook, Raggou. An expert plunderer, he takes full advantage of a world turned upside-down. For Raggou, marriage offers a means to avoid the halter. The rest of the troop is casually censured. This reveals the paradoxical way in which some aspects of cavalier culture revelled in the disreputable image parliamentarian tracts painted of royalists. When drinking the king's health became an illegal, politically charged pastime, taverns were celebrated as a site of sedition.[70] Disreputable behaviour, love of mischief and loyalty to the Crown merged as cavalier culture sought to identify itself as different from that of the parliamentarians. In so doing, cavalier culture established the commonwealth period as a carnivalesque space that was contained by a hope that political order would be restored at Charles's return. Within this context, the play appears to cynically celebrate the possibility that Raggou and his fellow troop members have exploited the civil war; where even the king returns money confiscated from parliamentarians because 'he had rather had his subjects heart than money' (V.i, sig. I2r), his troops may be forgiven for choosing the most personally advantageous or politically expedient course of action.

The Old Troop offers a cynical gloss on the commonwealth. Neither cavalier nor roundhead is wholly good. The king is unable to rely upon the natural order of the body politic and the accompanying due reverence and respect that guarantees loyalty. Consequently, even the rightful monarch has to resort to bribery.[71] Panegyric has failed to maintain the mythology of monarchy and generate loyalty; financial necessity therefore becomes the means through which loyalty may be temporarily purchased. To trust in someone's selfless honesty or faithfulness can lead only to discontent:

> BIDDY: Sir, I am naturally very merry, and shall be, if you will but do me the favour to think me very honest.
> LIEU[TENANT]: I shall do you a great favour, if I do, for I never thought any body so yet
>
> (II.i, sig. C4r)

Biddy is referring to her sexual chastity, but elicits a more general response from the lieutenant. In the pragmatic world of this play, there is no person worthy of praise. All possess vices in addition to their virtues. Unquestioning loyalty to the Crown cannot be rewarded; it never existed. Howard may offer an idealised vision of the noble cavalier through the construction of royalist couples, but this notion of honour is rejected by Lacy.

Remembering and reinventing the civil war

The Old Troop and *The Committee* represent two extremes of a debate about how royalists and parliamentarians could and should be perceived at the Restoration. Many other Restoration comedies, including John Wilson's *The Cheats* (1663) and George Etherege's *Comical Revenge* (1664), enter into discussions about political allegiance during the civil war and commonwealth. As Susan Wiseman has observed, when the public theatres reopened at the Restoration, they did not reappear invigorated and refreshed from a twenty-year absence to offer radical drama with a new sense of political topicality. Plays that do possess a political significance were informed by the commonwealth and the dramatic modes that were permitted under commonwealth governments: as a consequence, they are not exclusively influenced by the Restoration.[72] Since the political concerns of the commonwealth and Restoration were diverse, it is unsurprising that plays which engage with the political legacy of the commonwealth do not have a homogenised political conviction. Despite the Act of Indemnity and Oblivion's endeavour to end discussion of the recent past, the curiously compliant parliament's agreement to the terms of the Restoration, and the recording of the occasion in plays, ballads and panegyric, meant that the event could not be easily laid to rest.

As Charles II negotiated the various political crises of his reign, the point of Restoration began to be viewed nostalgically: for some, it was seen as a brief moment of political unity. There may have been a desire to forget the recent troubles, but the dramatic potential of the previous twenty years, combined with a desire felt by some to reimagine the Restoration as it ought to have been, meant that (for at least the first decade of the Restoration) playwrights were loath to consign civil war discourse and the idea of restoration to oblivion.[73]

Just before the Restoration, *The Rump* attempted to reject panegyric. However, Tatham could not dismiss notions of panegyric despite the prologue declaring that the play has a documentary function. The end of the second Rump Parliament may have been inevitable, but the writer of civic pageants could not lay panegyric constructs to rest so easily. Likewise, the Restoration settlement failed in its attempt to forget that the commonwealth had ever been. The fact that the Restoration was immortalised by panegyric writers means that the commonwealth could not be ignored. It does not necessarily follow that, in establishing a commonwealth, there would eventually be a restoration of monarchy. However, the Stuarts would never have needed restoring to the throne had there been no civil war, regicide and commonwealth to have removed them in the first place. Consequently, beneath all panegyric in praise of the Restoration lies the memory of the recent past. Attempts to forget the civil war and commonwealth were doomed to failure.

By returning to the commonwealth as the temporal setting of these comedies, Tatham, Howard and Lacy bring to the surface events that the Act of Indemnity and Oblivion tried to consign to the distant past. The fictional parliamentarians of Tatham's play face a dilemma over how to define themselves as the natural mode of government in the absence of monarchy. The restored government had an equally difficult task as it sought a means through which to eulogise the Restoration while simultaneously endeavouring to erase the collective memory of the previous twenty years. Although it would have been convenient for the restored government and the cavalier parliament to forget recent history, they could not succeed. Restoration politics and the panegyric mode were thus complicated by the historical events they wished to conceal.

Notes

1 *The Diary of Samuel Pepys*, ed. Robert Latham and William Matthews, 11 vols (London: Harper Collins, 1995), 1:89 (16 March 1660).
2 Pepys, *Diary*, 1:280 (1 November 1660).
3 Pepys, *Diary*, 1:79 (6 March 1660).
4 Pepys, *Diary*, (6 March 1660).
5 For a brief description of Edward Montagu's shift from supporter of Cromwell to advocate of the restored monarchy, see esp. pp. 73–9 of Claire Tomalin's *Samuel Pepys: The Unequalled Self* (London: Penguin, 2003).
6 John Patrick Montano observes that public opinion over who should govern was broadly neutral. Monarchical rule may have been viewed as a means of putting an end to extremism of any form in government (Montano, *Courting the Moderates, Ideology, Propaganda and the Emergence of Party, 1660–1678* (London: Associated University Presses, 2002), p. 72).
7 N. H. Keeble, *The Restoration: England in the 1660s* (Oxford: Blackwell, 2002), pp. 26–53; Tim Harris, *London Crowds in the Reign of Charles II: Propaganda and Politics from the Restoration until the Exclusion Crisis* (Cambridge: Cambridge University Press, 1987), chapter 3; Tim Harris, *Restoration: Charles II and His Kingdom* (London: Allen Lane, 2005), chapter 1; Paul Seaward, *The Cavalier Parliament and the Reconstruction of the Old Regime, 1661–1667* (Cambridge: Cambridge University Press, 1989), p. 1.
8 Pepys, *Diary*, 1:91 (19 March 1660).

Ideas of panegyric 183

9 Seaward, *Cavalier Parliament*, esp. chapter 6.
10 Nicholas Jose, *Ideas of the Restoration in English Literature* (London and Basingstoke: Macmillan, 1984), esp. p. 126.
11 J. Tatham, *The Rump: or the Mirrour of the Late Times* (London, 1660), IV.i, sig. F4r.
12 Derek Hughes, *English Drama: 1660–1700* (Oxford: Clarendon Press, 1996), p. 30.
13 Susan Wiseman, *Drama and Politics in the English Civil War* (Cambridge: Cambridge University Press, 1998), p. 187.
14 Hughes, *English Drama*, p. 30.
15 Michael Cordner, 'Sleeping with the enemy; or, Aphra Behn's *The Roundheads* and the political comedy of adultery', in Michael Cordner and Peter Holland (eds), *Players, Playwrights, Playhouses: Investigating Performance, 1660–1800* (Basingstoke: Palgrave, 2007), pp. 45–77 (p. 50).
16 Hughes, *English Drama*, p. 30.
17 Cordner, 'Sleeping with the enemy', pp. 50–1.
18 Wiseman, *Politics*, p. 187.
19 To prevent confusion, when discussing Tatham's rendering of these historical characters, I will adopt the name he gives them. In referring to the figures themselves, I will use their real names.
20 Trevor Royle, *Civil War: The Wars of the Three Kingdoms, 1638–1660* (London: Abacus, 2005), p. 733.
21 Austin Woolrych, *Britain in Revolution, 1625–1660* (Oxford: Oxford University Press, 2002), p. 741.
22 I.e. Herbert Morely, a member of the Rump Parliament. He was appointed as one of the seven Commissioners after Fleetwood was stripped of his commission as Commander in Chief of the army.
23 Woolrych, *Britain in Revolution*, p. 737.
24 *The Kings Cabinet Opened* (London, 1645); Karen Britland, *Drama at the Courts of Queen Henrietta Maria* (Cambridge: Cambridge University Press, 2006), pp. 188–9, 192–4 and 197–200.
25 For example, see Henry Neville's attack on royalists by figuring a royalist parliament of ladies, *The Ladies Parliament* ([London, 1647]) and *The Ladies, A Second Time, Assembled in Parliament* (1647); see also Wiseman, *Politics*, p. 180.
26 For some extensive studies, see Cordner; Elizabeth Bennett Kubek, '"Night mares of the commonwealth": royalist passion and female ambition in Aphra Behn's *The Roundheads*', *Restoration*, 17 (1993), 88–103; Susan Owen, '"Suspect my loyalty when I lose my virtue": sexual politics and party in Aphra Behn's Plays of the exclusion crisis, 1678–83', *Restoration*, 18 (1994),

37–47, and Anita Pancheco, 'Reading Toryism in Aphra Behn's cit-cuckolding comedies', *RES*, 55 (2004), 690–708.
27 Cordner, 'Sleeping with the enemy', p. 53.
28 Of course, Nedham gained some notoriety in the seventeenth century for being a double turncoat. Jonathan Scott has argued that this turncoating does not represent so much Nedham's lack of loyalty to Crown or parliament but a consistent set of political values that meant he would change allegiance to support whoever seemed more inclined to realise these values (Jonathan Scott, *Commonwealth Principles: Republican Writing of the English Revolution* (Cambridge: Cambridge University Press, 2004), pp. 241–7).
29 Hughes, *English Drama*, pp. 30–1.
30 Royalist propaganda played upon the idea of low-born parliamentarians usurping the authority of their betters. In reality, the parliamentarians (and royalists) were not a socially homogeneous group.
31 Hughes, *English Drama*, p. 30.
32 Royle, *Civil War*, p. 756. In his *ODNB* entry, Ronald Hutton suggests that Monck, always moderate, became increasingly exasperated with parliament, leading him to eventually support and help to implement the Restoration ('Monck, George, first duke of Albemarle (1608–1670)', *Oxford Dictionary of National Biography* (Oxford: Oxford University Press, Sept 2004) www.oxforddnb.com/view/article/18939 (accessed 28 July 2008)).
33 Wiseman, *Politics*, p. 187.
34 Wiseman, *Politics*, chapter 7, esp. pp. 181–6.
35 See, for example, John Tatham, *Londons Glory Represented By Time, Truth and Fame* (London, 1660).
36 Hughes, *English Drama*, pp. 30–1.
37 See, for example, Hero Chalmers, *Royalist Women Writers, 1650–1689* (Oxford: Oxford University Press, 2004), pp. 171–4 (esp. p. 172, n. 60).
38 Cordner, 'Sleeping with the enemy', pp. 55–6. Chalmers also observes a connection between *The Roundheads* and *The Committee* (*Royalist Women Writers*, pp. 172–4).
39 Seaward, *Cavalier Parliament*, pp. 52–4 and pp. 193–4. See also Woolrych's description of the Bishop Wars (*Britain in Revolution*, chapters 3 and 4).
40 Harris, *Restoration*, chapter 3.
41 John Kerrigan, *Archipelagic English: Literature, History and Politics, 1603–1707* (Cambridge: Cambridge University Press, 2008), pp. 282–5.
42 *Ravillac Redivivus: Being a Narrative of the Late Tryal of Mr James Mitchel*, 2nd edn (London: Walter Kettilby, 1682), sig. C1r. James Sharp, the Archbishop of St Andrews, was eventually murdered on 3 May 1679 (*Ravillac Redivivus*, sig. A2v and Harris, *Restoration*, p. 330).

Ideas of panegyric 185

43 *Ravillac Redivivus*, sig. B2r.
44 *Ravillac Redivivus*, sig. B2r.
45 *Ravillac Redivivus*, sig. L1r.
46 *Ravillac Redivivus*, sigs K2r–M2r, and *passim*.
47 See, for example, Chaucer's 'The Wife of Bath's Tale', where Alice asserts of Friars; 'Ther is noon oother incubus but he, / And he ne wol doon hem but dishonour'. (lines 880–8, in *Geoffrey Chaucer: The Canterbury Tales*, ed. A. C. Cawley (London: Everyman, 1958; repr. 2000).
48 Lucy Hutchinson, *Memoirs of the life of Colonel Hutchinson*, ed. N. H. Keeble (London: Phoenix Press, 2000), p. 208. See also pp. 209–10, 222–3, 230–2 and 278–9 for Hutchinson's observations on perceived Presbyterian duplicity.
49 *The Humble Desires and Propositions For a Safe and Well-Grounded Peace, Agreed Upon by the Mutuall Advice and Consent of the Parliaments of Both Kingdoms, United by Solemn League and Covenant* (London, 1644), sig. A2v.
50 Woolrych, *Britain in Revolution*, pp. 298–9.
51 C. V. Wedgwood, *The Trial of Charles I* (London: Folio Society, 1959), p. 19.
52 Sir Robert Howard, 'The Committee', in *Four New Plays* (London, 1665), sigs K2r–S4r (I.i, sig. L4r).
53 This oath acknowledged the commonwealth regime and, from January 1650, all men aged over eighteen were legally obliged to subscribe to it (Woolrych, *Britian in Revolution*, p. 452).
54 Margaret Cavendish, 'A true relation of my birth, breeding, and life', in *Natures Pictures Drawn by Fancies Pencil to the Life* (London, 1656), sigs. Aaa4v – Ddd4r (sig. Ccc2r). For further comments relating to the committee's refusal to grant Cavendish funds at the meeting in Goldsmith's hall, see Margaret Cavendish, *The Life of the Thrice Nobel High and Puissant Prince William Cavendish* (London, 1667), sig. T2r.
55 Woolrych argues that the dramatic events of the mid-seventeenth century were caused more through blunders than strategic planning (*Britain in Revolution*, p. 156).
56 *An Act of Free and General Pardon, Indempnity, and Oblivion* (London, 1660), sig. G2r.
57 The only example of a conviction in a London court for forcible taking and marriage I can find for the period relates to the abduction and marriage of a thirteen year-old girl in 1690 and is therefore too late to have had its genesis in the civil war and commonwealth period (*The Proceedings on the King and Queens Commissions of the Peace, and Oyer and Terminer and Gaol-Delivery of Newgate, held for the City of London, and County of Middlesex, at Justice-Hall in the Old-Bailey. On Wednesday, Thursday, Friday, Saturday and Wednesday, being 10th, 11th, 12, 13th and 17th Days of December, 1690* (1690). The trial

relates to the abduction of Mary Wharton by John Johnson, p. 5, column 2 – p. 6, column 1).
58 Edward Vallance notes that Digges and Burghley had made proposals for an oligarchy to take control. This was to ensure that government could continue if an assassination attempt on Elizabeth proved successful before she decided who her heir would be. A bill was presented to Parliament, but rejected (Vallance, *Revolutionary England and the National Covenant: State Oaths, Protestantism and the Political Nation* (Woodbridge: Boydell Press, 2005), pp. 24–5). Had this measure prove successful, it might have provided commonwealth leaders with the precedent that some desired.
59 Cordner, 'Sleeping with the enemy', p. 63.
60 See esp. chapter 8 of Seaward, *Cavalier Parliament*, and Keeble, *The Restoration*, pp. 82–4, for discussions of royalist discontent with the Restoration settlement.
61 This event generated many pamphlets. See, for example, *The Downe-fall of Dagon, or, the Taking Downe of Cheap-side Crosse this Second of May, 1643* (1643); *A Vindication of Cheapside Crosse Against the Roundheads* (Oxford, 1643).
62 For an example of this kind of propaganda see I. W., *The Bloody Prince, or a Declaration of the Most Cruell Practices of Prince Rupert, and the Rest of the Cavaliers in Fighting Against God, and the True Members of his Church* (London, 1643), esp. sig. B3r.
63 Pepys, *Diary*, 2:234 (16 December 1661).
64 Hughes, *English Drama*, p. 30; Cordner, 'Sleeping with the enemy', p. 60.
65 See Cowley's preface, *Cutter of Coleman Street* (London, 1663), sigs A2r–A3r.
66 J. Douglas Canfield, *Tricksters and Estates: On the Ideology of Restoration Comedy* (Lexington: University Press of Kentucky, 1997), p. 161; William Van Lennep, ed., *The London Stage, 1660–1800*, 11 vols (Carbondale: Southern Illinois University Press, 1968), 1:cvi.
67 John Lacy, *The Old Troop, or Monsieur Raggou* (London, 1672), I.i, sig. C1r.
68 Canfield, *Tricksters and Estates*, pp. 175–6.
69 This mode of allegorical personification emerged out of a tradition established by the morality plays of the medieval period and borrowed by panegyrical constructs.
70 Timothy Raylor, *Cavaliers, Clubs and Literary Culture: Sir John Mennes, James Smith and the Order of the Fancy* (London and Toronto: Associated University Presses, 1994), p. 192; Lois Potter, *Secret Rites and Secret Writings: Royalist Literature, 1641–1660* (Cambridge: Cambridge University Press, 1989), pp. 138–48.
71 Canfield draws similar conclusions (*Tricksters and Estates*, p. 176).

Ideas of panegyric

72 Wiseman, *Politics*, pp. 211–99.
73 Cordner suggests that Robert Howard's and George Villiers's *The Country Gentleman* (1669) neatly captures a shift in emphasis from comedies embracing topicality in the 1660s to rejecting it in the 1670s ('Sleeping with the enemy', p. 63).

Epilogue
Of 1688 and reinventing the past

In the decades and centuries that followed 1660, the civil war and commonwealth were continually remembered and reinvented. Representations of Charles I and Oliver Cromwell maintained a dramatic resonance through which ideas of kingship were repeatedly debated. In the eighteenth century, the regicide was used as an interpretative focal point for contemporary anxieties. Fifty-six years after the regicide, and seventeen years after England ejected its Catholic monarch in favour of the king's Protestant daughter and her Dutch husband, another play was published. Entitled *The Royal Martyr, King Charles I*, Alexander Fyfe's work offers a different image of royal martyrdom and mediates some of the criticism levied at Cromwell in play pamphlets printed from the late 1640s until 1660. However, the eighteenth-century view of Cromwell remained negative and the play echoes this negativity.[1]

In 1705, Cromwell was still believed to be the usurper and, as such, is represented in the play as adopting Machiavellian measures to achieve the regicide:

> Things just when execute against a Law,
> May many Clamours, many hazards draw.
> Such of us as are members of the *House*,
> Justice it self to Duty will induce:
> I must with such as are not on my side
> Threaten, Allure, by Policy divide,
> And that the People may be kept in aw,
> Be sure it have the colour of a Law.[2]

The regicide must have the appearance of legality, if only to pacify the populace. Although Charles remains an exemplary image of suffering royalty, the play acknowledges parliamentarian concerns that led to a rift between monarch and Commons. Knowing that there was no legal basis for trying the king, the 1705 representation of Cromwell views the regicide as necessary and morally just. Whereas negative depictions of Cromwell throughout the commonwealth period dramatised him as being purely motivated by a wish to gain power, by 1705 Cromwell was perceived as possessing some inclination to act for the public good. The utilitarian reasoning adopted to justify the regicide did not negate the belief that Cromwell was driven by a desire to fulfil personal ambition, but offers a narrative that acknowledges post-1688 views regarding authority.

Since 1649, perceptions of monarchy had altered to accept that an erring ruler could be deposed. Whether the deposer had the right to usurp the erstwhile monarch and take over governance of the kingdom, however, remained contentious. Fyfe's play questions the conqueror's right to rule, but does not come to any neat conclusions.[3] Politics had transformed much in the preceding forty-five years, and Fyfe's drama is different from the anonymous play pamphlets that preceded it.[4] *The Royal Martyr* accommodates the change in ideology that occurred at the beginning of the long eighteenth century to present a slightly alternative view of the trials and tribulations of Charles I.

The restoration of the monarchy in 1660 was greeted with much festivity, though some of this may have been orchestrated.[5] As we saw in the multiple views articulated in the comedies discussed in Chapter 5, there was not a uniform and joyful response to Restoration. Charles II's reign was marred by disputes and upon the succession of his brother in 1685, some of these controversies intensified. Throughout the various conflicts of the later seventeenth century, religion continued to be a matter of concern. When Charles I's second son, James, ascended the throne, the events that had caused the exclusion crisis in the latter years of Charles II's reign came to a head. James had converted to Catholicism and this conversion heralded fears of arbitrary government. These concerns were enforced when James's second wife, Mary of Modena, gave birth to a (Catholic) son and the baby boy automatically held right of succession over his (Anglican) elder sisters. Coinciding with 5 November, the date upon which (in 1605) Guy Fawkes and his Catholic co-conspirators intended to blow up parliament and thereby assassinate James I, William of Orange landed on English soil. His claimed purpose was diplomacy. However, the fact his landing took place in 1688, the centenary year of the Spanish Armada, meant that some were of the belief that his appearance signified long-standing English solidarity and strength in thwarting Catholic oppression. Furthermore, negotiating an amicable truce between James and the English parliament did not seem to be part of William's agenda: his entourage of diplomats comprised 10,692 regular infantry, 3,060 regular cavalry and various volunteers who felt the need to be part of the invasion.[6] When knowledge of William's landing reached James, he took the most sensible course of action for a man who had seen his father executed by edict of a disgruntled parliament. Perceiving that William's idea of diplomacy might involve a certain degree of harm against the person, James fled to the continent accompanied by his queen and son. Upon James's desertion, William and his wife, Mary, were duly enthroned as joint constitutional monarchs.

Although discussions about the nature of kingship and its relationship to parliament can be found throughout the seventeenth century and in earlier times, 1688 can be viewed as a turning point. The 1688 revolution limited royal absolutism, and the 1701 Act of Settlement confirmed these limits by addressing later seventeenth-century grievances and confirming the succession upon the descendants of James I's daughter, Elizabeth of Bohemia.[7] While the 1688 revolution should not be viewed as finishing the actions begun by the wars of the 1640s, the political and religious uncertainties of the mid-seventeenth century made the establishment of a limited monarchy possible.[8] The different revolutions each contributed to alterations in popular ideas about kingship.

Fyfe's play lingers upon images of Charles in the domestic sphere. Whereas during his lifetime (and especially in the 1640s) some perceived the close relationship Charles had with Henrietta Maria as dangerous, fifty years later the relationship is celebrated as emblematic of marital bliss:[9]

> KING: I have determin'd: To disswade forbear;
>   You'll, in the Glory, or Disaster, share:
>   Indeed, that Motive's strong; but cannot bait:
>   Let's altogether yield unto our Fate:
> QUEEN: Then, then, our strong Affections closely meet,
>   Love makes adventures fearless, Troubles sweet.
>
> (I.i, sig. B1r)

The image parliamentarians in the 1640s had depicted of an uxorious husband has been replaced. We are now presented with a loving husband and wife who mutually share in one another's misfortunes. This echoes

Epilogue

the way in which courtly masques of the 1630s celebrated the couple's happy union. It also modifies these ideas from the 1630s to accommodate post-halcyon days and some of the gestures to allegorical images of Charles and Henrietta Maria that were discussed in Chapter 4. As time progressed and the regicide became a cultural memory, the circumstances relating to the civil wars and their aftermath would be reimagined. Constructions of Charles were not the only images of monarchy to undergo a sentimental rebranding in the later seventeenth century. John Banks's plays about Elizabeth refigure her from the good militant queen Bess (who had previously been applauded by many roundheads) to depict her as a weak and feeble woman who, through duty, signs the death warrants of the man whom she loves and the cousin whom she admires.[10]

The private sphere is thus used by these later playwrights as a means of comprehending public actions. This is in contrast to *The Famous Tragedie*, *Cromwell's Conspiracy*, *The Rump* and the countless commonwealth satires where Cromwell is given a private relationship with Mrs Lambert. In these earlier pieces, the private sphere is used to suggest that personal intemperance can lead to intemperance in public actions.

The change in focus means that Fyfe's early eighteenth-century play can acknowledge that both Charles and Cromwell had flaws. At the same time, in this representation of the two men, each person is also afforded redemptive characteristics. Unlike in the earlier plays, there is a complex discussion about Cromwell in relation to the regicide. Ultimately, in permitting the trial and execution, Cromwell's actions are still perceived to be those of a tyrant. His dialogue with the Prince of Wales and future Charles II, however, demonstrates there is no easy way to define what grants a monarch the right to rule:

PRINCE: If injur'd Monarchs their known Rights may sue,
    What's Nature's Law? What's an Usurper's Due?
    For Crimes of such a dye, what can attone?
    A murther'd Father, and a banish'd Son!
CROM[WELL]: I took but up the Sword he could not wear,
    And since I'm Conqueror, I'll be his Heir.
    Titles to Crowns from civil Contracts Spring;
    It's *Law* that makes, and takes away a King.
    It's but in vain a Birth-right to pretend;
    For *publick safety* knows no private End.
PRINCE: You talk of *Law*, who Law have overthrown;

> My Subjects gave you what was not their own.
> Conquest! so murdering Robbers give't a Name;
> Where prosp'rous Villainy admits no Shame.
>
> (V.ii, sigs H4r–H4v)

And so the discussion continues, until a mournful Marquess of Montrose enters and provides a diversion through a sword fight with Cromwell. The argument for divine right is neatly counterbalanced by a call for constitutional monarchy, despite the Cromwell of the play also asserting his right to rule the conquered land. Such arguments and counter-arguments abounded during the 1650 engagement controversy,[11] and the publication in 1690 of John Locke's influential *Two Treatises on Government* demonstrates that debates about the right to govern and what defines rightful government continued following William and Mary's accession to the throne.[12]

Despite these discussions, the play still presents Charles as dying a royal martyr: Charles's sanctification is not disputed. His son may protect himself through fleeing the might of Cromwell's sword, but Charles is depicted as endeavouring to rescue his nations from conquest through sacrificing himself:

> I die the Peoples *Martyr*, here's the Cause,
> That in the Sword I'd not subject the *Laws*.
> You've run in this gross Error all along;
> For success never justifies a Wrong.
> Right Measures for the Kingdoms Peace pursue;
> Give *God*, his *Church*, and next my *Son* their Due.
>
> (V.i, sig. H2v)

By 1705, parallels with the regicide and the atonement are supplanted by a new dialogue. Charles dies failing to protect his subjects from the arbitrary government that Cromwell is going to inflict upon them. Church and state will be in disarray, and the nation can only hope for future stability:

> JUXON: Though for some time the wicked man prevail,
>   Under the Rod, the Patient must not fail,
>   Until the darting light dispel the cloud.
>
> (V.i, sig. G4r)

The righteous must look to a future happiness. Whether this happiness will occur at the restoration of the monarchy (or after death) is not stated.

Instead, it is confirmed that those who remain true to Anglicanism and their suffering monarch will get their just rewards.

The Royal Martyr ends at the point of regicide, which leaves the audience with thoughts about what happened next. Juxon's prophecy collides with the audience's knowledge of Cromwell's governance and the legacy of commonwealth and Restoration. The ambiguous space at the end of the play meets with distant memories of the event. In 1705, few people who had been adults at the time of the regicide were still living. By the time of the first production and publication of *King Charles the First* by William Havard in 1737, the numbers of people who had experienced the civil war would have dwindled considerably.

King Charles the First was billed as *An Historical Tragedy Written in Imitation of Shakespear*. In this play, eighteenth-century bardolatry meets with an historical reconstruction of the regicide. Martyrological debates are replaced by an account that makes claims of historical veracity and appropriates Shakespeare (who in the eighteenth century was crowned the national poet)[13] as the muse behind the rewriting of the nation's history. Since Shakespeare had become celebrated especially for his ability to craft tragedies and histories, the title page to Havard's play is a canny piece of marketing. However, this also points to an aesthetic connection between literature and history. The historical narrative needs to imitate Shakespeare's style as a way of enforcing its national significance. Regardless of the literary merits of Havard's text (or his success at producing a pastiche of his much admired predecessor), with Shakespeare as the force that underpins the text, it is afforded cultural validation as both a narrative of history and a theatrical production.

The play appears to have been very popular with contemporaries; large audiences came to see the play over three months at Lincoln's Inn Fields in 1737 and it enjoyed numerous revivals in London and at provincial theatres throughout the next seventy years. Some of its popularity might have been due to the author's connection with the Shakespeare Ladies' Club. David Garrick, in whose acting company Havard was to gain a reputation for being a reliable actor, applauded the Ladies' Club for their part in fostering interest in Shakespeare.[14] Emmett L. Avery observes that nearly all the Drury Lane revivals of Shakespeare in the 1730s had been produced due to the efforts of these women and the club had gained sufficient notoriety to be a useful selling point for Havard's play.[15]

As well as success on the London stage, the play also went into multiple printed editions throughout the eighteenth century and was also performed in the provinces. In Worcester in 1767, a young John Philip

Kemble played the part of the Duke of York, with his parents affording the production a certain degree of metadramatic familial dysfunctionality by playing the parts of General and Lady Fairfax.[16] It was in the provincial playhouse that the melancholy tale was also rumoured to have heralded calamity. At the end of a performance in Hull in 1777 or 1778, a young lady in the audience dropped dead. Some blamed the pathos of Havard's writing for this catastrophic event, while others attributed it to divine vengeance making an example of one profane theatregoer.[17] Whether as a cautionary tale relating to the perils of sitting through the play, or as an example of the extreme effects of observing the dramatisation of regicide, it would seem that watching a play about the death of Charles I could induce a powerful reaction. Almost a century after the 1688 revolution, an account of the trials and tribulations of Charles would be perceived by some as being sufficient to lead to the expiration of one accustomed to constitutional monarchy.

In his preface, Havard admits to having modified the historical account of the events that he is dramatising:

> And first, as to the Liberties I have taken with History, I hope I may be forgiven my introducing the Queen, who was in *France* at the Time I have laid the Action of the Play; but it being a Story barren of Female Characters, I was induc'd to make her appear ...
>
> Again, to heighten the Distress in the last Act, and to bring on One suppos'd to receive and convey the Advice better, that the King sends by him to his eldest Son *Charles*, *James* appears, who was at that time in *Holland* ...
>
> I am not conscious of any other Liberties I have taken, except heightening the Characters of *Fairfax* and his Lady, which has added a Warmth to the Piece, and in some measure supply'd the Want of Real Matter to constitute Five Acts: The other Persons in the *Drama*, are as strongly characteris'd, and as impartially, as I had Ability, and the shortness of time would permit.[18]

By 1737, Edward Hyde, first Earl of Clarendon's *History of the Rebellion and Civil Wars in England* had gone into multiple editions, and an astute reader could therefore compare the play with Clarendon's account. Havard argues that changes to the narrative are for theatrical purposes: the need of the contemporary theatre to have sufficient roles for women actors, the belief that the tale requires elaboration to make it last five acts, and a desire to increase the pathos of the piece led him to make the story fit for the eighteenth-century stage. While absolving himself of blame for deliberate historical inaccuracy, Havard also makes a claim for historical impartiality: a lack of bias that Hyde (who had once served as lord chancellor to Charles II) is unlikely to have possessed. For Francis Wilson, the most striking aspect of Havard's play is the neutrality of the political narrative.[19] However, while Havard may have sought to depoliticise his subject matter, the fact that the play is dedicated to the Duchess of Marlborough clouds matters.

The Duchess of Marlborough to whom the play is dedicated might be the wife of Charles Spencer rather than Sarah Churchill who was by 1737 dowager Duchess of Marlborough. Despite this, the dedication evokes the latter: a formidable woman who, before their very public falling out, had been Queen Anne's chief adviser. The Marlboroughs were connected to many prominent Whigs and were extremely active in party politics.[20] Havard implicitly aligns the play with Whig party politics, offering an alternative story to the Tory tale in Clarendon's text. However, a newspaper article dated 9 December 1731 alleges that Clarendon's royalist account of the civil wars had been amended to make it fit for the eighteenth-century reader. Condemning non-authorial revisions in general, the article justifies the amendments by stating that they were performed to make Clarendon's text more balanced:

> For if this History was published to serve the *Tory* and *High Church* Cause; if it became the Oracle of that Party, and was published with that View; if, in order to blacken and make odious the opposite Party, it was necessary to *defame* and *detract from* the Avowers of Resistance, and the Assertors of Liberty, against King *Charles* the First, why then these Insertions were not *needless*. Neither can the Heads, or Agents, of Faction be considered as *cool* and *deliberate* Men, when *Party Heats* run so extravagantly high, as at the Time when this History was published; nor can any Argument be drawn from the Distance of *Sixty Years*, that the History of *Charles the First* could not then be corrupted, any more than that the same Contests could not then continue, when we know they are hardly determined even at this Day.
> ...
> If then any of these Persons[21] did conspire to sophisticate and corrupt the Earl of *Clarendon's* History, I am *charitably* willing to believe, that they did not from any *Spight against Truth*, or from any *Malice against the Persons*, whose Characters they new modelled; but merely from an innocent, great, and laudable Design of rendring [sic] *mighty Services* to their *favourite Party*.[22]

The author of the article justifies amendments to Clarendon's text because the political conditions under which it is published require a different narrative to the royalist one penned by Clarendon. It is insufficient to print

Clarendon's relation of the civil wars, commonwealth and Restoration as this particular text is biased toward the Tory party. Havard may have modified his history to accommodate bigger parts for the women actors and to add to the overall pathos, but Clarendon's piece requires modification to acknowledge a new order in the body politic. This emphasises the fluidity of historical accounts: not only the poet but also the historian is permitted to be selective in how he or she narrates historical events. The article suggests that modifications were made for the good of the Whig party and endeavoured to neutralise what is perceived to be Tory propaganda. Through this action, Clarendon's piece is rendered less controversial, thereby maintaining balance in the body politic.

However, this does not necessarily lead to a politically neutral historical account, nor do the pains Havard takes to depoliticise his material lead to a politically neutral play. Havard's prologue begins on a patriotic note. Written 'By a friend' (sig. A5r), the prologue celebrates the author's dexterity as a historian-playwright:

> Murder avow'd by Law, he boldly paints;
> Heroes and Patriots, Hypocrits and Saints:
> Rebellion fighting for the Publick Good
> And Treason smiling in a Monarch's Blood,
> ...
>   When *Charles* submits to Faction's deadly Blow,
> What loyal Heart but shares the Monarch's Woe.
>   Nor less *Maria's* Grief, ye gentle Fair,
> Claims the sad Tribute of a tender Tear
> From *British* scenes to-night we hope Applause,
> And *Britons*, sure will aid a *British* cause.
>
>   (sig. A5r, italics inverted)

This quotation appeals to Britishness; it does not invoke ideas relating to Englishness. In so doing, it demonstrates how the 1707 Act of Union between England and Scotland changed the historical accounts from being one of trouble in the three kingdoms to a narrative of British affairs. To draw Henrietta Maria further into this 'British' story, her name is anglicised to 'Maria' and 'Henrietta' is dropped as an unnecessary Francophone prefix. While there are numerous documents from the seventeenth century that refer to Henrietta Maria as 'Queen Mary' or 'Maria' and her adopted court had often attempted to anglicise her name, Henrietta Maria resolutely retained her French name.[23] Through anglicising her name, Havard brings Henrietta Maria fully into the narrative and renders her grief emblematic of British sorrow that the civil wars led to the execution of the king. The regicide, in this post-1688 rendering of the event, becomes a legally sanctioned crime that, reluctantly, was committed to prevent tyranny. The Act of Union, the 1688 revolution and the regicide become connected as a teleological view of the previous ninety years is constructed. Rebellion, when the nation's liberty is at stake, is morally just. The execution of Charles, however, becomes a British tragedy, which obfuscates the understanding of regicide as a necessary way to depose a tyrant.[24]

A British tale therefore unfolds on stage, with a Machiavellian Cromwell and a brooding Fairfax failing to agree over the fate of the hapless Charles. Naseby becomes the focal point of royalist lamentation when, in the opening scene, Juxon and Richmond bewail the battle as the genesis of royalist misfortune. Following this, Cromwell enters, celebrates victory over Charles and applauds the dawn of a more democratic society:

> Now thro' the Maze of gloomy Policy,
> Has fire-ey'd Faction work'd her Way to Light
> And deck'd Ambition in the Robe of Power.
> Our Fears in *Charles's* Safety are remov'd,
> And but one Blow remains to fix our State –
> The lopping off his Head. No more the Royal Tree
> Shall, from Legitimacy's Root presume
> To sprout forth Tyrant Branches: Commonwealth
> Own no hereditary Right, unless worth
> Shine equal to our Birth: Wherefore at once
> Down with Nobility – The Commons rule!
> Avaunt Prerogative and Lineal Title,
> And be the Right to rise superior Merit.
>
> (I:i, sig. B2r)

A meritocracy is advocated above a hereditary right to rule, but the language is tenuously balanced. 'Faction', the entity to which (in the prologue) Charles has been forced to submit, is here rewarded. Ambition and faction, both terms which had negative connotations in the seventeenth and eighteenth centuries, are here celebrated and personified by Cromwell while the royal line is viewed as tyrannous. The rhetoric is antithetical and contradictory: 'legitimate' governance is tyrannous and usurpation is meritorious. Although applauding the removal of a tyrant, the two phantoms whom Cromwell invokes are not celebrated either. The appearance of the royal tree destabilises the passage further. The tree was important to Restoration iconography and the 'Royal Oak' feeds into cultural memory. Charles II hid in an oak tree before making an elaborate escape to the continent following an ill-advised plan to regain the Crown in 1651.[25] The audience's shared knowledge of the oak tree and its function as a sanctuary for royalty therefore meets the play's depiction of Cromwell and offers a mocking corrective to the tree surgery the aspiring protector proposes. The lopping of Charles I's head did not lead to the death of the royal tree; instead, the metaphorical imagery points to an extreme form of pruning, and ceases to mark the end of monarchical government.

Cromwell may applaud ambition and faction, but the play's dramatisation of Fairfax views these qualities negatively. Justice drives Fairfax's idealism: he sought justice against monarchical tyranny and is now seeking mercy from parliamentarian oppression. Knowing how to manipulate, Havard's Cromwell purposefully orchestrates the invasion of Scotland as a way of getting Fairfax to resign his commission and thereby give Cromwell sole command of the New Model Army. Fairfax ceases to be useful to Cromwell and is therefore coaxed out of authority in the army. The lord general's qualms about the regicide mean he must discreetly retire, while his wife is blamed for his misgivings:

> 'Tis the wife of *Fairfax*: Once as hearty,
> As zealous for the Cause, as *Cromwell's* self,
> And wrought her Lord to think so. Now, O Woman!
> Such is thy varying Nature, that the Waves
> Are not more fluctuating than thy Opinions,
> Nor sooner are displac'd. To her is owing
> The wayward Pity of her Vassal Lord.
> Oh! 'Tis certain Danger to have such a Woman.
> Who, when Man leaves himself to toy with her,
> Knows how to win, and practise on his Weakness,
>
> (III.i, sigs C4v–C5r)

In this passage (which renders women's inconstancy responsible for Fairfax's change of heart), we are presented with an image of a turncoating, controlling wife. In this 1737 interpretation of the regicide, the role of uxorious husband has been transferred from Charles to Fairfax. However, Fairfax and Lady Fairfax are ultimately dramatised as being united in their condemnation of the regicide and desire to remain untainted by it.

Epilogue

A thread that runs throughout the play is how future generations will view the regicide. Cromwell, focused upon the current moment, does not think about his posthumous reception. Fairfax, however, is keenly conscious of his legacy:

> Why did I conquer – to repent of Conquest;
> Who tho' I fought for Liberty alone,
> Will yet acquit me of the Guilt that follows?
> Will future Ages when they read my Page
> (Tho' *Charles* himself absolves me of the Deed)
> Spare me the Name of Regicide? O no!
> I shall be blacken'd with my Party's Crimes,
> And damn'd with my full Share, tho' innocent.
>
> (V.i, sig. E1v)

The play thus acquits Fairfax of any involvement in the regicide. This echoes the figure of a remorseful Fairfax depicted in some mid-seventeenth-century play pamphlets, but it also chimes with Fairfax's memoirs (published posthumously in 1699). Here Fairfax claimed that scheming army agitators circumvented his command, thereby bringing about Charles's death.[26] Fairfax, and those who published his memoirs, thus favoured being perceived as not being in sufficient command of his troops to being seen as playing an active role in the final stages of the civil wars. The play's account thus echoes the way that those who had inherited Fairfax's estate wished him to be remembered.

Fairfax is thus exonerated of playing a major part in the regicide, but he plays some key roles in the drama where, presented as a moderate parliamentarian, Fairfax embodies the post-1688 acceptance of a constitutional monarchy. Havard's depiction of Fairfax not only exonerates the lord general of his involvement in the regicide, but also offers a view of Charles as someone who needed to be deposed but ought not to have been executed: while a monarch who behaves despotically can be removed, he or she should be permitted to live. Fairfax also acts as a parallel to Charles. Both are concerned with their posthumous receptions and, despite perceiving governance very differently, are represented as being keen to see that justice is fairly given:

> KING: Deny'd to speak – Why have I liv'd to this?
>   When I had Power, the meanest of my Subjects,
>   Not heard by me, wou'd straight arraign my Justice,

And brand me with the hated Name of Tyrant.
Will future Ages, looking back to this,
Credit this Record? They will rather deem it
The black invective of a partial Pen
And curse his Mem'ry that libell'd *England*.

(IV.ii, sig. D6r)

The play may be able to adapt the account of Fairfax's behaviour as found in his memoirs and thereby absolve the lord general of involvement in the regicide, but no alternative history can provide a counter-narrative regarding the trial of Charles. Instead, a desire for the historical record to be inaccurate is preferred to the idea that the trial fails to adhere to habeas corpus.

Charles is thus sentenced. Before the final scene upon the scaffold, he imparts advice to the future James II:

When I am dead, look on thy Brother *Charles*,
Not as thy Brother only, but thy King;
...
If Heav'n restores him to his lawful Crown,
Let him wreak no Revenge upon his Foes,
...
Let him maintain his Pow'r, but not increase it;
The String Prerogative, when strain'd too high,
Cracks, like the tortur'd Chord of Harmony,
And spoils the Consort between King and Subject;

(V.ii, sig. E4v)

The play attributes to Charles the basis of the Restoration settlement and the Act of Indemnity and Oblivion. Revenge at the Restoration can only weaken monarchical rule and should therefore be avoided as much as possible. Reviewing his career, Charles warns against arbitrary government and encourages his offspring to champion constitutional monarchy. The balance of power should be carefully shared between monarch and parliament. Although Havard claims in the preface that James was included in the narrative as he would be a better messenger than the Duke of Gloucester for Charles's final advice to the Prince of Wales, his appearance implicitly brings 1688 into the story. The belief that James sought to increase monarchical authority partly led to his deposition: since James failed to heed the memory of his father's fate, he could and should be removed from office.

After taking leave of some of his children, Charles thus goes to his death. Reviewing civil war and regicide in the final lines of the play, Juxon presents them as a necessary evil:

> Thus fell *Charles!*
> A Monument of Shame to the present Age –
> A Warning to the future: His Example
> May prove this Maxim's Truth to all Mankind;
> The Subject's Reverence, and the Prince's Love,
> Grasping, and grasp'd, walk Hand in Hand together,
> Strengthened by Union; then, the King's Command
> Is lost in the Obedience of the Subject;
> The King, unask'd, confirm's the People's Rights,
> And by the willing Gift prevents the Claim:
>
> (V.iii, sig. E6r)

Charles's fate becomes a cautionary tale about what happens when the bond between monarch and subject is broken. The monarch's right to rule rests with the people and not in hereditary right. Notions of the monarch ruling as God's anointed vice-regent on earth have been replaced by ideas of a contractual agreement between monarch and subject. The regicide has been rewritten to accommodate and celebrate ideas of constitutional monarchy.

Havard's play thus ends, he hopes, without causing '*Offence to* Whig *or* Tory' (Epilogue, sig. F1r). The British tragedy presented by Havard vaunts its political impartiality. These references to party politics, however, do not depoliticise the narrative, but instead point to eighteenth-century political anxieties. While the play does not engage with eighteenth-century party politics, these political parties are anachronistically mapped on to the regicide. Cromwell, who in the play is supported by Bradshaw and Ireton, astutely manipulates party politics, while Fairfax, Juxon and Richmond are unable to exert their influence and gain a pardon for Charles. Although later historians have rightly identified the popish plot and exclusion crisis as the point where political parties were emerging, the play implicitly locates faction during the civil wars as causing the emergence of party.

Established political parties were incomprehensible to many in the seventeenth century. However, the proliferation of royalist and parliamentarian newsbooks in the 1640s demonstrates that ideas relating to faction as a dangerous beast within the body politic were well established and, as we saw in Chapter 4, drama responded to anxieties regarding faction at the Restoration. These newsbooks also shaped historical interpretation by reporting on and rewriting the civil war. An understanding of the execution and the events that led to war was produced mainly through both the printed material that was produced throughout the latter half of the seventeenth century and the printing of Clarendon's formidable *History of the Rebellion* in the early eighteenth century. These texts all contribute to the cultural memory of civil war and ideas of what it meant to be a royalist or a parliamentarian. These ideas fed into nineteenth-century historical accounts of the regicide.

In some respects, these views of seventeenth-century England were useful to Whig historiography, which appropriated the past as a means of justifying and applauding the present. Whig historiography dominated historical studies in the nineteenth and early twentieth centuries. It presented a teleological view of history as a way of showing how the past created the conditions of the present. In these readings, the abdication of James II in 1688 and the establishment of a monarchy whose powers are limited by constitution becomes the definitive point at which revolution has occurred. This suggests that the political divisions and perceived anxieties about holiday pastimes that prevailed before the Restoration represent an extreme reaction to the various social changes as the three kingdoms moved towards constitutional monarchy: social and political schisms become more fraught as society and authority is redefined. Herbert Butterfield criticised these narratives for anachronistically assuming that value judgements in the present are identical to those of the past, and censured the strong political bias that informed this type of scholarship. From the 1970s, revisionist historiography challenged the Whiggish tendency to create grand narratives of history. However, as Peter Lake and Steve Pincus have observed, revisionism's 'focus on court-centered elite politics and ideological consensus is exactly replicated in the nineteenth- and earlier twentieth-century Whig accounts of the later seventeenth century'.[27] Lake and Pincus suggest that Whig and revisionist interpretations of history correlate, but the epistemological and ideological concepts that underpin each reading of history are radically different.

As a young man, the eminent nineteenth-century historian Thomas Babington Macaulay commented that official history in the eighteenth century painted a negative image of Cromwell, but there still continued a popular tradition that celebrated Cromwellian rule.[28] When he came to pen his *History of England* (vol. I, 1849), Macaulay wrote an account that

Epilogue

was to redeem Cromwell from some of the more overt charges of tyranny. However, the image he paints of the godly is, as Percy Scholes pointed out in the 1930s, 'an eloquent catalogue of imaginary attributes, constituting a perfect picture of the "Stage puritan"'.[29] In discussing the unresolved religious tensions of the early seventeenth century, Macaulay presents an image of the 'precise puritan', which is the diametrical opposite of the fun-loving cavalier. Locating persecution of breakaway sects in the sixteenth century as the reason for strongly held convictions in the early seventeenth, Macaulay presents a teleological view of the build up to civil war and regicide. Macaulay also suggests a causal connection between the Elizabethan settlement and the emergence of puritan austerity: had there not been such a divergence of ecclesiastical opinion after the Reformation, the godly would not have dogmatically looked to the Old Testament and Hebrew Scriptures for guidance through their suffering. Macaulay claims that 'rules ... which would have appeared insupportable to the free and joyous spirit of Luther, and contemptible to the serene and philosophical intellect of Zwingle [sic], threw over all life a more than monastic gloom'.[30] Post-Reformation, Protestants broke into smaller factions and forgot the fundamental principles that were behind the Reformation. Schisms in the church led to divisions in the state and, eventually, an aversion to monarchical rule and holiday pastimes.

The 'Stage Puritan' thus, in Macaulay's historical narrative, becomes the *de facto* image of puritanism. Whatever the historical reality, popular images of puritans as hypocritically austere figures gained credibility. These images were promulgated in the Restoration. Charles II (who generally maintained a tolerance toward religious factions to the consternation of his government) appreciated humour that attacked puritan Protestantism such as Jonson's *Bartholomew Fair* (1614), a play that was revived at least seven times before 1666.[31] These revivals were not without their critics, proving that anti-Presbyterian satire did not please all members of the Restoration audience.[32] The fact it was often revived also suggests that this type of comedy had a broad appeal, which had the potential to be lucrative for playwrights wishing to copy the successful formula. Revivals of some Jacobean comedies and, as we saw in Chapter 5, new plays aligned the godly with radical parliamentarians to present them as figures of fun and this continued in the later seventeenth century. Whether or not it was (as Macaulay asserted) 'a sin to touch the virginals', the image of the godly as presented in many seventeenth-century plays and in the print culture of the civil war and commonwealth gained credibility.[33]

Of course, as Scholes pointed out many decades ago and Martin Butler and Margot Heinemann reasserted in the 1980s, this image suited a political agenda.[34] Although the theatres were officially closed and some festivities ceased, not all holiday pastimes were censured. What we have seen in this book are some of the continuities and discontinuities in theatrical practice in the seventeenth century. Perhaps one of clearest pieces of evidence for these continuities comes from the print culture of music scores during the protectorate. In the 1650s, John Playford specialised in publishing music scores.[35] The introduction to *A Musicall Banquet* (1651) even advertises music tutors in the City of London for those seeking instruction:

> Thus having briefely set downe these few necessary and easie principles of the theorick part of Musick, I shall wish you good successe in the practick part, which will soon bee obtained by the helpe of an able Master, this City being at present furnished with many excellent and able Masters in the Art and Science, some of whose names for information of such as desire to become Practitioners therein, I have heere inserted.

For the Voyce or Viole.		For the Organ or Viginall.
Mr. Henry Lawes.	Mr. Edward Colman.	Mr. Richard Portman.
Mr. Charles Colman.	Captaine Cooke.	Mr. Christopher Gibbons.
Mr. William Webb.	Mr. Henry Farabosco.	Mr. Randall Jewet.
Mr. John Birtenshaw.	Mr. John Harding.	Mr. John Cobb.
Mr. George Husdon.	Mr. Jeremy Savile.	Mr. John Hinkston.
Mr. Thomas Bates.	Mr. John Esto.	Mr. Brian.
Mr. Stephen Bing.	Mr. William Paget.	Mr. Benjamin Sandley.
Mr. Thomas Maylard.	Mr. Gregory.	Mr. Benjamin Rogers.
Cum multis aliis.		Cum multis aliis.[36]

Music and dancing were not banned under the commonwealth and protectorate, and (as we have seen) drama continued to function in spite of the ordinances for theatre closure. In fact, Henry Lawes, Edward Coleman and Captain Henry Cook all sang in, or wrote music for, performances of *The Siege of Rhodes* in 1656.[37] Despite this, the construction of supporters of the commonwealth having animosity to holiday pastime, as presented in play pamphlets, drama and other pamphlets, has proved difficult to erase. Whatever the historical fact, the historical fiction produced enduring images that would be modified to suit the concerns of the current historical moment. History and myth merged as the mythos of the civil wars, regicide, commonwealth, protectorate and Restoration continued to be rewritten and reinvented.

Royalists, republicans and supporters of the protectorate used drama to produce enduring images of the civil war period. The neat dichotomies, like the martyred king usurped by a Machiavellian Cromwell, or the fun-loving cavalier jovially battling the precise puritan parliamentarian, continued and became more dichotomous in their representations. Davenant's protectorate entertainments, discussed in Chapter 3, do not negate these images; rather, they add to the rich patchwork of dramatic renderings of Cromwell through celebrating protectorate foreign policy. The 1647 and 1648 ordinances for theatre closure politicised the very act of producing drama, and therefore writers emphatically used dramatic conventions for political ends. However, there would also be aesthetic legacies for drama as a consequence of the civil wars.

At the Restoration, the performance of playtexts in the playhouse was very different from how drama was staged in the Elizabethan and early Stuart playhouse. Perhaps Davenant's protectorate masques had a greater aesthetic legacy than their political context would suggest. In transferring the court masque to the public stage, Davenant introduced novelties such as the proscenium arch, scenery and women actors. These innovations were retained and built upon as exiled royalists (who were accustomed to these staging conventions in continental theatre houses and at the early Stuart court) returned to England. Although heroic drama was a short-lived fashion on the early Restoration stage, other forms of drama were being revived and modified.

When the theatres reopened, the two managers of the theatre companies inherited earlier playtexts. Revivals of Elizabethan and early seventeenth-century plays were common: the King's Company, under the management of Thomas Killigrew, in particular staged many revivals on account of inheriting the majority of the old playtexts.[38] Adaptations of these plays meant that tropes from earlier drama would be revised and made fit for the Restoration theatre space.[39] The idea of drama may have been used during the commonwealth as a means of rewriting the historical moment, but earlier drama and ideas borrowed from earlier drama were now being performed in a revised theatrical space. Restoration stage practitioners were keenly aware of earlier drama and, likewise, the protectorate stage borrowed heavily from knowledge of the masque. Drama may have been used to reinvent the recent past, but theatrical performance space was also reinvented as a consequence of the recent past.

As I have argued, the 1642 ordinance for theatre closure shut the playhouse because playgoing was incompatible with a time of crisis, but the 1647 and 1648 ordinances turned the writing, production and printing of drama into a political act. Play pamphlets were used in the 1640s and 1650s to construct reductive images of Cromwell and Charles, and Davenant reinvented the Stuart court masque to turn the form into a way of celebrating Cromwellian foreign policy on the protectorate stage. In the early Restoration, heroic drama was similarly used as a means through which to discuss ideas of kingship, and the comic mode was appropriated to reflect upon the civil war, commonwealth and Restoration. These ideas would not end in 1672, but continued to occupy playwrights and dramatists in the eighteenth century and beyond. While the performing and production of drama no longer had such overt political connotations, the appeal and possibilities of fictionalising the civil wars through the medium of drama endured.[40] The images constructed in drama during the 1640s, 1650s and 1660s and the way they were used to (re)write the civil war, commonwealth and Restoration represented the beginnings of a narrative that would alter to suit changing political and cultural climates.

Notes

1. See Blair Worden, *Roundhead Reputations: The English Civil Wars and the Passions of Posterity* (London: Penguin, 2001).
2. [Alexander Fyfe], *The Royal Martyr, K. Charles I. An Opera* (1705), III:i, sig. E4v.
3. The title page asserts that the play is an 'opera'. I have not come across any musical score for the piece, or evidence that any music ever existed, so I can only assume that opera here means 'work'. I am also unaware of any performance of the drama taking place. Perhaps it was conceived as musical drama, but the text was never transformed into a libretto.
4. See Chapter 2.
5. Tim Harris, *London Crowds in the Reign of Charles II: Propaganda and Politics from the Restoration until the Exclusion Crisis* (Cambridge: Cambridge University Press, 1987), pp. 36–52.
6. Tim Harris, *Revolution: The Great Crisis of the British Monarchy, 1685–1720* (London: Allen Lane, 2006), p. 274. I am indebted to Harris's account in the following paragraphs.
7. Harris, *Revolution*, pp. 493–4.
8. Harris, *Revolution*, pp. 512–17.

9 Francis P. Wilson has identified a handful of post-regicide elegiac poems that focus upon the idea of Charles's grief-stricken family and sentimentalise Henrietta Maria's role as a widow ('"That Memorable Scene": The image of King Charles the First in seventeenth and eighteenth century literature' (Unpublished doctoral thesis, University of York, 1993), pp. 47–9). Nevertheless, Henrietta Maria's influence over her husband would still be regarded with suspicion by many in her adopted country, and 'contemptuous fear of … Henrietta Maria' continued to be a 'national pastime' throughout the Restoration (p. 125).

10 See John Banks, *The Unhappy Favourite or the Earl of Essex* (London, 1682); *The Island Queen, or the Death of Mary, Queen of Scotland* (London, 1682), and Elizabeth's cameo in his *Vertue Betray'd: or, Anna Bullen* (London, 1682). Michael Dobson and Nicola J. Watson discuss this sentimentalising of Elizabeth in the long eighteenth century (*England's Elizabeth An Afterlife in Fame and Fantasy* (Oxford: Oxford University Press, 2002), pp. 88–102). John Watkins suggests an alternative reading, which argues that early Restoration representations of Elizabeth emphasise anxieties in regard to influential Catholics at court, whereas the sentimental rebranding of Elizabeth in Banks's plays engages with Whig rhetoric to offer a critique of absolutism. *Representing Elizabeth in Stuart England: Literature, History, Sovereignty* (Cambridge: Cambridge University Press, 2002), esp. pp. 108–87. Julia Walker demonstrates that not all posthumous representations of Elizabeth in the seventeenth century were positive. See 'Bones of contention: posthumous images of Elizabeth and Stuart politics', in Julia M. Walker (ed.), *Dissing Elizabeth: Negative Images of Gloriana* (Durham, NC, and London: Duke University Press, 1998), pp. 252–76.

11 See Quentin Skinner, 'conquest and consent: Thomas Hobbes and the engagement controversy', in G. E. Aylmer (ed.), *The Interregnum and the Quest of Settlement 1646–1660* (London and Basingstoke: Macmillan, 1972), pp. 78–98, for a discussion of justifications for subscribing to *de facto* power during the engagement controversy. Edward Vallance offers a revisionist account through focusing upon Anglican responses to the controversy ('Oaths, casuistry, and equivocation: Anglican responses to the engagement controversy', *The Historical Journal*, 44 (2001), 59–77).

12 Locke's first treatise is a direct response to Robert Filmer's advocacy of absolutist primogeniture, *Patriarcha, or the Natural Power of Kings* (first published 1680, written c. 1638/39 (see Peter Laslett's introduction to John Locke, *Two Treatises of Government* (Cambridge: Cambridge University Press, 1988)). Although elements of Locke's *Treatises* were written before the 1688 revolution, the printing of the text suggests a shift in focus in the 1690s.

13 Michael Dobson, *The Making of the National Poet: Shakespeare, Adaptation and Authorship, 1660–1769* (Oxford: Clarendon Press, 1994).
14 Dobson, *Making*, p. 148.
15 Emmett L. Avery, 'The Shakespeare ladies club', *Shakespeare Quarterly*, 7 (1956), 153–8 (154).
16 James Boaden, *Memoir of the Life of John Philip Kemble esq: including a history of the stage, from the time of Garrick to the present period*, 2 vols (London: Longman, Hurst, Rees, Orme, Brown and Green, 1825), 2:4. See also p. 336; Philip H. Highfill, Jr, Kalman A. Burnim and Edward A. Langhans, *A Biographical Dictionary of Actors, Actresses, Musicians, Dancers, Managers and Other Stage Personnel in London, 1660–1800*, 16 vols (Carbondale: Southern Illinois University Press, 1973–93), 8:336.
17 Tate Wilkinson, *The Wandering Patentee; or, a History of the Yorkshire Theatres, from 1770 to the Present Time*, 4 vols (London, 1795), 2:7–8.
18 *King Charles I: An Historical Tragedy Written in Imitation of Shakespear* (Dublin, 1737), sigs A4r–A4v.
19 Francis P. Wilson, 'That memorable scene', p. 329.
20 Although Sarah Churchill's daughter, Henrietta (who had succeeded to the ducal title in her own right and held the title until her death in 1733), was known as a great patron of the arts (and, aged forty-two, gave birth to the child of William Congreve – a playwright and Whig MP), the Marlboroughs were more commonly recognised for their political intriguing.
21 I.e., Bishop Smallridge, Dr Aldrich and the Bishop of Rochester, the three men whom the article attributes with amending Clarendon's text.
22 Francis Walsingham, 'Reflections on a paper said to be lately printed at Paris, and now reprinted in London, entitled, The Late Bishop of Rochester's vindication of Bishop Smallridge, Dr. Aldrich, and Himself, from the charge against them, relating to the publication of Lord Clarendon's History', *The Free Briton*, 106 (9 December 1731), no pagination [fol. 1r].
23 Karen Britland, *Drama at the Courts of Queen Henrietta Maria* (Cambridge: Cambridge University Press, 2006), pp. 18–19.
24 This in turn invokes the memory of 1688 as exemplifying how to remove a cantankerous king. In so doing, the play emphasises the representation of 1688 as a 'bloodless revolution' that replaced James II as monarch with his daughter and nephew.
25 Austin Woolrych, *Britain in Revolution, 1625–1660* (Oxford: Oxford University Press, 2002), pp. 497–9; Trevor Royle, *Civil War: The Wars of the Three Kingdoms, 1638–1660* (London: Abacus, 2005), p. 602.
26 *Short Memorials of Thomas Lord Fairfax, Written by Himself* (London, 1699).

27 Herbert Butterfield, *The Whig Interpretation of History* (London: G. Bell, 1931); Peter Lake and Steve Pincus, 'Rethinking the public sphere in early modern England', *Journal of British Studies*, 45 (2006), 270–92 (271).
28 See Worden, *Roundhead Reputations*, pp. 216–17.
29 Percy A. Scholes, *The Puritans and Music in England and New England: A Contribution to the Cultural History of Two Nations* (Oxford: Oxford University Press, 1934), p. 103.
30 Charles Harding Firth, ed., *The History of England from the Accession of James the Second by Lord Macaulay*, 6 vols (London: Macmillian, 1913), 1:70.
31 Paul Seaward, *The Cavalier Parliament and the Reconstruction of the Old Regime, 1661–1667* (Cambridge: Cambridge University Press, 1989), p. 33; Dobson, *Making of the National Poet*, p. 24.
32 See Michael Cordner, 'Zeal-of-the-Land-Busy restored', in Martin Butler (ed.), *Re-presenting Ben Jonson: Text, History, Performance* (London: Macmillan, 1999), pp. 174–92 (pp. 179–81); see also Frances Teague, *The Curious History of Bartholomew Fair* (London and Toronto: Associated University Presses, 1985), pp. 61–78.
33 For Macaulay's extended list of 'outlawed' pastimes, see Macaulay, *History of England*, 1:68–71.
34 See Scholes's energetic dismissal of many of his 'good friends' findings in relation to seventeenth-century attitudes to music, *The Puritans and Music*, esp. chapter 1; Martin Butler, *Theatre and Crisis, 1632–1642* (Cambridge: Cambridge University Press, 1984); Margot Heinemann, *Puritanism and Theatre: Thomas Middleton and Opposition Drama Under the Early Stuarts* (Cambridge: Cambridge University Press, 1980).
35 Scholes, *The Puritans and Music*, chapter 8.
36 *A Musicall Banquet, Set forth in three choice varieties of Musick* (London, 1651), sig. A4r.
37 [William Davenant], *The Siege of Rhodes* (London, 1656), sig. G1r.
38 Paulina Kewes, *Authorship and Appropriation: Writing for the Stage in England, 1660–1710* (Oxford: Clarendon Press, 1998), p. 13.
39 For some studies into Restoration stage adaptations, see Dobson, *The Making of the National Poet*; Kewes, *Authorship and Appropriation*.
40 For twenty-first-century screenplays that demonstrate how the civil war continues to be dramatised, see *To Kill a King*, dir. by Mike Barker (2003); *The Devil's Whore*, dir. Marc Munden (2008), Jerome de Groot, '"Welcome to Babylon": performing and screening the English revolution', in Mark Thornton Burnett and Adrian Streete (eds), *Filming and Performing Renaissance History* (Basingstoke: Palgrave Macmillan, 2011), pp. 65–82.

Bibliography

Primary texts

Printed books

An Account of the Last Houres of the Late Renowned Oliver Lord Protector (London: Robert Ibbitson, 1659)

An Act of Free and General Pardon, Indempnity, and Oblivion (London: John Bill and Christopher Barker, 1660)

The Actors Remonstrance, or Complaint: for the Silencing of their Profession, and Banishment from their Severall Play-Houses. (London: Edw[ard] Nickson, 1643)

Arsy Versy: or, The Second Martyrdom of the Rump (1660)

A Bartholomew Faire (London: Richard Harper, 1641)

A Bartholomew Fairing (London: 1649)

The Bible: Authorised King James Version with Apocrypha, ed. Robert Carroll and Stephen Prickett (Oxford: Oxford University Press, 1997)

The Book of Common Prayer (London: 1662)

The Case is Altered, Or Dreadful News from Hell (London: John Andrews, [1660])

The Character of a London Diurnall (1644 [February 1645])

A Coffin for King Charles: A Crowne for Cromwell: A Pit for the People. ([1649])

A Conference Between the Ghost of the Rump and Tom Tell-Troth ([1660])

A Conference held Between the Old Protector and the New Lord General Truly Reported by Hugh Peters (London: 1660)

The Court Career, Death Shaddow'd to life. Or Shadowes of Life and Death. A Pasquil Dialogue (1659)

Cromwell's Conspiracy (London: 1660)

A Declaration of the Lords and Commons Assembled in Parliament, for the Appeasing and Quietting of all Unlawfull Tumults and Insurrections in the Severall Counties of England, and Dominion of Wales. Die Veneris, Septemb. 2. 1642 (London: John Wright, 1642)

Bibliography

A Declaration of the Prince Paltsgrave to the High Court of Parliament, Concerning the Cause of his departure out of England in These Times of Distractions (J. Greene, 1642)

A Dialogue Betwixt the Ghosts of Charls the I, Late King of England: And Oliver The Late Usurping Protector (London: 1659)

The Discontented Conference Betwixt The Two Great Associates, William Archbishop of Canterbury, and Thomas Late Earle of Strafford (1642)

The Disease of the House: or the State Mountebanck: Administering Physick to a Sick Parliament (1649)

The Downe-fall of Dagon, or, the Taking Downe of Cheap-side Crosse this Second of May, 1643 (Thomas Wilson, 1643)

Eikon Alethine (London: 1649)

Eikon Basilike (London: 1649)

The English-Devil: Or Cromwel and his Monstrous Witch Discovered at White-Hall (London: Robert Wood for George Horton, 1660)

The Famous Tragedie of King Charles I (1649)

The Famous Tragedie of the Life and Death of Mris Rump Shewing How She was Brought to Bed of a Monster (London: Theodorus Microcosmus, 1660)

Fifth Report of the Royal Commission on Historical Manuscripts, 2 vols (London: George Edward Eyre and William Spottiswoode, 1876)

'First Ordinance of the Long Parliament Against Stage-Plays and Interludes, September 2 1642', in W. C. Hazlitt (ed.), *The English Drama and Stage Under the Tudor and Stuart Princes, 1543–1664, Illustrated by a Series of Documents Treatises and Poems, with a Preface and Index* (London: Roxburghe Library, 1869), p. 63

A Full and Exact Relation of the Horride Murder Committed Upon the Body of Col. Rainsborough, the Persons that Did it and the Cause Thereof (London: R. A., 1648)

The Heads of a Conference Delivered by M. A.: Pymm, at a Committee of Both Houses, Junii 24. 1641 (1641)

Hell's Higher Court of Justice; or The Triall of the Three Politick Ghosts, Viz. Oliver Cromwell, King of Sweden a Cardinal Mazarine (London, 1661)

The History of the Grand Rebellion ... Digested into Verse, 3 vols (London: J. Morphew, 1713)

The History of the Second Death of the Rump ([1660])

The Humble Desires and Propositions For a Safe and Well-Grounded Peace, Agreed Upon by the Mutuall Advice and Consent of the Parliaments of Both Kingdoms, United by Solemn League and Covenant. (London: Edw. Husbands, 1644)

The Kings Cabinet Opened (London: Robert Bostock, 1645)

The Kings Majesties His Declaration to His Subjects, Concerning Lawfull Sports to be Used (London: Bonham Norton and John Bill, 1618)

The Kings Majesties His Declaration to His Subjects, Concerning Lawfull Sports to bee Used (London: Robert Barker, 1633)

The Kings Majesties His Declaration to His Subjects, Concerning Lawfull Sports to bee Used (London: Robert Barker, 1634)

The Kings Majesties Resolutions, And the Parliaments Determinations, Concerning the Request of the French and Spanish Embassadors. With the Names and Charge of the 47. of the House of Commons, Appointed for the Committee, till the Parliament Sit Againe (London: B. Alsop, 1641)

A Letter, in which the Arguments of the Annotator, and Three Other Speeches Upon their Majestie's Letters Published at London, are Examined and Answered (1645)

The Life and Death of King Charles the Martyr, Parallel'd with out Saviour in all his Sufferings (London, 1649)

The Life and Death of Mris Rump. And the Fatal End of Her Base-Born Brat of Destruction (London: Thedorus Microcosmos, 1660)

In Memoriam Thomæ Rainsbrough, Pro Populo, & Parliamento, Chiliarchæ Fortisim ([1648])

Merculicu Militaris, or the Armies Scout, Communicating from all parts of England, Scotland, & Ireland, all Martiall Enterprizes, Designs and Successes ... From Tuesday, Novem. 14. to Tuesday Novem. 21 1648 ([London], 1648)

A Messenger from the Dead, or Conference Full of Stupendious Horrour, Heard Distinctly, and by Alternate Voyces, by Many as That Time Present. Between the Ghosts of Henry the 8. and Charls the First of England, in Windsor-Chappel, Where They Were Both Buried (London, 1658)

A Musicall Banquet, Set forth in Three Choice Varieties of Musick (London: T. H. for John Benson, and John Playford, 1651)

A New Bull-Bayting: or, A Match Play'd at the Town-Bull of Ely (1649)

A New Meeting of Ghosts At Tyburn (London, 1660 [1661])

A New Play Called Canterburie His Change of Diot (1641)

An Ordinance of the Commons Assembled in Parliament for the Utter Suppression and Absolving of all Stage Players and Interludes (London: John Wright, 1647)

An Ordinance of the Lords and Commons Assembled in Parliament, for the Utter Suppression and Abolishing of all Stage-Playes and Interludes. With the Penalties to be inflicted upon the Actors and Spectators, Herein Exprest. Die Veneris 11 Februarii 1647 (London: John Wright, 1648)

A Parly Between The Ghosts of the Late Protector and the King of Sweden, at their Meeting in Hell (London: Lo. Whimbleton, 1660)

A Perfect Relation of the Forme and Governement of the Kirke of Scotland (1641)

A Phanatick Play (London, 1660)

Bibliography 213

The Proceedings on the King and Queens Commissions of the Peace, and Oyer and Terminer and Gaol-Delivery of Newgate, Held for the City of London, and County of Middlesex, at Justice-Hall in the Old-Bailey. On Wednesday, Thursday, Friday, Saturday and Wednesday, Being 10th, 11th, 12, 13th and 17th Days of December, 1690 (1690)

Ravillac Redivivus: Being a Narrative of the Late Tryal of Mr James Mitchel a Conventical Preacher, who was Executed the 18th of January 1677 For an Attempt Which he Made on the Sacred Person of the Arch-Bishop of St. Andrews. To Which is Annexed, an Account of the Tryal of that Most Wicked Pharisee Major Thomas Weir, Who Was Executed for Adultery, Incest and Bestiality, 2nd edn (London: Walter Kettilby, 1682)

The Remarkable Funeral of Cheapside-Crosse in London (London: Robert Hodgekinsonne, 1642)

The Resolution of the Round-heads to Pull Down Cheap-side (1642)

The Scottish Politike Presbyter, Slaine by an English Independent. Or, The Independents Victory Over the Presbyterian Party (1647)

'Second Measure of the Long Parliament Directed to the Suppression of Theatrical Performances in England. October 22, 1647', in W. C. Hazlitt (eds.), *The English Drama and Stage Under the Tudor and Stuart Princes, 1543–1664, Illustrated by a Series of Documents Treatises and Poems, with a Preface and Index* (London: Roxburghe Library, 1869), pp. 64–5

Sir Francis Drake Revivd (London: Nicholas Bourne, 1653)

Sr. Tho. Widdringtons Speech at a Conference Betweene Both Houses, on Tuesday the 20. of July 1641. At the Transmission of the Impeachment Against Matthew Wren Doctor in Divinity, Late Bishop of Norwich, and Now Bishop of Ely (London: E. G. for R. Best, 1641)

Sir William Parkins Speech to the House of Commons in Parliament, Concerning the Present Establishment of Church Government, July 5th 1641 (1641)

The Tragical Actors or the Martydome of the Late King Charles ([1660])

The Traytors Tragedy: or their Great Plot and Treasonable Design Discovered (London: R. Cotton, 1660)

Tyrannicall-Government Anatomized (London, 1642 [1643])

A Vindication of Cheapside Crosse Against the Roundheads (Oxford, 1643)

Women Will Have Their Will, or Give Christmas His Due (London: E. P. for W. G., 1648)

Allen, William [pseud.], *Killing, no Murder* (London, 1659)

Alsop, Bernard, *The Weekly Account: Number 5, October 4 1643* (London, 1643)

Arber, E., ed., *A Transcript of the Registers of the Worshipful Company of Stationers, 1640–1708 AD*, 3 vols (London, 1913–14)

Banks, John, *Vertue Betray'd: or, Anna Bullen* (London: Bentley and M. Magnes, 1682)
—— *The Unhappy Favourite or the Earl of Essex* (London: Richard Bentley and Mary Magnes, 1682)
—— *The Island Queen, or the Death of Mary, Queen of Scotland* (London: R. Bentley, 1682)
Bawcutt, N. W., ed., *The Control and Censorship of Caroline Drama: The Records of Sir Henry Herbert, Master of the Revels, 1623–73* (Oxford: Oxford University Press, 1996)
Bayly, Tho[mas], *The Golden Apophthegms of His Royall Majesty King Charles I* (London: John Clowes, 1660)
Beaumont, Francis and John Fletcher, *Comedies and Tragedies* (London: Humphrey Robinson and Humphrey Moseley, 1647)
——, *Philaster, or, Love Lies a Bleeding* (London, 1652)
[——] *Fifty Comedies and Tragedies* (London: J. Macock, for John Martyn, Henry Herringman, Richard Marriot, 1679)
de la Bédoyère, Guy, ed., *The Diary of John Evelyn* (Woodbridge: Boydell Press, 1995)
Behn, Aphra, *The Roundheads, or the Good Old Cause* (London: D. Brown and H. Rhodes, 1682)
Black, Joseph (ed.), *The Martin Marprelate Tracts* (Cambridge: Cambridge University Press, 2008)
[Boyle, Roger,] Earl of Orrery, *The History of King Henry the Fifth. And the Tragedy of Mustapha, Son of Solyman the Magnificent* (London: H. Herringman, 1668)
—— *Two New Tragedies. The Black Prince, and Tryphon* (London: H. Herringman, 1672)
Britanicus, Mercurius [pseud.], *The Copie of A Letter Written by Mercurius Britanicus to Mercurus Civicus* ([1644])
—— *Mercurius Britanicus, His Apologie to All Well-Affected People. Together with an Humble Addresse to the High Court of Paliament* (London: R. W., 1645)
Britannophilus, Alethophilus Basiluphilus [pseud.], *Cromwell's Recall* (1649)
Brome, Richard, *Five New Plays* (London: Humphrey Moseley, Richard Marriot, and Thomas Dring, 1653)
Brooks, Thomas, *The Glorious Day of the Saints Appearance; Calling for a Glorious Conversation from all Beleevers* (London: M. S. for Rapha Harford and Matthew Simmons, 1648)
Browne, Richard, *The Several Speeches Made to the Honorable Sir Richard Brown Lord Mayor of the City of London: on Monday the Twenty Ninth Day of October, in the Twelfth Year of His Majesties Most Happy Reign Anno Dom 1660* (London: R. Wood, 1660)

[Buchanan, George,] *Tyrannicall-government Anatomized* (London: John Field, 1642 [1643])
Bunyan, John, *The Pilgrim's Progress*, ed. Roger Sharrock (London: Penguin, 1987)
[Butler, Samuel,] *Hudibras. In Three Parts* (London: W. Rogers, 1684)
Carpenter, Richard, *A New Play Call'd The Pragmatical Jesuit New-Leven'd* (London: Printed for N. R., (London, [1665])
Cavendish, Margaret, 'A true relation of my birth, breeding, and life', in *Natures Pictures Drawn by Fancies Pencil to the Life* (London: J. Martin and J. Allestrye, 1656)
[———] 'Bell In Campo', in *Playes written by the Thrice Noble Illustrions and Excellent Princess, the Lady Marchioness of Nesocastle* (London: A. Warren, for John Martyn, James Allestry and Tho. Dicas, 1662)
——— *The Life of the Thrice Nobel High and Puissant Prince William Cavendish* (London: A. Maxwell, 1667)
Cawley, A. C., ed., *Geoffrey Chaucer The Canterbury Tales* (London: Everyman, 1958; repr. 2000)
Chan, Mary, and Jamie C. Kassler, eds, *Roger North's Cursory Notes of Musicke (c. 1698–1703) Physical, Psychological and Critical Theory* (Kensington, New South Wales: Unisearch Ltd, 1986)
——— *Roger North's 'The Musical Grammarian 1728'* (Cambridge: Cambridge University Press, 1990)
Coates, Willson H., Anne Steel Young and Vernon F. Snow, eds, *The Private Journals of the Long Parliament*, 3 vols (New Haven and London: Yale University Press, 1982), 1
Cowley, Abraham, *Cutter of Coleman Street* (London: Henry Herringman, 1663)
——— *The Guardian* (London: John Holden, 1650)
[Davenant, William], *Salmacida Spolia* (London: T. H. for Thomas Walkley, 1639)
——— *The First Days Entertainment at Rutland-House* (London: J. M. for H. Herringman, 1656)
[———] *The Siege of Rhodes* (London: J. M. for Henry Herringman, 1656)
——— *The Cruelty of the Spaniards in Peru* (London: Henry Herringman, 1658)
——— *The History of Sir Francis Drake* (London: Henry Herringman, 1659)
——— *The Siege of Rhodes: the First and Second Parts* (London: Henry Herringman, 1663)
——— *The Siege of Rhodes: the First and Second Parts* (London: Henry Herringman, 1670)
——— *The Play House to be Let* in *The Works of Sr William Davenant* (London: 1673) sig I4r–Q1r

—— *Gondibert*, ed. David F. Gladish (Oxford: Oxford University Press, 1971)
Duffet, T[homas], *The Mock-Tempest: Or the Enchanted Castle* (London: William Cademan, 1675)
Durfey, Thomas, *The Royalist* (London: Jos[eph] Hindmarsh, 1682)
[Fairfax, Thomas], *Short Memorials of Thomas Lord Fairfax, Written by Himself* (London: Ri[chard] Chiswell, 1699)
Filmer, Robert, *The Anarchy of a Limited or Mixed Monarchy* (1648)
—— *Patriarcha: or the Natural Power of Kings* (London: Walter Davis, 1680)
Fleckno[e], Richard, *Ariadne, Deserted by Theseus, and Found and Courted by Bacchus* (London, 1654)
—— *Love's Dominion* (London, 1654)
—— *The Marriage of Oceanus and Brittania* (1659)
—— *Heroick Portraits With Other Miscellary Pieces, Made, and Dedicate to His Majesty* (London: Ralph Wood, 1660)
—— *Love's Kingdom a Pastoral Trage-Comedy* (London: R. Wood, 1664)
Ford, John, *Comedies, Tragi-Comedies and Tragaedies* (London, 1652)
[Fyfe, Alexander], *The Royal Martyr, K. Charles I. An Opera* (1705)
Goodwin, Jo[hn], *Anticavalieriasme, or, Truth Pleading as well the Necessity, As the Lawfulnesse of this Present Warre, for the Suppressing of that Butcherly Brood of Cavaliering Incendiaries, who are now Hammering England, to Make an Ireland of it* (London: Henry Overton, 1643)
Gosson, Stephen, *The Schoole of Abuse* (London: Thomas Woodcocke, 1579)
Gouge, William, *Of Domesticall Duties, Eight Treatises*, 3rd edn (London: George Miller, 1634)
Griffith, Matthew, *Bethal: Or a Forme For Families* (London: Jacob Bloom, 1633)
Hakluyt, Richard, *Voyages and Discoveries*, ed. Jack Beeching (Harmondsworth: Penguin, 1972)
Harrington, James, *The Commonwealth of Oceana*, ed. Henry Morley (London: George Routledge and Sons, 1887)
[Havard, William], *King Charles I: An Historical Tragedy Written in Imitation of Shakespear* (Dublin: J. Jones, 1737)
[Hewitt, John], *The True and exact Speech and Prayer of Doctor John Hewytt Upon the Scaffold on Tower-hill* ([1658])
Hobbes, Thomas, *Leviathan*, ed. J. C. A. Gaskin (Oxford: Oxford University Press, 1996)
Howard, Edward, *The Change of Crownes* ed. Frederick S. Boas (London: Oxford University Press, 1949)
—— *The Womens Conquest* (London, 1671)
Howard, Robert, 'The Committee,' in *Four New Plays* (London: Henry Herringman, 1665)

―――― *The Great Favourite, or the Duke of Lerma* (London: Henry Herringman, 1668)

Howell, James, *A Winter Dreame* (1649)

Hutchinson, Lucy, *Memoirs of the life of Colonel Hutchinson*, ed. N. H. Keeble (London: Phoenix Press, 2000)

[Hyde, Edward], *The History of the Rebellion and Civil Wars in England*, 3 vols (Oxford: printed at the Theatre, 1732)

Jonson, Benjamin, 'Lovers Made Men', in *The Works of Benjamin Jonson. The Second Volume* (London: Richard Meighen, 1640)

―――― 'A Masque Presented in the House of the Right Honorable the Lord Haye', in *The Works of Benjamin Jonson. The Second Volume* (London: Richard Meighen, 1640)

Jeffs, Robin *et al.* (eds), *The English Revolution III: Newsbooks I: Oxford Royalist*, notes by Peter Thomas, 4 vols (London: Cornmarket Press, 1971)

Kirkman, Francis, *The Presbyterian Lash. Or, Noctroff's Maid Whip* (London: 1661)

Lacy, John, *The Old Troop, or Monsieur Raggou* (London: William Crook and Thomas Dring, 1672)

Langbaine, Gerard, *Momus Triumphans: or, the Plagiaries of the English Stage* (London: N. C., 1688)

Latham, Robert, and William Matthews (eds), *The Diary of Samuel Pepys*, 11 vols (London: Harper Collins, 1995)

[Leslie, Henry], *The Martyrdome of King Charles, or his Conformity with Christ in his Suffering* (The Hague: Samuel Brown, 1649)

[Lilburne, John], *A Whip for the Present House of Lords, or The Levellers Levelled* (London, 1648)

Lindley, David (ed.), *Court Masques* (Oxford: Oxford University Press, 1995)

Locke, John, *Two Treatises of Government*, ed. Peter Laslett (Cambridge: Cambridge University Press, 1988)

Locke, Matthew, and Christopher Gibbons, *Cupid and Death*, ed. Edward J. Dent, 2nd rev. edn (London: Stainter and Bell, 1974)

Loveday, Samual, *An Answer to the Lamentation of Cheap-side Crosse. Together with the Reasons Why so Many Doe Desire the Downfall of it, and all Such Popish Reliques* (London: T. A., [1642])

[Macaulay, T. B.], *The History of England from the Accession of James the Second*, ed. Charles Harding Firth, 6 vols (London: Macmillian, 1913), 1

Maclean, Gerald, ed., *The Return of the King: An Anthology of English Poems Commemorating the Restoration of Charles II* (Electronic Text Center: University of Virginia Library, 1999), http://etext.virginia.edu/toc/modeng/public/MacKing.html (accessed 23 January 2013)

Marprelate, Martin [pseud.], *The Protestatyon of Martin Marprelat* ([1589])
—— *The Just Censure and Reproofe of Martin Junior* ([1589])
Marvell, Andrew, *The Complete Poems*, ed. Elizabeth Story Donno (London: Penguin, 1996)
Melancholicus, Mercurius [pseud.], *The Armies Letanie, Imploring the Blessing of God on the Present Proceedings of the Armie* (1647)
—— *Ding Dong, Or Sr. Pitifull Parliament On His Death-Bed* (1648)
—— *Mistress Parliament her Gossipping* (1648)
—— *Mistress Parliament Brought to Bed of a Monstrous Childe of Reformation* (1648)
—— *Mistress Parliament Presented in her Bed* (1648)
—— *The Parliament Arraigned, Convicted; Wants Nothing but Execution* (1648)
—— *Mrs. Parliament her invitation of Mrs. London, to a Thanksgiving dinner* (1648)
—— *The Cuckoo's-Nest At Westminster, or the Parlement Between the Two Lady-Birds, Quean Fairfax, and Lady Cromwell* (1648)
—— *A Nose-Gay for the House of Commons* (1648)
—— *The Parliaments Thanks to The Citie: For Their Kind Compliance in all their Reasons From Time to Time Committed Against His Majesties Honour, Crowne and Dignitie* (1648)
—— *Craftie Cromwell: or, Oliver Ordering our New State* (1648)
Middleton, Thomas, *A Game at Chess*, ed. T. H. Howard-Hill (Manchester: Manchester University Press, 1993)
[Milton, John], *A Declaration of His Highness, by the Advice of His Council; Setting Forth, on Behalf of the Commonwealth, the Justice of their Cause Against Spain, 26 October 1655* (London: Henry Hill and John Field, 1655)
—— *Eikonoklastes*, in Don M. Wolfe et al. (eds), *The Complete Prose Works of John Milton* 8 vols (New Haven and London: Yale University Press, 1962), 3:331–601
Montaigne, Michel de, *The Complete Essays*, trans. M. A. Screech (London: Penguin, 1987)
Moon, Man in the [pseud.], *A Tragi-Comedy Called New-Market-Fayre or a Parliament Out-Cry: of State-Commodities Set to Sale* (1648 [1649])
—— *A Tragi-Comedy Called New-Market-Fayre or a Parliament Out-Cry of State-Commodities Set to Sale*, 3rd edn (1649)
—— *A Tragi-Comedy Called New-Market-Fayre or a Parliament Out-Cry of State-Commodities Set to Sale* (London: E. Crowch, 1661)
—— *A Tragi-Comedy Called New-Market-Fayre or Mrs. Parliaments New Figaryes* (1649)
[Nashe, Thomas,] *The Returne of the renowned Cavaliero Paquill of England from the Other Side the Seas, and His Meeting with Marforius at London Upon the Royall Exchange* (1589)

―― 'Somwhat to reade for them that list', in *Syr P. S. His Astrophel and Stella* (London: Thomas Newman, 1591)
A Countercuffe Given to Martin Junior: by the Venturous, Hardiem and Renowned Pasquill of England, Cavaliero (1589)
―― *Mar-Martine* ([1589])
―― *A Myrror for Martinists* (London: John Wolfe for T. T., 1590)
[Neville, Henry], *The Ladies Parliament* ([London, 1647])
―― *The Ladies, A Second Time, Assembled in Parliament* (1647)
Northbrook, John, *Spiritus est Vicarius Christi in Terra. A Treatise Wherein Dicing, Dauncing, Vaine Playes or Enterluds With Other Idle Pastimes [et]c. Commonly Used on the Sabboth Day, are Reproved by the Authoritie of the Word of God and Auntient Writers* (London: H. Bynneman, for George Byshop, 1577)
Ogilby, John, *The Fables of Æsop Paraphras'd in Verse, and Adorn'd with Sculpture* (London: Thomas Warren for Andrew Crook, 1651)
―― *The Fables of Æsop Paraphras'd in Verse, and Adorn'd with Sculpture*, 3rd edn (London: printed by the author, 1673)
Otway, Thomas, 'The Soldiers' Fortune', in *Four Restoration Marriage Plays* ed. Michael Cordner (Oxford: Oxford University Press, 1995)
Overton, Richard, *New Lambeth Fayre* (London: R. O. and G. D., 1642)
―― *Articles of High Treason Exhibited Against Cheap-side Crosse* (London: R. Overton, 1642)
[Ovid], *The. XV Bookes of P. Ovidius Naso, Entytuled Metamorphosis, Translated Oute of Latin into English Meeter, by Arthur Golding Gentleman* (London: Willyam Seres, [1567])
P[hilips], J[ohn], *The Tears of the Indians* (London: J. C. for Nath. Brook, 1656)
de Pizan, Christine, *The Book of the Body Politic*, ed. Kate Langdon Forhan (Cambridge: Cambridge University Press, 1994)
Pragmaticus, Mercurius [pseud.], *The Second Part of Cratfy Cromwell or Oliver in his Glory as King* (London, 1648)
Price, Laurence, *A New Dialogue Between Dick of Kent, and Wat the Welch-man* (London: John Andrews, 1654)
Prynne, William, *Histrio-mastix* (London: E. A. and W. I. for Michael Sparke, 1633), facsimile edn, with a preface by Arthur Freeman (New York and London: Garland Publishing Inc., 1974)
―― *The Levellers Levelled to the Very Ground* (London: T. B. for Michael Spark, 1647)
[――] *Beheaded, Dr John Hewytts Ghost* (London, 1659)
[Rainolds, John], *Th'overthrow of Stage-Playes, by the Way of Controversie Betwixt D. Gager and D. Rainoldes Wherein All the Reasons that Can be Made for Them are Notably Refuted* (1599)

[Rudyerd, Benjamin], *The Speeches of Sr. Benjamin Rudyer in the High Court of Parliament* (1640)

[———], *The Speeches of Sr. Bejamin Rudyer in the High Court of Parliament* (1641)

Rymer, Thomas, *Edgar, or the English Monarch* (London: Richard Tonson, 1678)

Ryves, Bruno, ed., *The First Week. Mercurius Rusticus, or the Cuntries Complaint of the Murthers, Robberies, Plundring, and Other Outrages, Committed, By the Rebells, on his Majesties Faithfull Subjects* (1643)

S., I., *The Picture of a New Courtier, Drawn in a Conference, Between Mr. Timeserver and Mr. Plain-heart* (1656)

S., M. M., *The Spanish Colonie* (London: William Brome, 1583)

Sabol, Andrew J. (ed.), *Four Hundred Songs and Dances from the Stuart Masque With a Supplement of Sixteen Additional Pieces* (Hanover and London: University Press of New England, 1978)

Sadler, Anthony, *The Subjects Joy for the Kings Restoration, Cheerfully Made Known in a Sacred Masque Gratefully* (London: James Davis, 1660)

[Saltmarsh, John, and Henry Ironmonger Walker, eds,] *The 20th. Weeke. Perfect Occurrences of Parliament And Chief Collections of Letters from the Armie* (London: Andrew Coe, 1645)

[Savile, George], Marquis of Halifax, *The Lady's New Year Gift: or, Advice to a Daughter* (London: Randal Taylor, 1688)

Sheppard, S[amuel], *The Committee-Man Curried* (1647)

——— *The Second Part of the Committee-Man Curried* (1647)

[———] *The Joviall Crew, or The Devill Turn'd Ranter* (London: W. Ley, 1651)

Shirley, James, *The Triumph of Peace* (London: John Norton for William Cooke, 1633)

——— *Cupid and Death* (London: T. W. for J. Cook and J. Baker, 1653)

——— *The Imposture*, in *Six New Playes* (London: Humphrey Robinson and Humphrey Moseley, 1653)

[———] *Cupid and Death A Private Entertainment, Represented with Scenes, Variety of Dancing, Musick, Both Vocall and Instrumentall* (London: John Crooke and John Playford, 1659)

Southerne, Thomas, 'The Wives' Excuse; Or, Cuckolds Make Themselves', in Michael Cordner (ed.), *Four Restoration Marriage Plays*, (Oxford: Oxford University Press, 1995)

Spalding, Ruth, ed., *The Diary of Bulstrode Whitelock 1605–1675* (Oxford: Oxford University Press, 1990)

Spencer, Jane, ed., *Aphra Behn: The Rover and Other Plays* (Oxford: Oxford University Press, 1995)

Spenser, Edmund, *The Faerie Queene*, in Tim Cook (ed.), *The Works of Edmund Spenser* (Ware: Wordsworth, 1995)

Bibliography

―― *A View of the State of Ireland*, ed. Andrew Hadfield and Willy Maley (Oxford: Blackwell, 1997)
Swedenberg, H. T. *et al.*, eds, *The Works of John Dryden*, 20 vols (Berkeley, Los Angeles and London: University of California Press, 1961–2000)
Tatham, J., *The Rump: or the Mirrour of the Late Times* (London: W. Godbid for R. Bloome, 1660)
―― *Londons Glory Represented by Time, Truth and Fame: at the Magnificent Triumphs and Entertainment of His most Sacred Majesty Charls the II* (London: William Godbid, 1660)
Taylor, John, *A Swarme of Sectaries, and Schismatiques* (1641)
[Villiers, George (Duke of Buckingham)], *The Rehearsal* (London: Thomas Dring, 1673)
W., I., *The Bloody Prince, or a Declaration of the Most Cruell Practices of Prince Rupert, and the Rest of the Cavaliers in Fighting Against God, and the True Members of his Church* (London, 1643)
Walsingham, Francis, 'Reflections on a Paper said to be lately printed at Paris, and now reprinted in London, entitled, The Late Bishop of Rochester's Vindication of Bishop Smallridge, Dr. Aldrich, and Himself, from the Charge against them, relating to the Publication of Lord Clarendon's History', *The Free Brito*, 106 (9 December 1731)
Whately, William, *A Bride-Bush, or a Direction for Married Persons* (London: Bernard Alsop, 1623)
[Whitelock, Bulstrode], *Memorials of English Affairs* (London: Nathaniel Ponder, 1682)
Wilkinson, Tate, *The Wandering Patentee; or, a History of the Yorkshire Theatres, from 1770 to the Present Time*, 4 vols (London: Wilson, Spence and Mawman, 1795)
[Wilson, John], *The Cheats* (London: G. Beddell, T. Collins, and Cha. Adams, 1664)
Wolfe, Don M., *et al.*, eds, *Complete Prose Works of John Milton*, 8 vols (New Haven: Yale University Press, 1953–82
Wortley, Francis, *Lines Dedicated to Fame and Truth* (York: Stephen Bulkley, 1642)
Wright, Leonard, *A Friendly Admonition to Martine Marprelate and his Mates* (London: John Wolfe, 1590)

Manuscripts and unprinted works
The Confinement (Bodleian Library MS Rawlinson B.165 fols 104r–105v)
Diary, Chiefly of Public Events, by Joseph Williamson, from 4 March to 11 December 1668, full and important; containing many items of Court and Parliamentary news (PRO, SP 29/231)

An Elegie upon the Death of our Soveraign Lord King Charles the Martyr, [1650] (BL Thomason E:594 (10) MS fol. 1)

Fraser, James, *Triennial Travels*, 2 vols (University of Aberdeen MS 2538/1)

Howard, Edward, *The Change of Crownes* (Folger MS Add 948/V.b. 329)

J[ordan], T[homas], *Cupid His Coronation* (Bodleian Library MS Rawlinson B.165 fols 107r–113v)

Secondary texts

Published works

Adamson, John, *The Noble Revolt: The Overthrow of Charles I* (London: Weidenfeld and Nicolson, 2007)

Arendt, Hannah *The Human Condition*, 2nd edn (Chicago: The University of Chicago Press, 1998)

Asch, Ronald G., 'Wentworth, Thomas, first earl of Strafford (1593–1641)', *Oxford Dictionary of National Biography*, Oxford University Press, 2004; online edn, Oct 2009, www.oxforddnb.com/view/article/29056 (accessed 5 January 2012)

Astington, John H., *English Court Theatre, 1558–1642* (Cambridge: Cambridge University Press, 1999)

Attridge, Derek, 'Dryden's dilemma, or, Racine refashioned: the problem of the English dramatic couplet', *Yearbook of English Studies*, 9 (1979), 55–77

Avery, Emmett L., 'The Shakespeare ladies club', *Shakespeare Quarterly*, 7 (1956), 153–8

Bannard, Yorke, 'Music of the commonwealth: a corrected chapter in musical history', *Music and Letters*, 3 (1922), 394–401

Barbeau, Anne T., *The Intellectual Design of John Dryden's Heroic Plays* (New Haven and London: Yale University Press, 1970)

Beal, Peter, 'Massinger at bay: unpublished verses in a war of the theatres', *Yearbook of English Studies*, 10 (1980), 190–203

Bennett, Gillian, 'Ghost and witch in the sixteenth and seventeenth centuries', *Folklore*, 97 (1986), 3–14

Bitot, Michel, '"Alterations in a commonwealth": disturbing voices in caroline drama', *Cahiers Elisabethains*, 47 (1995), 79–86

Boaden, James, *Memoir of the Life of John Philip Kemble esq: including a history of the stage, from the time of Garrick to the present period*, 2 vols (London: Longman, Hurst, Rees, Orme, Brown and Green, 1825)

Britland, Karen, *Drama at the Courts of Queen Henrietta Maria* (Cambridge: Cambridge University Press, 2006)

Brotton, Jerry, *The Sale of the Late King's Goods: Charles I and His Art Collection* (Basingstoke and Oxford: Macmillan, 2006)

Brown, Laura, 'The ideology of restoration poetic form: John Dryden', *Publications of the Modern Languages Association of America*, 97 (1982), 395–407

Butler, Martin, *Theatre and Crisis, 1632–1642* (Cambridge: Cambridge University Press, 1984)

Butterfield, Herbert, *The Whig Interpretation of History* (London: G. Bell, 1931)

Bywaters, David, 'Representations of the interregnum and restoration in English drama of the early 1660s', *Review of English Studies* advanced access, published 18 April 2008 (16 pp.)

Caldwell, Tanya, *Time to Begin Anew: Dryden's 'Georgics' and 'Aeneis'* (London: Associated University Presses, 2000)

Canfield, J. Douglas, 'The significance of the Restoration rhymed heroic play', *Eighteenth-Century Studies*, 13 (1979), 49–62

—— *Tricksters and Estates: On the Ideology of Restoration Comedy* (Lexington: University of Kentucky Press, 1997)

Chalmers, Hero, *Royalist Women Writers, 1650–1689* (Oxford: Oxford University Press, 2004)

Clare, Janet, 'The production and reception of Davenant's *Cruelty of the Spaniards in Peru*', *Modern Language Review*, 89 (1994), 832–41

—— *Drama of the English Republic: 1649–1660* (Manchester: Manchester University Press, 2002)

Clark, Ira, 'Shirley, James (*bap.* 1596, *d.* 1666)', *Oxford Dictionary of National Biography*, (Oxford: Oxford University Press, 2004) www.oxforddnb.com/view/article/25427 (accessed 8 December 2007)

Clark, William S., 'The sources of the Restoration heroic play', *Review of English Studies*, 4 (1928), 49–63

Clegg, Cyndia Susan, *Press Censorship in Elizabethan England* (Cambridge: Cambridge University Press, 1997)

—— *Press Censorship in Jacobean England* (Cambridge: Cambridge University Press, 2001)

—— *Press Censorship in Caroline England* (Cambridge: Cambridge University Press, 2008)

Cogswell, Thomas, and Peter Lake, 'Buckingham does the Globe: *Henry VIII* and the politics of popularity in the 1620s', *Shakespeare Quarterly*, 60 (2009), 253–78

Cordner, Michael, 'Zeal-of-the-Land-Busy restored', in Martin Butler (ed.), *Re-presenting Ben Jonson: Text, History, Performance* (London: Macmillan, 1999), pp. 174–92

—— 'Sleeping with the enemy; or, Aphra Behn's *The Roundheads* and the political comedy of adultery', in Michael Cordner and Peter Holland (eds), *Players,*

Playwrights, Playhouses: Investigating Performance, 1660–1800 (Basingstoke: Palgrave, 2007), pp. 45–77

Corns, Thomas N., ed., *The Royal Image: Representations of Charles I* (Cambridge: Cambridge University Press, 1999)

Cowen, Brian, 'English coffeehouses and French salons: rethinking Habermas, gender and sociability in early modern French and British historiography', in Angela Vanhaelen and Joseph Ward (eds), *Making Space Public in Early Modern Europe: Performance, Geography, Privacy* (New York and London: Routledge, 2013), pp. 41–53

Cressy, David, 'Remembrancers of the revolution: histories and historiographies of the 1640s', in Paulina Kewes (ed.), *The Uses of History in Early Modern England* (San Marino: Huntington Library, 2006), pp. 253–64

Dharwadker, Aparna, 'Class, authorship, and the social intertexture of genre in Restoration theater', *Studies in English Literature*, 37 (1997), 461–82

Dimmock, Matthew, *Mythologies of the Prophet Muhammad in Early Modern English Culture* (Cambridge: Cambridge University Press, 2013)

Dobson, Michael, *The Making of the National Poet: Shakespeare, Adaptation and Authorship, 1660–1769* (Oxford: Clarendon Press, 1994)

Dobson, Michael, and Nicola J. Watson, *England's Elizabeth An Afterlife in Fame and Fantasy* (Oxford: Oxford University Press, 2002)

Edmond, Mary, *Rare Sir William Davenant: Poet Laureate, Playwright, Civil War General, Restoration Theatre Man* (Manchester: Manchester University Press, 1987)

Erne, Lukas, *Shakespeare as Literary Dramatist* (Cambridge: Cambridge University Press, 2003)

Falkner, James, 'Churchill, Sarah, duchess of Marlborough (1660–1744)', *Oxford Dictionary of National Biography* (Oxford: Oxford University Press, 2004; online edn, Jan 2008) www.oxforddnb.com/view/article/5405 (accessed 15 September 2008)

Farmer, Alan B., and Zachary Lesser, *DEEP: Database of Early English Playbooks*, http://deep.sas.upenn.edu (accessed 31 March 2009)

Ferdinand, C. Y., 'Herringman, Henry (*bap.* 1628, *d.* 1704)', rev. in *Oxford Dictionary of National Biography* (Oxford, 2004; online ed. Jan 2008), www.oxforddnb.com/view/article/37538 (accessed 12 October 2008).

Fincham, Kenneth, and Peter Lake, 'The ecclesiastical policy of King James I', *The Journal of British Studies*, 24 (1985), 169–207

Firth, C. H., 'Sir William Davenant and the revival of drama during the protectorate', *English Historical Review*, 18 (1903), 319–21

—— (ed.), *The History of England from the Accession of James the Second by Lord Macaulay*, 6 vols (London: Macmillian, 1913

Fisher, Alan S., 'Daring to be absurd: the paradoxes of *The Conquest of Granada*', *Studies in Philology*, 73 (1976), 414–39

Fitzmaurice, Andrew, 'The civic solution to the crisis of English colonization, 1609–1625', *The Historical Journal*, 42 (1999), 25–51

Fox, Adam, 'Ballads, libels, and popular ridicule in Jacobean England', *Past and Present*, 145 (1994), 47–83

—— *Oral and Literate Culture in England, 1500–1700* (Oxford: Oxford University Press, 2000)

Fraser, Antonia, *Cromwell: Our Chief of Men* (London: Bookclub Associates, 1974; repr. 1977)

—— *The Weaker Vessel: Woman's Lot in Seventeenth Century England* (London: Phoenix Press, 1984; repr. 2002)

Fraser, Nancy, 'Rethinking the public sphere: a contribution to the critique of actually existing democracy', in Craig Calhoun (ed.), *Habermas and the Public Sphere* (Cambridge, MA, and London: MIT Press, 1992), pp. 109–42

Gagen, Jean, 'Love and honor in Dryden's heroic plays', *Publications of the Modern Languages Association of America*, 77 (1962), 208–20

Gardiner, Samuel Rawson, *History of the Commonwealth and Protectorate 1649–1656*, 4 vols (London: Longman, Green and Co., 1903)

Garganigo, Alex, 'The heroic drama's legend of good women', *Criticism*, 3 (2003), 483–505

Gentles, Ian J., 'Fairfax, Thomas, third Lord Fairfax of Cameron (1612–1671)', in *Oxford Dictionary of National Biography* (Oxford: Oxford University Press, 2004) www.oxforddnb.com/view/article/9092 (accessed 10 August 2007)

—— 'Rainborowe, Thomas (*d.* 1648)', in *Oxford Dictionary of National Biography* (Oxford: Oxford University Press, 2004), www.oxforddnb.com/view/article/23020 (accessed 12 December 2006)

Gordon, Scott Paul, *The Power of the Passive Self in English Literature, 1660–1770* (Cambridge: Cambridge University Press, 2002)

Gough, Melinda J. 'Courtly *comédiantes*: Henrietta Maria and amateur women's stage plays in France and England', in Pamella Allen Brown and Peter Parolin (eds), *Women Players in England, 1500–1660* (Aldershot: Ashgate, 2005), pp. 193–215

de Groot, Jerome, *Royalist Identities* (Basingstoke: Palgrave Macmillan, 2004)

—— '"Welcome to Babylon": performing and screening the English revolution', in Mark Thornton Burnett and Adrian Streete (eds), *Filming and Performing Renaissance History* (Basingstoke: Palgrave Macmillan, 2011), pp. 65–82

Guest, Harriet, *Small Change: Women, Learning, Patriotism, 1750–1810* (Chicago and London: University of Chicago Press, 2000)

Gurr, Andrew, *The Shakespearian Stage 1574–1642*, 3rd edn (Cambridge: Cambridge University Press, 1992)
Habermas, Jürgen, *The Structural Transformation of the Public Sphere*, trans. Thomas Burger (Cambridge: Polity Press, 1992)
Halasz, Alexandra, *The Marketplace of Print: Pamphlets and the Public Sphere in Early Modern England* (Cambridge: Cambridge University Press, 1997)
Harbage, Alfred, *Cavalier Drama: An Historical and Critical Supplement to the Study of the Elizabethan and Restoration Stage* (London: Oxford University Press, 1936)
Harbage, Alfred (revised by S. Schoenbaum and Sylvia Stoler Wagonheim), *The Annals of English Drama 975–1700*, 3rd edn (London: Routledge, 1989)
Harris, Michael, and Alan J. Lee, eds, *The Press in English Society from the Seventeenth to Nineteenth Centuries* (London: Associated University Presses, 1986)
Harris, Tim, *London Crowds in the Reign of Charles II: Propaganda and Politics from the Restoration until the Exclusion Crisis* (Cambridge: Cambridge University Press, 1987)
—— *Restoration: Charles II and His Kingdoms, 1660–1685* (London: Allen Lane, 2005)
—— *Revolution: The Great Crisis of the British Monarchy, 1685–1720* (London: Allen Lane, 2006)
Healy, Robert M., 'The Jews in seventeenth-century Protestant thought', *Church History*, 46 (1977), 63–79
Heinemann, Margot, *Puritanism and Theatre: Thomas Middleton and Opposition Drama Under the Early Stuarts* (Cambridge: Cambridge University Press, 1980)
Hermes, Katherine, 'Fifth Monarchists', in Francis J. Bremer and Tom Webster (eds), *Puritans and Puritanism in Europe and America*, 2 vols (Santa Barbara: ABC-CLIO), 1:398–99
Highfill, Philip H. Jr, Burnim, Kalman A. and Langhans, Edward A., *A Biographical Dictionary of Actors Actresses, Musicians, Dancers, Managers and Other Stage Personnell in London, 1660–1800*, 16 vols (Carbondale: Southern Illinois University Press, 1973–93)
Hill, Christopher, *The World Turned Upside Down: Radical Ideas During the English Revolution* (Harmondsworth: Penguin, 1975; repr. 1982)
—— *The Century of Revolution 1603–1740*, 2nd edn (London and New York: Routledge, 1980)
Holstun, James, 'Ehud's dagger: patronage, tyrannicide, and "Killing No Murder"', *Cultural Critique*, 22 (1992), 99–142
—— (ed.), *Pamphlet Wars: Prose in the English Revolution* (London: Frank Cass, 1992)

Hotson, Leslie, *The Commonwealth and Restoration Stage* (Cambridge, MA.: Harvard University Press, 1928)
Hourani, Albert, *Islam in European Thought* (Cambridge: Cambridge University Press, 1991)
Howe, Elizabeth, *The First English Actresses, 1660–1700* (Cambridge: Cambridge University Press, 1992)
Hughes, Derek, *Dryden's Heroic Plays* (London and Basingstoke: Macmillan, 1981)
—— *English Drama: 1660–1700* (Oxford: Clarendon Press, 1996)
Hume, Robert, *The Development of English Drama in the Late 17th Century* (Oxford: Clarendon Press, 1976)
—— 'Fleckno [Flecknoe], Richard', *Grove Music Online*, ed. L. Macy, www.grovemusic.com (accessed 21 May 2008)
Hutson, Lorna, *The Usurer's Daughter: Male Friendship and Fictions of Women in 16th Century England* (London: Routledge, 1994)
Hutton, Ronald, 'Monck, George, first duke of Albemarle (1608–1670)', *Oxford Dictionary of National Biography* (Oxford: Oxford University Press, Sept 2004) www.oxforddnb.com/view/article/18939 (accessed 28 July 2008)
Irving, Washington, *Chronicle of the Conquest of Granada* (1829), e-book, Project Gutenberg, www.gutenberg.org/etext/3293
Jacob, James R., and Timothy Raylor, 'Opera and obedience: Thomas Hobbes and "a proposition for advancement of morality" by Sir William Davenant', *The Seventeenth Century*, 6 (1991), 205–50
Jenner, Mark, 'The roasting of the rump: scatology and the body politic in Restoration England', *Past and Present*, 177 (2002), 84–120
Jones, Ann Rosalind, and Peter Stallybrass, *Renaissance Clothing and the Materials of Memory* (Cambridge: Cambridge University Press, 2000)
Jose, Nicolas, *Ideas of the Restoration in English Literature* (London and Basingstoke: Macmillan, 1984)
Kastan, David Scott, 'Performances and playbooks: the closing of the theatres and the politics of drama', in Kevin Sharpe and Steven N. Zwicker (eds), *Reading, Society and Politics in Early Modern England* (Cambridge: Cambridge University Press, 2003), pp. 167–84
Keeble, N. H., *The Restoration: England in the 1660s* (Oxford: Blackwell, 2002)
Kerrigan, John, *Archipelagic English: Literature, History and Politics, 1603–1707* (Cambridge: Cambridge University Press, 2008)
Ketcham, Michael G., 'Setting and self-presentation in the restoration and early eighteenth century', *Studies in English Literature*, 23 (1983), 399–412
Kewes, Paulina, *Authorship and Appropriation: Writing for the Stage in England, 1660–1710* (Oxford: Clarendon Press, 1998)

Kishlansky, Mark, *A Monarchy Transformed: Britain 1603–1714* (London: Penguin, 1996)

Knoppers, Laura Lunger, 'The politics of portraiture: Oliver Cromwell and the plain style', *Renaissance Quarterly*, 51 (1998), 1282–319

—— *Constructing Cromwell: Ceremony, Portrait and Print, 1645–1661* (Cambridge: Cambridge University Press, 2000)

Korda, Natasha, *Shakespeare's Domestic Economies: Gender and Property in Early Modern England* (Philadelphia: University of Pennsylvannia Press, 2002)

Kubek, Elizabeth Bennett, '"Night mares of the commonwealth": royalist passion and female ambition in Aphra Behn's *The Roundheads*', *Restoration*, 17 (1993), 88–103

Lacey, Andrew, *The Cult of Charles the Martyr* (Woodbridge: Boydell Press, 2003)

Lake, P. G., 'Constitutional consensus and puritan opposition in the 1620s: Thomas Scott and the Spanish Match', *The Historical Journal*, 25 (1982), 805–25

Lake, Peter, and Steve Pincus, 'Rethinking the public sphere in early modern England', *Journal of British Studies*, 45 (2006), 270–92

Lamont, William, 'Prynne, William (1600–1669)', *Oxford Dictionary of National Biography* (Oxford: Oxford University Press, September 2004; online edn, January 2008) www.oxforddnb.com/view/article/22854 (accessed 12 October 2008)

Law, Richard, 'The heroic ethos in Dryden's heroic plays', *Studies in English Literature*, 23 (1983), 389–98

Lefkowitz, Murray, 'Masque: Commonwealth (1649–60)', *Grove Music Online* (Oxford: Oxford University Press, 2006) www.grovemusic.com/shared/views/article.html?section=music.17996.4 (accessed 14 September 2006)

Lesser, Zachary, *Renaissance Drama and the Politics of Publication: Readings in the English Book Trade* (Cambridge: Cambridge University Press, 2004)

Levinas, Emmanuel, *On Thinking-of-the-Other Entre Nous*, trans. Michael B. Smith and Barbara Harshav (London: The Athlone Press, 1998)

Lewcock, Dawn, *Sir William Davenant, the Court Masque, and the English Seventeenth-Century Scenic Stage c. 1605-c. 1700* (Amhurst: Cambria Press, 2008)

Lewis, Jayne Elizabeth, *The English Fable: Aesop and Literary Culture, 1651–1740* (Cambridge: Cambridge University Press, 1996)

Limon, Jerzy, *Masque of Stuart Culture* (London: Associated University Presses, 1990)

Lindenbaum, Peter, 'Publishers' booklists in late seventeenth-century London', *The Library: The Transactions of the Bibliographical Society*, 7 (2010), 381–404

Lindley, David, ed., *The Court Masque* (Manchester: Manchester University Press, 1984)
Loewenstein, David, *Milton and the Drama of History: Historical Vision, Iconoclasm, and the Literary Imagination* (Cambridge: Cambridge University Press, 1990)
Loftis, John, ed., *The Revels History of Drama in English*, 8 vols (London: Methuen, 1976)
Loxley, James, *Royalism and Poetry in the English Civil Wars* (Basingstoke: Macmillan, 1997)
Lukács, Georg, *The Historical Novel*, trans. Hannah and Stanley Mitchell (London: Merlin Press, 1962; repr. 1989)
Maclean, Gerald M., *The Rise of Oriental Travel: English Visitors to the Ottoman Empire, 1580–1720* (Basingstoke: Palgrave Macmillan, 2004)
Maguire, Nancy Klein, 'The theatrical mask/masque of politics: the case of Charles I', *The Journal of British Studies*, 28 (1989), 1–22
—— *Regicide and Restoration: English Tragicomedy, 1660–1671* (Cambridge: Cambridge University Press, 1992)
Mah, Harold, 'Phantasies of the public sphere: rethinking the Habermas of historians', *The Journal of Modern History*, 72 (2000), 153–82
Manley, Lawrence, *Literature and Culture in Early Modern London* (Cambridge: Cambridge University Press, 1995)
Marcus, Leah S., *The Politics of Mirth: Jonson, Herrick, Marvell and the Defense of Old Holiday Pastimes* (Chicago and London: University of Chicago Press, 1986)
Marshall, Alan, 'Williamson, Sir Joseph (1633–1701)', *Oxford Dictionary of National Biography*, Oxford University Press, 2004; online edn, Jan 2008 www.oxforddnb.com/view/article/29571 (accessed 9 March 2011)
Marshall, Rosalind K., *The Winter Queen: The Life of Elizabeth of Bohemia, 1596–1662* (Edinburgh: Scottish National Portrait Gallery, 1998)
Massai, Sonia, *Shakespeare and the Rise of the Editor* (Cambridge: Cambridge University Press, 2007)
Mayer Brown, Howard *et al.*, 'Opera, 1: Early opera, 1600–90: Humanist court opera', *Grove Music Online* (Oxford: Oxford University Press, 2007) www.grovemusic.com/shared/views/article.html?section=music.40726.3.1 (accessed 8 December 2007)
McElligott, Jason, 'Roger Morrice and the reputation of the *Eikon Basilike* in the 1680s', *The Library*, 6 (2005), 119–32
—— *Royalism, Print and Censorship in Revolutionary England* (Woodbridge: Boydell and Brewer, 2007)
McFadden, George, 'Political satire in *The Rehearsal*', *Yearbook of English Studies*, 4 (1974), 120–8

McGirr, Elaine, *Heroic Mode and Political Crisis, 1660–1745* (Newark: University of Delaware Press, 2009)

McManus, Clare, *Women on the Renaissance Stage: Anna of Denmark and Female Masquing Culture in the Stuart Court (1590–1619)* (Manchester: Manchester University Press, 2002)

McRae, Andrew, *Literature, Satire and the Early Stuart State* (Cambridge: Cambridge University Press, 2004)

Mitchell, W. J. T., *Iconology: Image, Text, Ideology* (Chicago and London: University of Chicago Press, 1986)

Montano, John Patrick, *Courting the Moderates: Ideology, Propaganda and the Emergence of Party, 1660–1678* (London: Associated University Presses, 2002)

Morrill, John, ed., *Oliver Cromwell and the English Revolution* (London and New York: Longman, 1990)

——— 'The suffering people: English Quakers and their neighbours c.1650 – c.1700', *Past and Present*, 188 (2005), 71–103

Mullaney, Stephen, 'What's Hamlet to Habermas? Spatial literacy, theatrical publication, and the publics of early modern public stage', in Angela Vanhaelen and Joseph Ward (eds), *Making Space Public in Early Modern Europe: Performance, Geography, Privacy* (New York and London: Routledge, 2013), pp. 17–40

Nevitt, Marcus, *Women and the Pamphlet Culture of Revolutionary England, 1640–1660* (Aldershot: Ashgate, 2006)

Nicholls, Mark, and Penry Williams, 'Ralegh, Sir Walter (1554–1618)', in *Oxford Dictionary of National Biography* (Oxford: Oxford University Press, 2004) www.oxforddnb.com/view/article/23039 (accessed 13 December 2007)

Nicoll, Allardyce, 'Political plays of the Restoration', *Modern Language Review*, 16 (1921), 224–42

Noonan, Kathleen M., '"The cruell pressure of an enraged, barbarous people": Irish and English identity in seventeenth-century policy and propaganda', *The Historical Journal*, 41 (1998), 151–77

Norbrook, David, *Writing the English Republic: Poetry, Rhetoric and Politics* (Cambridge: Cambridge University Press, 1999)

O'Day, Rosemary, *Women's Agency in Early Modern Britain and the American Colonies* (Harlow: Pearson Education, 2007)

O'Malley, Thomas, 'Religion and the newspaper press, 1660–1685: a study of the *London Gazette*', in Michael Harris and Alan J. Lee (eds), *The Press in English Society from the Seventeenth to Nineteenth Centuries* (London: Associated University Presses, 1986), pp. 25–46

Ollard, Richard, *The Image of the King: Charles I and Charles II* (London: Hodder and Stoughton, 1979)

Orgel, Stephen, *The Illusion of Power: Political Theatre in the English Renaissance* (Berkeley: University of California Press, 1975)

Orgel, Stephen, and Roy Strong, *Inigo Jones and the Theatre of the Stuart Court*, 2 vols (Berkeley and Los Angeles: University of California Press, 1973)

Orr, Bridget, *Empire on the English Stage, 1660–1714* (Cambridge: Cambridge University Press, 2001)

Orrell, John, *The Theatres of Inigo Jones and John Webb* (Cambridge: Cambridge University Press, 1985)

Owen, Susan, '"Suspect my loyalty when I lose my virtue": sexual politics and party in Aphra Behn's plays of the exclusion crisis, 1678–83', *Restoration*, 18 (1994), 37–47

—— *Restoration Theatre and Crisis* (Oxford: Oxford University Press, 1996)

Palisca, Claude V., *Baroque Music*, 3rd edn (Englewood Cliffs, NJ: Prentice Hall, 1991)

Pancheco, Anita, 'Reading Toryism in Aphra Behn's cit-cuckolding comedies', *Research in English Studies*, 55 (2004), 690–708

Parker, Geoffrey, ed., *The Thirty Years' War*, 2nd edn (London: Routledge, 1997)

Parry, Graham, *The Golden Age Restored: The Culture of the Stuart Court, 1603–42* (Manchester: Manchester University Press, 1981)

—— *The Seventeenth Century: The Intellectual and Cultural Context of English Literature, 1603–1700* (London and New York: Longman, 1989)

Patrides, C. A., '"The bloody and cruell Turke": the background of a Renaissance commonplace', *Studies in the Renaissance*, 10 (1963), 126–35

Patterson, Annabel, *Censorship and Interpretation: the Conditions of Writing and Reading in Early Modern England* (Madison: University of Wisconsin Press, 1984)

—— *Fables of Power: Aesopian Writing and Political History* (Durham, NC, and London: Duke University Press, 1991)

Paulson, Ronald, *The Fictions of Satire* (Baltimore: Johns Hopkins University Press, 1967)

Peacey, J. T., 'Hewitt, John (*bap.* 1614, *d.* 1658)', in *Oxford Dictionary of National Biography* (Oxford: Oxford University Press, 2004) www.oxforddnb.com/view/article/13147 (accessed 2 December 2006)

—— 'The management of civil war newspapers: auteurs, entrepreneurs and editorial control', *The Seventeenth Century*, 21 (2006), 99–127

Pierce, Helen, 'Images, representation and counter representation', in Joad Raymoned (ed.), *The Oxford History of Popular Print Culture, vol.1: Beginnings to 1660* (Oxford: Oxford University Press, 2011), pp. 263–79

Pincus, Steven C. A., *Protestantism and Patriotism: Ideologies and the Making of English Foreign Policy, 1650–1668* (Cambridge: Cambridge University Press, 1996)

Plett, Heinrich F., *Rhetoric and Renaissance Culture* (New York and Berlin: Walter de Gruyter, 2004)
Poston, Mervyn L., 'The origin of the English heroic play', *Modern Language Review*, 16 (1921), 18–22
Potter, Lois, ed., *The Revels History of Drama in English*, 8 vols (London: Methuen, 1981)
—— *Secret Rites and Secret Writings: Royalist Literature, 1641–1660* (Cambridge: Cambridge University Press, 1989)
Poynting, Sarah, 'Charles I's letters to Jane Whorwood', *The Seventeenth Century*, 21 (2006), 128–40
Prendergast, Arthur H. D., 'The masque of the seventeenth century, its origin and development', *Proceedings of the Musical Association*, 23 Sess. (1896–1897), 113–31
Price, Curtis A., *Music in the Restoration Theatre: With a Catalogue of Instrumental Music in the Plays 1665–1713* (Ann Arbor: UMI Research Press, 1979)
Pritchard, Allan, 'George Wither and the sale of the estate of Charles I', *Modern Philology*, 77 (1980), 370–81
Raffield, Paul, 'A discredited priesthood: the fallings of common lawyers and their representation in seventeenth century satirical drama', *Law and Literature*, 17 (2003), 365–95
Randall, Dale B. J. *Winter Fruit: English Drama 1642–1660* (Lexington: The University Press of Kentucky, 1995)
Rankin, Mark, Christopher Highley and John N. King, eds, *Henry VIII and His Afterlives* (Cambridge: Cambridge University Press, 2009)
Raylor, Timothy, *Cavaliers, Clubs and Literary Culture: Sir John Mennes, James Smith and the Order of the Fancy* (London and Toronto: Associated University Presses, 1994)
Raymond, Joad, *The Invention of the Newspaper: English Newsbooks 1641–1649* (Oxford: Clarendon Press, 1996)
—— *Pamphlets and Pamphleteering in Early Modern Britain* (Cambridge: Cambridge University Press, 2003)
Raymond, Joad, ed., *News, Newspapers and Society in Early Modern Britain* (London: Frank Cass Publishers, 1999)
Richardson, R. C., *Images of Oliver Cromwell: Essays for and by Roger Howell, Jr* (Manchester and New York: Manchester University Press, 1993)
Rickard, Jane, *Authorship and Authority: The Writings of James VI and I* (Manchester: Manchester University Press, 2007)
Rommelse, Gijs, *The Second Anglo-Dutch War (1665–1667): Raison d'état, Mercantilism and Maritime Strife* (Hilversum: Uitgeverij Verloren, 2006)

Royle, Trevor, *Civil War: The Wars of the Three Kingdoms, 1638–1660* (London: Abacus, 2005)

Sambrook, James, 'Godolphin, Henrietta, suo jure duchess of Marlborough (1681–1733)', *Oxford Dictionary of National Biography* (Oxford: Oxford University Press, online edn, Jan 2008) www.oxforddnb.com/view/article/92329 (accessed 15 September 2008)

Sauer, Elizabeth, *'Paper Contestations' and Textual Communities in England, 1640–1675* (Toronto: University of Toronto Press, 2005)

—— 'Closet drama and the case of *Tyrannicall-Government Anatomized*', in Marta Straznicky (ed.), *The Book of the Play: Playwrights, Stationers, and Readers in Early Modern England*, (Amhurst and Boston: University of Massachusetts Press, 2006), pp. 80–95

Schiffer, Edward, 'Sir William Davenant: the loyal scout lost at sea', *English Literary History*, 59 (1992), 553–76

Scholes, Percy A., *The Puritans and Music in England and New England: A Contribution to the Cultural History of Two Nations* (Oxford: Oxford University Press, 1934)

Scott, Jonathan, *Commonwealth Principles: Republican Writing of the English Revolution* (Cambridge: Cambridge University Press, 2004)

Seaward, Paul, *The Cavalier Parliament and the Reconstruction of the Old Regime, 1661–1667* (Cambridge: Cambridge University Press, 1989)

Selden, R., 'Juvenal and Restoration modes of translation', *Modern Language Review*, 68 (1973), 481–93

Shaughnessy, Robert, 'Havard, William (1710–1778)', *Oxford Dictionary of National Biography* (Oxford: Oxford University Press, 2004) www.oxforddnb.com/view/article/12622 (accessed 15 September 2008)

Sherwood, Roy, *The Court of Oliver Cromwell* (London: Croom Helm Ltd, 1977)

Shohet, Lauren, 'The masque in/as print', in Marta Straznicky (ed.), *The Book of the Play: Playwrights, Stationers, and Readers in Early Modern England* (Amhurst and Boston: University of Massachusetts Press, 2006), pp. 176–202

—— *Reading Masques: The English Masque and Public Culture in the Seventeenth Century* (Oxford: Oxford University Press, 2010)

Sirluck, Ernest, 'Shakespeare and Jonson among the pamphleteers of the first civil war: some unreported seventeenth-century allusions', *Modern Philology*, 3 (1955), 88–99

Skinner, Quentin, 'Conquest and consent: Thomas Hobbes and the engagement controversy', in G. E. Aylmer (ed.), *The Interregnum and the Quest of Settlement 1646–1660* (London and Basingstoke: Macmillan, 1972), pp. 78–98

Smith, Jeremy L., *Thomas East and Music Publishing in Renaissance England* (New York: Oxford University Press, 2003)
Smith, Nigel, *Literature and Revolution in England 1640–1660* (New Haven and London: Yale University Press, 1994)
—— *Andrew Marvell: The Chameleon* (New Haven and London: Yale University Press, 2010)
Smuts, R. Malcolm, *Court Culture and the Origins of a Royalist Tradition in Early Stuart England* (Pennsylvania: University of Philadelphia Press, 1987)
Smyth, Adam, '"Reade in one age and understood i'th'next": recycling satire in the mid-seventeenth century', *Huntington Library Quarterly*, 69 (2006), 67–82
The Society of King Charles the Martyr, www.skcm.org/SKCM/skcm_main.html (accessed 4 June 2009)
Spink, Ian, *English Song: Dowland to Purcell* (London: B. T. Bastford, 1974)
——, *Henry Lawes: Cavalier Songwriter* (Oxford: Oxford University Press, 2000)
Stephenson, Joseph F., 'On the markings in the manuscript of *Sir John Van Olden Barnavelt*', *Notes and Queries*, 53 (2006), 522–4
Teague, Frances, *The Curious History of Bartholomew Fair* (London and Toronto: Associated University Presses, 1985)
Thomas, P. W., *Sir John Berkenhead, 1617–1679: A Royalist Career in Politics and Polemics* (Oxford: Oxford University Press, 1969)
Thompson, Ayanna, *Performing Race and Torture on the Early Modern Stage* (New York and London: Routledge, 2008)
Tomalin, Claire, *Samuel Pepys: The Unequalled Self* (London: Penguin, 2003)
Tomlinson, Sophie, *Women on Stage in Stuart Drama* (Cambridge: Cambridge University Press, 2005)
Treitler, Leo, ed., *Strunk's Source Readings in Music History*, revised edn (New York and London: W. W. Norton and Company, 1998)
Tupper, James W., 'The relation of the heroic play to the romances of Beaumont and Fletcher', *Publications of the Modern Language Association of America*, 20 (1905), 584–621
Turner, James Grantham, *One Flesh: Paradisal Marriage and Sexual Relations in the Age of Milton* (Oxford: Oxford University Press, 1987)
Underdown, David, *Royalist Conspiracy in England, 1649–1660* (New Haven: Yale University Press, 1960)
Vallance, Edward, 'Oaths, casuistry, and equivocation: Anglican responses to the engagement controversy', *The Historical Journal*, 44 (2001), 59–77
—— *Revolutionary England and the National Covenant: State Oaths, Protestantism and the Political Nation* (Woodbridge: Boydell Press, 2005)
Van Lennep, William, ed., *The London Stage, 1660–1800*, 11 vols (Carbondale: Southern Illinois University Press, 1968)

Venuti, Lawrence, *Our Halcyon Days: English Pre-revolutionary Texts and Postmodern Culture* (London: University of Wisconsin Press, 1989)
Wainwright, Jonathan, *Musical Patronage in Seventeenth-century England: Christopher, First Baron Hatton (1605–70)* (Aldershot and Brookfield: Scolar Press, 1997)
Waith, Eugene M., 'The voice of Mr Bayes', *Studies in English Literature*, 3 (1963), 335–43
Walker, Julia, 'Bones of contention: posthumous images of Elizabeth and Stuart politics', in Julia M. Walker (ed.), *Dissing Elizabeth: Negative Images of Gloriana* (Durham, NC, and London: Duke University Press, 1998), pp. 252–76
——— *Elizabeth I as Icon: 1603–2003* (Basingstoke: Palgrave Macmillan, 2004)
Wallace, John M., 'Dryden and history: a problem in allegorical reading', *English Literary History*, 36 (1969), 265–90
Walls, Peter, *Music in the English Courtly Masque* (Oxford: Oxford University Press, 1996)
Warner, Michael, 'Publics and counterpublics', *Public Culture*, 14 (2002), 49–90
Watkins, John, *Representing Elizabeth in Stuart England: Literature, History, Sovereignty* (Cambridge: Cambridge University Press, 2002)
Watt, Tessa, *Cheap Print and Popular Piety, 1550–1640* (Cambridge: Cambridge University Press, 1993)
Wedgwood, C. V., *The King's Peace* (London: Collins, 1955)
——— *The Trial of Charles I* (London: Folio Society, 1959)
——— *Oliver Cromwell and the Elizabethan Inheritance*, Neale Lectures in History Series (London: Jonathan Cape, 1970)
West, Michael, 'Dryden's ambivalence as a translator of heroic themes', *Huntington Library Quarterly*, 36 (1973), 347–66
White, Eric Walter, *The Rise of English Opera* (London: John Lehmann Ltd, 1951)
Wilcher, Robert, 'Moseley, Humphrey (b. in or before 1603, d. 1661)', in *Oxford Dictionary of National Biography* (Oxford: Oxford University Press, 2004) www.oxforddnb.com/view/article/19390 (accessed 12 October 2008)
Williamson, Arthur H., 'An empire to end empire: the dynamic of early modern British expansion', in Pauline Kewes (ed.), *The Uses of History in Early Modern England* (San Marino: Huntington Library, 2006), pp. 223–52
Willie, Rachel, 'Sacrificial kings and martyred rebels: Charles and Rainborowe Beatified', *Études Épistémè*, 20 (2011), *Catastrophe: Literary Representations of the Regicide in 16th and 17th-century Europe*, http://revue.etudes-episteme. org/?sacrificial-kings-and-martyred (accessed 6 June 2012)
——— 'Viewing the paper stage: civil war, print, theatre and the public sphere', in Angela Vanhaelen and Joseph Ward (eds), *Making Space Public in Early*

Modern Europe: Performance, Geography, Privacy (New York and London: Routledge, 2013), pp. 54–75

Wiseman, Susan, *Drama and Politics in the English Civil War* (Cambridge: Cambridge University Press, 1998)

—— 'Pamphlet plays in the civil war news market: genre, politics and "context"', in Joad Raymond (ed.), *News, Newspapers and Society in Early Modern Britain* (London: Frank Cass Publishers, 1999), pp. 66–83

Woolf, D. R., *Reading History in Early Modern England* (Cambridge: Cambridge University Press, 2000)

—— 'Howell, James (1594?–1666)', *Oxford Dictionary of National Biography* (Oxford: Oxford University Press, Sept 2004; online edn, Jan 2008) www.oxforddnb.com/view/article/13974 (accessed 2 January 2009)

Woolrych, Austin, *Britain in Revolution, 1625–1660* (Oxford: Oxford University Press, 2002)

Worden, Blair, *Roundhead Reputations: The English Civil Wars and the Passions of Posterity* (London: Penguin, 2001)

Wright, Louis B., 'The reading of plays during the puritan revolution', *The Huntington Library Bulletin*, 6 (1934), 73–108

Zwicker, Steven N., 'Is there such a thing as Restoration literature?', *Huntington Library Quarterly*, 69 (2006), 425–49

Unpublished works

Wilson, Francis P., '"That memorable scene": the image of King Charles the First in seventeenth and eighteenth century literature' (Unpublished doctoral thesis, University of York, 1993)

Index

Act of Indemnity and Oblivion 173–4, 181–2
Actors Remonstrance, The 9, 36
Act of Settlement 190
Act of Union 56, 196–7
Aesop 19, 84–5, 148
Anna of Denmark 83, 111 n.21
Anne, Queen 195
Arendt, Hannah 32, 35, 45
Attridge, Derrick 133

Banks, John 191
Barbeau, Anne 137–8
Beaumont, Francis and John Fletcher 14–15, 30
  first folio 29, 31
Behn, Aphra 14
  The Roundheads 162, 166–7
Bennet, Henry, Earl of Arlington 146
body natural 67, 69–70, 72–3
body politic 19, 39, 41, 46, 61, 66–73
Boyle, Roger 132–3, 151
  The Black Prince 132
Buchanan 37, 101
  Tyrannicall-Government Anatomized 37
Bunyan, John
  The Pilgrim's Progress 178
Butler, Martin 204

Canfield, Douglas 178
cavaliers 29, 31, 180
  representations 1–4, 17, 20, 159, 162, 169–80, 205
Cavendish, Margaret 171–3
  Bell in Campo 129
Cavendish, William 94
Channen, Luke 83–4
Charles I 58, 62, 87–9, 99–100, 121–2, 130, 162
  ghostly representations 65–6, 68–73
  in the eighteenth century 188–201
  personal rule 67
  represented as martyr 17–18, 35, 40, 42, 52–5, 64–6, 187–93
  represented as tyrant 33
  trial and execution 5, 58–61, 67
Charles II 10–14, 58, 117, 128, 132–6, 139–40, 150, 180, 198, 203
  in exile 72–3
  reign 13, 143, 181, 189
  and the Restoration 157–9, 180
Charles X of Sweden 63
Churchill, Sarah, Duchess of Malborough 195
cit-cuckolding comedy 166–7
city comedy 175
civil wars 5–7, 29, 33, 35, 39, 43, 58, 60–2, 67, 69, 70, 94, 121–2, 131, 147

civil wars (*cont.*)
  cultural memory 17, 53, 71, 99–100, 117, 129, 137, 143, 146, 147, 171–2, 175, 180–2, 195–9, 201–6
  re-enactment (1645) 1–5, 17
Clare, Janet 3, 99, 124–5
Cokaine, Aston 31
Coleman, Catherine 128
Coleman, Edward 204
colonialism 96–107
Committee of Sequestration 169, 171
  satirised 169–74
constitutional monarchy 58, 70, 190, 192, 194, 199–202
Cook, Henry 204
Cordner, Michael 160, 167
Counter-Reformation 59, 62, 96, 102, 105, 107, 139
Cowley, Abraham 175
  Cutter of Coleman Street 175–7
  The Guardian 175
Cressy, David 2
Cromwell, Oliver
  afterlife 42–3, 61–8, 73–4, 157–65, 198–203, 205
  enjoyer of holiday pastimes 6, 94, 204–5
  figured as Machiavellian tyrant 14, 18, 33–41, 53–68, 71–3, 163, 198, 197
  foreign policy 19, 29, 34, 55–7, 62–3, 95–109, 123
  lord protector 57–8, 71, 164, 172
  perceived sexual virility 41, 54–5, 162
  posthumous execution 73–5
Cromwell, Richard
  62, 119, 157–8, 164

Davenant, William 7, 18–20, 29, 80, 82, 85, 89–103, 108–9, 117–22, 124–36, 150, 205–6
  The Cruelty of the Spaniards in Peru 18–19, 94, 96–103, 105–8, 131, 139, 144
  The First Days Entertainment at Rutland House 90–1, 94

Gondibert 125–7, 133
The History of Sir Francis Drake 18, 94, 103, 106–8, 131
  letter to Thurloe 94–5, 119
The Playhouse to be Let 90
  Restoration theatre manager 18, 109, 119–20, 135, 205
The Siege of Rhodes (1656) 7, 19, 92–4, 109, 120, 122–4, 127, 204
The Siege of Rhodes (1663) 19, 120–1, 127–32, 134–6
Declaration of Sports 95
Drake, Francis 101–2
drolls 8
Dryden, John 14, 19, 29, 118, 133–41, 144, 146–7, 150–1, 160
  The Conquest of Granada 19, 118, 133–4, 136–46, 150
  Defence of the Epilogue. Or, An Essay on the Dramatique Poetry of the Last Age 133, 145
  Of Heroique Playes 133–5

Edward VI 100–1
Elizabeth I 38, 69, 100–2, 104, 191, 203
Elizabeth of Bohemia 130–2
engagement controversy 192
Evelyn, John 93
exclusion crisis 17, 139, 166, 189, 201

fables 84–5, 148–9
Fairfax, Thomas 41, 57, 60, 68, 194, 197–201
fairs 8–9, 18, 52–4, 203
France 25, 91, 96, 124, 133, 139, 194, Frederick, Elector of the Palatinate 131
Fyfe, Alexander 188–91
  The Royal Martyr, King Charles I 188–91

Garganigo, Alex 140
Garrick, David 193
Gibbons, Christopher 81, 204
'Glorious' revolution 17, 139, 188–90, 194, 197, 199–200, 202
Grand Remonstrance 62

gunpowder plot 131
Gwyn, Nell 136–7, 140, 145

Habermas, Jürgen 18, 25–7, 32, 43
Hakluyt, Richard 101–2
Halasz, Alexandra 26
Havard, William 193,
   King Charles I 193–201
Heinemann, Margot 7, 204
Henrietta Maria 7, 87–8, 94, 98–9,
   121–2, 128–32, 136, 150, 162,
   190–1, 196–7
Henry VIII 38, 42, 68–72, 100
Herbert, Henry 9, 12, 119–20
Herringman, Henry 29
heroic drama 19, 109, 117–18, 132–7,
   141, 143, 145–51, 159, 172, 202,
   205, 206
Hobbes, Thomas 126
   Leviathan 27, 68, 99
holiday pastimes 1–3, 6, 8, 52, 95,
   202–5
Howard, Edward 9, 11–12, 14
   The Change of Crowns 9–13, 14,
   15–17,
   The Usurper 14
   The Womens Conquest 15
Howard, Robert 14, 20, 133, 151
   The Committee 159, 167–74, 176,
   180
   The Great Favourite or the Duke of
   Lerma 133
Hughes, Derek 159, 160
Hyde, Edward, Earl of Clarendon 13,
   118–19, 135
   History of the Rebellion 194–6, 202

James II 10, 17, 139, 189–90, 200–2
James VI and I 87, 95, 101, 131, 189
Jones, Inigo 81–2, 108
Jonson, Ben 13, 14, 15, 81–2, 93, 133,
   203
   Bartholomew Fair 203
   Epicoene 13
   Lovers Made Men 93
Jordan, Thomas, 81
   Cupid his Coronation 81

Kemble, John Philip 193–4
Killigrew, Thomas 119, 135, 205
kingship 4, 19, 20, 52, 70–2, 83, 122,
   132, 137–9, 142–3, 145–6, 150–1,
   160, 188, 190, 206
   body natural 67, 69–70, 72–3
   body politic 19, 39, 41, 46, 61,
   66–73
   in the masque 4, 6, 80–2, 86–8, 99,
   103, 107, 108, 109, 122, 190–1
Kirkman, Francis 15, 93
Knoppers, Laura 35, 40, 42, 59, 62
Korda, Natasha 89
Kyd, Thomas 124
   The Tragedye of Solyman and
   Perseda 124–5, 127

Lacy, John 10–12, 14, 177
   performs in *The Change of Crowns*
   10–12, 14
   The Old Troop 20, 159, 175, 177–80,
   182
Lake, Peter 202
Lambert, John 56, 161–3, 165
Lanier, Nicholas 93,
Laud, William, Archbishop of
   Canterbury 36–7, 40, 53
   execution 61, 66–8, 72
   perceived Catholicism 53, 59
   reforms in church worship 59,
   69–70
Lawes, Henry 93, 204
Lawes, William 93
Leake, William 30, 31
leveller 37, 41, 53, 57–8
Levinas, Emmanuel 44–6
Locke, John 192
   Two Treatises on Government 192
Locke, Matthew 81
London 11–13, 18, 25, 26, 53, 57,
   90, 94, 108, 109, 119, 128, 147,
   159–60, 166–7, 193, 204
Lukács, Georg 108

Macaulay, Thomas Babington 202
   History of England 202–3
Machiavelli 58, 66, 73, 74

Machiavellian 16, 18, 52, 58, 66, 74, 189–90, 197, 205
Maguire, Nancy Klein 13
Marvell, Andrew 6, 55–6
Mary III 190, 192
Mary of Modena 189
Mary Queen of Scots 66, 68–9
masque 4, 6, 18–19, 52, 80–109, 117–18, 120–5, 135–6, 150, 164, 191, 205–6
Master of the Revels 9, 12, 119,
May Day 1–3, 6, 8, 20
McFadden, George 146
Middleton, Thomas 7–8,
A Game at Chess 12
Milton, John 35, 96–7, 122
and *Eikon Basilike* 35–6
Mitchell, James 168–9
Monck, George 64, 166
Moseley, Humphrey 29, 31
Mullaney, Steven 26

Nashe, Thomas 28
Netherlands, The 13, 96, 121, 139
New Model Army 5, 55, 57–9, 96, 97, 100, 105–6, 144, 198
Newsbook 3, 26–7, 36–9, 202
parliamentarian 1–3, 5, 201–2
royalist 29, 37–8, 75

Oates, Titus 167
Ogilby, John 19, 84–5, 148
opera 80, 82, 90–3, 119
ordinances for theatre closure 4–6, 8, 9, 12, 30–1, 36, 204–5
ordinance for theatre closure (1642) 4, 5, 206
ordinance for theatre closure (1647) 4–6, 17, 205–6
ordinance for theatre closure (1648) 4–6, 8, 205–6

panegyric 19, 34, 40, 55, 74, 109, 137, 157, 159–67, 174, 178, 180–2
paper stage 18, 20, 27–35, 37–9, 41–6, 55, 63, 75, 159,
Astrophil and Stella 28

parliament 26, 36–41, 56–61, 66–7, 71–2, 75, 94, 100, 125, 140, 144, 157–60, 165–6, 169, 171, 174, 181, 189–90, 200
Cavalier Parliament 182
Long Parliament 66–7, 72, 157–60
Rump Parliament 60, 98, 117, 160–1, 163, 181
Pepys, Samuel 10–14, 73, 130–1, 157–9, 176
attends plays 10–14, 130–1, 176
documents the Restoration 157–9
Philips, John 97
Pincus, Steve 202
play pamphlets 3–4, 8–9, 17–19, 27–8, 33–43, 52–66, 73–5, 80, 159, 164, 188, 189, 199, 204, 206
A Bartholomew Fairing 54–7
The Case is Altered or Dreadful News from Hell 63–4
A Conference held Between the Old Protector and the New Lord General 64
The Court Career 73
Craftie Cromwell 37, 58–60
A Dialogue Betwixt the Ghosts of Charles the I Late King of England: and Oliver the Late Usurping Protector 42, 65–8, 74
Hell's Higher Court of Justice 74
A Messenger from the Dead 42, 68–73
Mistress Parliament pamphlets 37, 40–1, 148, 170
A New Bull-Bayting 41
A New Meeting of Ghosts at Tyburn 42, 73–4
New Lambeth Fayre 53
A Parly Between the Ghosts of the Late Protector and the King of Sweden 62–3
The Picture of a New Courtier 33–4
The Second Part of Crafty Cromwell 27, 60, 65
The Second Part of New Market Fair 54–5, 63

Index

A Tragi-comedy called New-Market Fayre 53
The Tragicall Actors 40
Playford, John 204
A Musical Banquet 204
playhouse 5–8, 12–14, 25–7, 30–2, 36, 38, 46, 89–90, 93, 94, 108–9, 128–9, 150, 194, 205, 206
playtext 12, 14–15, 18, 26–7, 29, 31, 33, 36, 43, 46, 205
popish plot 17, 139, 140, 167, 201
Potter, Lois 75, 86, 125
Pride's Purge 60
printers 29–30, 38, 46, 83–4, 88
  Henry Herringman 29
  William Leake 30, 31
  Humphrey Moseley 29, 31
  Humphrey Robinson 29
Prynne, William 7, 88, 94
public sphere 4, 18, 25–7, 32, 35–7, 43–6, 60
Putney Debates 5, 58, 147

Ralegh, Walter 106–7
Raymond, Joad 37, 59
recitative 90–3, 134
reopening of the theatres 6, 12–14, 89, 118–19, 128, 150, 181, 205
Reformation 62, 67, 203
religion 41, 53, 54, 59, 65, 69–71, 101, 123–4, 138, 167, 169, 171, 179, 189, 190, 203
  Calvinism 67
  Catholicism 53, 58–9, 62, 67, 69, 71, 98, 100, 101, 106, 123, 128, 138–40, 188–90
  Episcopacy 8, 53, 59, 61, 168–9
  Islam 101, 117, 123–4, 130, 138–9
  Presbyterianism 59, 60, 69, 167–9, 171, 203
  Protestantism 59, 62, 71, 98, 100, 101, 104, 106–7, 123, 131, 139, 188, 203
  Puritanism 4, 6–7, 119, 134, 176, 203
Restoration 3–6, 9–10, 12–20, 29, 42, 65, 73–4, 84, 86, 89, 94, 98, 108–9, 117–21, 125, 127–30, 132–7, 140, 143–4, 147, 150–1, 157–67, 172, 174–5, 181–2, 189, 193, 196, 198, 202, 203, 205, 206
Restoration settlement 169, 200
Robinson, Humphrey 29
roundhead 1–4, 17, 20, 157–8, 178–80, 191
Rupert of the Rhine 131–2

Sadler, Anthony 109
satire 37–42, 46, 55, 59, 146, 147, 160, 174–5, 178, 191, 203
Scholes, Percy 203–4
Shakespeare Ladies' Club 193
Shirley, James 14, 15–16, 19, 81–9, 108–9
  Cupid and Death (1653) 19, 81–9
  Cupid and Death (1659) 81, 86
  The Triumph of Peace 88–9
Smith, Nigel 39
Solemn League and Covenant 144, 169–71
Spain 8, 34, 59, 96–7, 102, 105, 107, 123, 138–40, 142–5
Spanish Armada 97, 102, 189
Spenser, Edmund 133
Stationers' Register 26–7, 93, 118, 120

Tatham, John 20, 159–64, 166–7, 170, 181–2
  The Rump 20, 159–67, 181, 191
Thomason, George 26
Thurloe, John 94–5, 119
Tomlinson, Sophie 128–9
Tory 195–6, 201
Turk 117, 123–5, 130, 132

Vaz, Lopez 101–2, 104, 106
Villiers, George, First Duke of Buckingham 38
Villiers, George, Second Duke of Buckingham 118, 146
  The Rehearsal 19, 118, 146–50

Webb, John 108, 131
Wedgwood, C.V. 169

Wentworth, Thomas, Earl of Strafford 61, 65–8, 72
western design 96, 97, 99
Whig 195–6, 201
Whig historiography 202–3
Whitelock, Bulstrode 122
William of Orange 189–93
Wilson, Francis 195

Wiseman, Susan 3, 5, 36, 87, 98, 130, 160, 166, 181
woman actor 7, 108, 128, 150, 194, 196, 205
   Catherine Coleman 128
Woolrych, Austin 169

Zwicker, Steven 9

EU authorised representative for GPSR:
Easy Access System Europe, Mustamäe tee 50,
10621 Tallinn, Estonia
gpsr.requests@easproject.com

www.ingramcontent.com/pod-product-compliance
Lightning Source LLC
Chambersburg PA
CBHW070237240426
43673CB00044B/1822